Successful Self-Leadership

Successful Self-Leadership

An Inside-Out Approach in Seven Steps

Tim Baker

Successful Self-Leadership: An Inside-Out Approach in Seven Steps

Copyright © Business Expert Press, LLC, 2025

Cover design by Charlene Kronstedt

Interior design by Exeter Premedia Services Private Ltd., Chennai, India

All rights reserved. No part of this publication may be reproduced, stored in a retrieval system, or transmitted in any form or by any means—electronic, mechanical, photocopy, recording, or any other except for brief quotations, not to exceed 400 words, without the prior permission of the publisher.

First published in 2025 by
Business Expert Press, LLC
222 East 46th Street, New York, NY 10017
www.businessexpertpress.com

ISBN-13: 978-1-63742-622-7 (paperback)
ISBN-13: 978-1-63742-623-4 (e-book)

Business Expert Press Human Resource Management and Organizational Behavior Collection

First edition: 2025

10 9 8 7 6 5 4 3 2 1

To Bill King, an excellent teacher who believed in me.

Description

Great leaders all share a common secret: they prioritize personal development.

Successful Self-Leadership: An Inside-Out Approach in Seven Steps is not your typical leadership guide. Its seven diagnostic tools for each practice make it unique, providing practical and immediately applicable resources. This book incorporates the latest research to help you **unlock your potential** and prepare for the journey of self-leadership, ensuring that you are well-equipped to apply the knowledge in your daily life.

Dr. Tim Baker shares his unique *Self-Leadership Development Framework*, which consists of seven personal leadership practices, including The Inner and Outer Game, which separates the good from the great leaders.

At its core, the book focuses on the concept of self-awareness, first taught by Socrates and foundational to genuine leadership. It introduces seven unique practices essential for today's leaders, equipping you with the tools to **tap into your inner potential.**

The book emphasizes that deep self-awareness, the journey of genuinely understanding oneself, is not a one-time destination but a continuous, engaging process that leaders should commit to. This understanding is crucial to **personal and leadership success,** and the book will guide you in staying engaged and committed to this process.

Successful Self-Leadership: An Inside-Out Approach in Seven Steps promises

- greater self-awareness
- more confidence
- superior focus and
- dynamic interpersonal skills.

Begin your path to greatness today—because the best investment you can make is in yourself. **Your journey starts now!**

Leadership expert Marshall Goldsmith called **Dr. Tim Baker "one of today's most influential HR experts."** With 18 successful books, Dr. Baker is a leadership expert and is constantly in global demand as a coach, consultant, and speaker. He was recently voted **as "One of the 50 Most Talented Global Training and Development Leaders"** by the World HRD Congress. (www.winnersatwork.com.au).

Contents

Testimonials xi
Introduction xiii

PART I **Understanding Self-Leadership** 1

Chapter 1 Self-Leadership Is the Foundation for a Great Life 3
Chapter 2 The Seven Practices of Self-Leadership 13

PART II **The Inner Game** 25

Chapter 3 Practice #1: Know Thyself 27
Chapter 4 Four Simple and Proven Ways to Develop
               Self-Awareness 37
Chapter 5 Practice #2: Discover True North 45
Chapter 6 Why Should You Lead Anyone? 55
Chapter 7 Practice #3: Build Strengths 63
Chapter 8 Leading in a Digital World 73
Chapter 9 Practice #4: Keep Growing 85
Chapter 10 Leadership Growth Framework 95

PART III **The Outer Game** 107

Chapter 11 Practice #5: Show Intent 109
Chapter 12 Eight Characteristics of Intentional Leaders 119
Chapter 13 Practice #6: Self-Regulate 129
Chapter 14 13 Proven Ways to Boost Emotional Self-Regulation 139
Chapter 15 Practice #7: Be Curious 149
Chapter 16 Unleashing the Power of Inquisitiveness 159

Conclusion 171
Appendices 175
Appendix A Are You a Peacock, Bull, Owl, or Lamb? 177

Appendix B Life Values Inventory 184
Appendix C Digital Leadership Development Profile 191
Appendix D Influencing Capabilities Profile 208
Appendix E Reflections on Leadership Intention 216
Appendix F Self-Regulation Appraisal 220
Appendix G Curiosity Inventory 225
Notes 231
References 241
About the Author 251
Index 253

Testimonials

"*Successful Self-Leadership is the latest book by Dr. Tim Baker, a renowned expert, author, and coach specializing in leadership, organizational performance, and culture change. He has written 18 books on these subjects. As the Chief Executive Officer of Lockyer Valley Regional Council, I have witnessed Dr. Baker in action as he led our organization through a journey of leadership development and cultural transformation, resulting in improved staff engagement and productivity.*

In his new book, Dr. Baker posits that true leadership originates from within us. He emphasizes the importance of cultivating constructive habits such as goal setting, self-reflection, and seeking feedback from peers. While leadership can be taught to some degree, developing our own self-leadership behaviors can elevate us to a new level. This personal growth enhances self-awareness, improves our ability to self-regulate behavior, fosters self-motivation, and encourages ownership of our own development.

I highly recommend this book to anyone in a leadership position and to anyone interested in self-improvement."—**Ian Church, CEO, Lockyer Valley Regional Council Lockyer Valley Regional Council**

"*Tim's way of summarising 2,000 years of leadership lessons and then putting that learning into a structured plan for our contemporary time is amazing. Following his seven practices will enhance your leadership success. His 'out of the box' thinking is essential for all leaders in our contemporary workplaces.*"
—**Mark Shaw, NEOS HR**

Introduction

Embark on an extraordinary journey of resilience, empowerment, and transformation with Viktor Frankl's (1984) gripping narrative in *Man's Search for Meaning*.[1] Delve into his awe-inspiring survival of the Holocaust, where amidst unimaginable suffering, he not only endured but thrived, illuminating the power of self-leadership in the darkest of times.

Frankl's story is a testament to the indomitable human spirit, where he not only survived the horrors of Nazi concentration camps but also exemplified self-leadership practices that are as relevant today as they were then. Anchored by his unwavering values, Frankl found meaning and purpose amid chaos, guiding his actions with resilience and determination.

His journey epitomizes self-leadership—the ability to navigate life's challenges with purpose, integrity, and strength. As we delve deeper into Frankl's experience, we uncover a profound self-understanding, the mastery of emotions, and the relentless pursuit of growth.

The concept of *self-leadership* emerged within organizational management literature, pioneered by Charles Manz in 1986.[2] He delineated self-leadership as a holistic self-influence paradigm, encompassing the ability to motivate oneself toward tasks that naturally inspire and effectively manage tasks that lack inherent motivation.

Self-leadership embodies seizing control over one's thoughts, emotions, and actions to live a better life. It hinges on a profound understanding of oneself, the establishment of meaningful objectives, and initiative-taking behavior aligned with those objectives. Self-leadership entails charting one's course through life's vicissitudes with purpose and grit, akin to steering one's ship through tumultuous seas.

Self-awareness, self-regulation, and self-motivation are central to the practice of self-leadership. Self-awareness involves discerning one's strengths, weaknesses, values, and motivations, laying the groundwork for informed decision making and connection with long-term aspirations. Meanwhile, self-regulation empowers individuals to navigate impulses, emotions, and behaviors, fostering focus, resilience, and adaptability in pursuing goals. Additionally, self-motivation propels individuals to set ambitious yet achievable objectives, nurturing a positive mindset and seeking avenues for development.

Engaging in self-leadership necessitates discipline, introspection, and a growth-oriented mindset. It entails cultivating constructive habits such as goal setting, self-reflection, and soliciting feedback from peers. Moreover, it involves assuming accountability for one's actions and decisions, recognizing that personal success and responsibility go hand in hand.

Is it worth all that?

Self-leadership empowers individuals to craft their destinies, guiding their lives with purpose, integrity, and resilience. The journey of self-discovery, growth, and transformation engenders greater fulfillment and efficacy across all spheres of life.

Why does self-leadership matter in the realm of effective management? It is the cornerstone for managers to survive and thrive in their roles. Through self-leadership, managers cultivate the essential qualities and behaviors to inspire, motivate, and guide their teams toward success.

Here are four overarching benefits for managers.

First, self-leadership amplifies self-awareness, enabling managers to discern their strengths and areas for growth. With this deeper understanding, managers can harness their talents while pinpointing areas ripe for development. This heightened self-awareness allows managers to adapt their leadership styles to suit various situations and individuals, fostering a more inclusive and supportive work environment.

Second, self-leadership enriches one's capacity to self-regulate, enabling better management of emotions, reactions, and behaviors, especially in high-pressure or uncertain scenarios. This ability to maintain composure and focus provides stability and direction for their teams. By modeling self-regulation, managers set a positive example, encouraging resilience and adaptability among their employees.

Third, self-leadership ignites self-motivation, propelling managers to continuously pursue excellence and inspiring their teams to do the same. Motivated managers set ambitious yet achievable goals, demonstrating a steadfast commitment to personal and organizational success. Their enthusiasm and passion are catalysts, infusing their teams with purpose and dedication and driving performance and innovation.

Lastly, self-leadership empowers managers to take ownership of their development and growth. By actively seeking feedback, learning opportunities, and mentorship, self-led managers continually refine their leadership skills and expand their interpersonal impact.

Self-leadership is indispensable for managers to cultivate the qualities and behaviors essential for outstanding leadership. Managers can inspire, empower, and guide their teams toward achieving success through mastery of self-awareness, self-regulation, and self-motivation.

While the literature on leading others abounds, the focus on self-leadership must be more extensive. *Successful Self-Leadership: An Inside-Out Approach in Seven Steps* stands out among its peers with its unique *Self-Leadership Development Framework*. This framework, comprising seven self-leadership practices, serves as a guiding light for personal and professional growth. Coupled with diagnostic tools for each practice, readers gain deeper insights into their current mindset and behaviors, paving the way for leveraging strengths and mitigating weaknesses.

Part I of the book offers a comprehensive exploration of self-leadership, introducing readers to the seven practices and providing a roadmap for their development. Part II delves into the four practices of The Inner Game, focusing on self-discovery, setting direction, leveraging strengths, and continuous growth. In Part III, we explore The Outer Game's three practices: intentionality, self-regulation, and curiosity. Additionally, seven diagnostics are included for each practice to offer deeper insights into your growth as a leader and an individual.

Embark on the transformative journey of self-leadership. Let's dive in and unlock your potential within. I asked, "Is it worth all that?"

Answer: Yes, it is!

PART I
Understanding Self-Leadership

CHAPTER 1

Self-Leadership Is the Foundation for a Great Life

Leadership is as much about who you are as it is about what you do.

Abraham Lincoln, the 16th President of the United States, believed in leading by example. He thought a leader should have strong moral principles, be willing to take risks and be prepared to learn from failures and mistakes.

Lincoln was known for his integrity, honesty, and compassion. He believed a leader should act in the best interests of the people they serve. Lincoln was prepared to make tough choices that benefited the nation, even when these decisions were unpopular.

A famous quote attributed to Lincoln is, "I am not bound to win, but I am bound to be true..." (Neilsen and Sirke, 2016)[1] *This comment sums up his commitment to self-leadership. Lincoln understood that leaders should be true to their values and act with integrity, regardless of the outcome.*

He was a life-long learner. Lincoln was a voracious reader, a skilled orator, and open to learning from the many setbacks he endured throughout his life. He did not fear new challenges and always looked for ways to improve himself and his leadership capabilities.

Lincoln's commitment to self-leadership helped him become one of the most revered leaders in American history. His integrity, honesty, and willingness to take risks and learn from failure continue to inspire leaders worldwide.

Self-leadership is the basis for exceptional leadership. Over the past two decades, I have coached thousands of leaders in 13 countries. I have observed that extraordinary leaders are obsessed with personal development. Great leaders are always looking for ways to improve. The opposite is true, too. Underperforming leaders also have one thing in common: They neglect their personal development and have stopped growing.

Leadership is as much about who you are as it is about what you do. Outstanding leadership—such as that exemplified by Lincoln—requires extraordinary action. A great leader's accomplishments stem from cultivating impressive character traits, such as courage and empathy. Exceptional achievements come from a unique mindset. We will explore seven practices of self-leadership that separate the ordinary from the extraordinary leader.

Before exploring these practices, we need to define self-leadership.

What Is Self-Leadership?

Developing leadership potential starts from within. However, the books we read, the seminars we attend, and the workshops we participate in teach us that leadership is a set of prescribed tactics and strategies to learn, such as driving a car. Although leadership skills obtained from training are undoubtedly valuable and necessary—without the proper mindset—these capabilities are not applied or are poorly executed.

Traditional leadership training focuses mainly on the way a manager interacts with others. The implication is that what a leader does (and does not do) holds the key to their success. For example, the leader learns to listen and be decisive. As valuable as these behaviors are, applying these skills involves more than what is learned in the training room.

Leadership training focuses on the outer game, whereas self-leadership begins with the inner game. Self-leadership is based on the premise that how we think shapes our behavior. Being self-aware, reflective, and continuously learning is the basis of self-leadership, which is *inside-out* leadership.

Here is an illustration of what I mean.

Franco thinks he is a good listener. However, those who work with him know that Franco does not listen. He is impatient and jumps in without taking the time to understand others' points of view entirely. Franco's boss decides to send him on a communication training course, thinking this will *fix* the problem. However, due to a lack of self-awareness, it is unlikely that Franco will apply the lessons learned from this training, even though they are relevant to his development.

Building leadership capability is marketed as a series of techniques to be acquired. However, with sufficient self-understanding, these training programs are more effective at changing behavior. Furthermore, if the participant in these courses does not have the aptitude for self-learning, everything stays the same in their external environment. Sustainable behavior change begins from within.

Take Edwina, for example. Jenny, her boss, enrolls her in a delegation course. Jenny tells Edwina that she is taking on too much and needs to delegate more tasks to her team. The course prescribes valuable techniques for delegating. Edwina enjoys the program. However, Jenny notices that she still needs to assign tasks to her team after a few weeks. It is business as usual for Edwina.

Why?

She is a control freak—her team sees Edwina as a micromanager. Real behavior change will only occur for Edwina when she fully understands her reluctance to delegate work to the team. Edwina does not trust her team members to complete the job, so she jumps in and does the work herself. Learning to delegate does not solve Edwina's lack of trust in her team.

Overcoming Obstacles

Many outstanding leaders I have worked with have overcome significant personal obstacles. A few are painfully shy, and others suffer from what psychologists Clance and Imes (1978) called *imposter syndrome.*"[2] These impressive leaders adopted an inside-out approach to overcome these barriers. In other words, they worked to be more outgoing and confident. Self-confidence cannot be learned from a book or podcast—it is an inside job.

Here are five examples of the power of self-leadership to overcome significant barriers.

Malala Yousafzai is a Pakistani activist for female education and the youngest Nobel Prize laureate. The Taliban shot her in the head in 2012 for speaking out against their restrictions on education for girls. However, she survived and advocated for women's education and empowerment.

Nelson Mandela was a South African anti-apartheid revolutionary who became the country's first black president. He spent 27 years in prison for his activism. However, upon his release, he continued to fight for equality and reconciliation between South Africa's different racial groups. Mandela demonstrated zero bitterness and did not harbor feelings of revenge toward his prisoners.

The British theoretical physicist and cosmologist Stephen Hawking passed away on March 14, 2018, at 76. Hawking made groundbreaking contributions to our understanding of the universe. He was diagnosed with a motor neuron disease at the age of 21, which gradually left him paralyzed. However, he continued to work and communicate through a speech-generating device until his death.

The British author and philanthropist J. K. Rowling is best known for writing the Harry Potter series. She struggled with depression and poverty as a single mother before the success of her books, which have since sold over 500 million copies worldwide.

Nick Vujicic is an Australian motivational speaker who was born with tetra-amelia syndrome, a rare disorder that left him without arms or legs. Despite this, he has become a successful speaker and author, inspiring others to overcome obstacles and live life to the fullest.

These leaders applied inside-out leadership.

Self-leadership is not only about overcoming shortcomings and barriers. It is also about discovering and using one's strengths to be a better leader. One of the seven practices is build Strengths, which we cover in Chapters 7 and 8.

Many people are promoted to leadership roles because of their superior technical capabilities. They may be outstanding accountants or brilliant engineers. Technically, they are competent problem solvers but probably need better leaders. Nonetheless, they are promoted to leadership based on their technical know-how.

For instance, the assumption is that a sound engineer will make a good leader of engineers. However, this is only sometimes the case.

The transition will only happen when the technically capable engineer invests similar time and energy into developing themselves. The technically competent engineer can grow into a skilled leader with a readiness to self-reflect, heightened self-awareness, and practice. This is the journey of self-leadership.

When I enrolled in my first undergraduate degree many moons ago, I chose electives that did not require me to give a presentation for assessment. At the time, I was scared stiff of speaking in public! I read Carnegie's (1998) famous book, *How to Win Friends & Influence People*, in my late teens.[3] Carnegie said it is unavoidable to go through life without learning to speak in public, whether at a funeral, wedding, or other occasion. So, he suggested learning the necessary skills of public speaking. I thought at the time: *Good God, is there another way?* With a sigh of resignation and trepidation, I joined Toastmasters.[*] Despite being scared, I would front up and participate in the program every week. I stuck with it. It was a life-changing decision. Now I get paid to speak all over the world.

With a *growth mindset*—a concept we explore in Chapter 9—and hours and hours of practice, you can overcome a limitation, whether in public speaking or something else.

To be a good leader, one needs a cheerful outlook, an uncompromising set of beliefs, and an unwavering determination to succeed. John Quincy Adams, the sixth President of the United States, served from 1825 to 1829. He was the son of the second U.S. President, John Adams. John Quincy Adams said, "If your actions inspire others to dream more, learn more, do more, you are a leader" (White, 2023).[4] Leadership is about inspiring others to fulfill their potential and achieve their goals—it is not a trick or tactic—it is a state of mind. It starts with self-leadership.

---

[*]Toastmasters International is a nonprofit educational organization that builds confidence and teaches public speaking skills through a worldwide network of clubs that meet online and in person, www.toastmasters.org/About.

> ## Where the Rubber Meets the Road
>
> **What Others Say About Self-Leadership**
>
> Self-leadership is widely recognized as an essential component of effective leadership. Here are a few quotes from leadership experts illustrating the importance of self-leadership:
>
> > Personal leadership (Self-Leadership) is the process of keeping your vision and values before you and aligning your life to be congruent with them.
> > —Stephen Covey
>
> > Self-leadership is the practice of intentionally influencing your thinking, feeling, and actions towards your objectives.
> > —Andrew Bryant
>
> > Being a self-leader is to serve as chief, captain, or CEO of one's own life.
> > —Peter Drucker
>
> > *Leadership is about creating a vision and inspiring others to work towards itt. But it starts with personal leadership—knowing who you are, what you stand for, and what you want to achieve.*
> > —Simon Sinek (Bryant and Kazan, 2012)[5]

The Basis of a Successful Life

Self-leadership is the basis for a successful life. It is the ability to take control of your life and steer it in your desired direction. More specifically, self-leadership is the capability to lead oneself effectively, to take control of one's life, to make intentional decisions, and to take responsibility for one's thoughts and behavior.

Being a self-leader starts with greater self-awareness, identifying your values, and forming a personal vision of success. Self-leadership requires self-discipline, self-motivation, self-confidence, and positive relationships with oneself and others. Self-leadership is about being the best version of oneself.

Successful Self-Leadership: An Inside-Out Approach in Seven Steps will help you harness your innate talents to be a dynamic leader and better human being. With a drive to learn and grow, the journey of self-leadership is transformative.

Self-leadership means taking ownership of your life—with no excuses—to learn new ways of thinking and doing. Whether in your personal or professional life, self-leadership is the cornerstone for achieving your maximum potential and living a fulfilling life.

Are you up for this? Do you believe it is possible to take charge of your life? In the pages, I will provide my Self-leadership Development Framework, which covers seven powerful practices.

Locus of Control

Psychologist Rotter (1992) coined the term *locus of control* in 1950.[6] According to Rotter, locus of control is the degree of power one assumes they have over the events of their lives. A person with an *internal* locus of control believes that their actions and decisions impact their life. On the other hand, an *external* locus of control is based on the belief that outside factors, such as luck or fate, determine one's life. Most people have a mix of internal and external locus of control. Nonetheless, to embrace the idea of self-leadership requires an internal locus of control. It would be best if you believed in the idea that it is possible to take charge of changing your life for the better.

Moreover, when you exercise self-leadership, you decide to shape your destiny. Instead of only reacting to external events and circumstances, you proactively live by your standards, values, goals, and priorities. By committing to taking personal responsibility for your life, you will inevitably be happier, more fulfilled, and more purposeful.

Gaining a deeper understanding of oneself is liberating. It is invigorating to understand who you are and what makes you tick. Self-understanding includes being more in touch with your emotions, thoughts, and the behavioral effects on others. Being more self-aware equips you to manage your feelings, make better decisions, and be more persuasive.

Greater self-awareness benefits you in all walks of life, not just at work. However, self-awareness is deceptive. We know ourselves better than we do. It is like mindfulness. If we are conscious of being present, we are not present! However, having a deeper understanding of who we are means we have a more authentic relationship with ourselves. Being more in touch with our inner life strengthens our interpersonal relationships, too.

Self-leadership enhances vital leadership skills: Setting goals, managing time and priorities, and learning continuously, to name three. When you set clear and achievable goals, you can better prioritize time and focus your efforts on what matters most. You improve your ability to juggle personal and professional responsibilities. Adopting a growth mindset means being in a perpetual state of progress.

Furthermore, applied self-leadership helps you be more resilient and adaptable—attributes vital for functioning effectively in our warp-speed and ever-changing world. When you take ownership of your life, you are more resilient to setbacks and more flexible to change. In other words, with a clearer sense of purpose and direction, you are more equipped to navigate the inevitable challenges of modern life.

Finally, by practicing self-leadership, you lead by example. When people around you see you developing personally, they are inspired. By being self-aware, goal-focused, and committed to learning continuously, you pave the way for team members to do the same.

In summary, practicing self-leadership benefits you and those you lead for many reasons. It permits us to take control of our lives, be more mindful, and build sound self-management habits. We become more fearless and flexible. We set a fitting example for others to follow. Self-leadership is the foundation for achieving our full potential and living a fulfilling life.

Are you ready?

In the next chapter, I will introduce the seven self-leadership practices.

Top 10 Points

1. Self-leadership is the foundation for exceptional leadership.
2. Developing leadership potential starts from within.
3. Leadership training focuses on the outer game, whereas self-leadership begins with the inner game.
4. Self-leadership is not only about overcoming shortcomings and barriers. It is also about discovering and using one's strengths to be a better leader.
5. To be a good leader, one needs a cheerful outlook, uncompromising beliefs, and unwavering determination to succeed.
6. Being a self-leader starts with greater self-awareness, identifying your values, and forming a personal vision of success.
7. Greater self-awareness benefits you in all walks of life, not just at work.
8. Self-leadership enhances vital leadership skills, such as setting goals, managing time and priorities, and learning continuously.
9. Applied self-leadership helps you be more resilient and adaptable—attributes vital for functioning effectively in our warp-speed and ever-changing world.
10. By practicing self-leadership, you lead by example.

CHAPTER 2

The Seven Practices of Self-Leadership

A positive, crystal-clear intention is bound to be inspirational—it engages the hearts and minds of others to contribute their best.

> *The great management consultant Peter Drucker stated that self-leadership is "... the only leadership that's going to matter in the 21st century." Bill Butler states, "Self-leadership extracts your potential and polishes it." J.D. Meier from Microsoft says, "What makes self-leadership so powerful is that it applies to you. It's personal. It's you at your best. Self-leadership is a way to lead yourself from the inside out...."*
>
> —(Meier).[1]

I hope you understand self-leadership and its benefits, so I will briefly define the seven self-leadership practices in this chapter. These practices form the self-leadership development framework, which, as I indicated in the Introduction, offers the blueprint for guiding and informing you on your leadership journey.

In Parts II and III, each practice is devoted to two chapters. The first chapter defines the practice, drawing on relevant perspectives from research. The second chapter offers practical tools for each practice. The appendices are diagnostics designed to assist you in gaining further insight into your development. Part II focuses on four practices in the framework classified as The Inner Game. Part III examines the other three practices impacting The Outer Game.

Figure 2.1 is the Self-leadership Development Framework.

Figure 2.1 Self-leadership development framework

Why seven practices? Why these practices? Moreover, why this sequence? These are the questions I will address first. I have explored the research and identified the most mentioned practices of self-leadership. That does not mean that other practices beyond these seven are not relevant. However, the journey of self-leadership development must begin somewhere. My framework offers a manageable plan of action for your personal growth.

You will notice that the seven practices are in two rows—four in the top and three in the bottom. I have made a broad distinction between the personal and interpersonal practices of self-leadership. Personal practices originate from inner reflection and self-examination. For instance, to *Build Strengths*, one must reflect on their innate talents before turning them into strengths. I refer to these personal practices illustrated in the top row as The Inner Game; they originate from personal reflection. As illustrated in Figure 2.1, The Inner Game practices are *Know Thyself, Discover True North, Build Strengths*, and *Keep Growing*.

Interpersonal self-leadership practices directly on others. Moreover, they influence the quality of a leader's working relationship with those they interact with. For instance, to *Be Curious*, a leader typically asks questions of others. The three practices in the bottom row of the framework are The Outer Game; that is, they affect interpersonal interactions. *Show Intent, Self-Regulate*, and *Be Curious* make up The Outer Game.

The seven practices combine personal and interpersonal traits. However, all these practices start from within. Applying the three practices of The Outer Game openly affects the quality of a leader's interpersonal interactions. Using the four practices of The Inner Game will also impact working relationships, but more indirectly. Each practice is a mix of personal and interpersonal orientation.

However, in the interests of clarity, we will look at each practice separately. It will be easier to apply each practice consciously.

The bottom line: All seven practices are relevant to your leadership growth and development.

There is some logic in the framework's sequence of going from left to right. Each practice builds upon the previous practices to some extent. For example, being more self-aware (Know Thyself) is the basis for being transparent about leadership priorities (Discover True North). However, given that all seven practices are relevant, you can begin your personal leadership journey anywhere in the framework.

For the remainder of this chapter, I will briefly define each practice in the self-leadership development framework's sequence.

Know Thyself

Know Thyself (being self-aware) is an ancient aphorism attributed to several Greek philosophers, including Socrates, Pythagoras, and Chilon of Sparta. The saying originated in ancient Greece and has been widely used in diverse cultures.

Self-awareness is consciously recognizing and understanding one's thoughts, emotions, strengths, weaknesses, values, and behaviors. Knowing oneself involves an ongoing, reflective process where one gains insights into one's motivations and reactions. Self-awareness is foundational to self-leadership, enabling one to make purposeful decisions, set meaningful goals, and successfully navigate challenges.

One of the primary benefits of practicing self-awareness is identifying and leveraging your talents (Build Strengths). By understanding your unique skills and capabilities, you can use these assets intentionally. Simultaneously, heightened self-awareness helps you to recognize areas for improvement. This can be a prompt for learning and development (Keep Growing).

Self-awareness is central to emotional intelligence (EQ). Individuals who cultivate greater self-awareness can easily navigate their emotions (Self-Regulate). With greater emotional resilience, one can make better decisions under pressure. Also, with heightened self-awareness, a leader can empathize with team members' perspectives, strengthening interpersonal relationships and team dynamics.

Self-awareness also plays a crucial role in goal setting (Show Intent). Individuals who understand their values can align them with their goals. In other words, a self-aware leader can pursue a path that resonates with their authentic selves (Discover True North). This alignment fosters a sense of purpose and fulfillment, driving sustained motivation. Knowing oneself is a transformative journey that equips you to lead yourself and others with authenticity, resilience, and purpose. Knowing oneself enhances personal and professional growth, positively influences decisions, and creates a supportive and high-performing work environment.

Know Thyself is the first practice of the Inner Game in the self-leadership development framework and is covered in Chapters 3 and 4.

Discover True North

Discover True North involves individuals identifying and aligning their core values and personal vision with their thoughts and actions. True North serves as an internal compass, guiding leaders in decision-making, goal-setting, and overall direction. This practice is rooted in the idea that authentic leadership is about knowing and behaving consistently with one's fundamental principles and aspirations.

The practice of Discover True North begins with introspection and reflection (Know Thyself). Self-discovery unearths the values and guiding principles that resonate with the leader. A deeper self-understanding is the basis upon which they can lead themselves and others.

One of the primary benefits of discovering one's true north is the clarity and consistency it brings to a leader's decision-making. Leaders who live by their values and mission make choices consistent with their authentic selves. Apart from the personal satisfaction this brings, true north also contributes to integrity and trustworthiness in the leader's working relationships (Show Intent).

Another benefit of this practice is setting meaningful goals. By knowing their true north, leaders can establish objectives that resonate with their values and contribute to their overarching purpose. Discovering their genuine north fosters commitment to their goals and direction, providing purpose and motivation to team members.

What is more, this practice builds resilience in the face of adversity. When leaders encounter obstacles, the clarity of their guiding principles helps them stay focused and navigate difficulties with clarity and determination (Self-Regulation).

The practice of Discover True North empowers one to lead oneself authentically, make aligned decisions, set meaningful goals, and navigate challenges with resilience. This practice contributes to a more purposeful and fulfilling personal and professional life.

Discover True North is the second practice of the Inner Game in the framework and is covered in Chapters 5 and 6.

Build Strengths

Building strengths involves deliberately identifying, developing, and leveraging unique talents. Instead of dwelling on weaknesses, this practice encourages individuals to build upon their capabilities to maximize personal and professional effectiveness. Build Strengths, apart from the intentional efforts to amplify one's innate talents, encompasses self-awareness (Know Thyself) and continuous learning (Keep Growing).

One of the primary benefits of building strengths is optimizing a leader's performance. By understanding and emphasizing their natural aptitudes, leaders can excel in tasks and responsibilities consistent with their strengths. This boosts confidence, increases motivation, and fosters a sense of accomplishment.

Furthermore, this practice builds self-esteem. As leaders exercise their strengths, they develop a deeper appreciation for their unique qualities and contributions. This self-affirmation engenders a more positive outlook, builds resilience in adversity, and encourages the leader to take on new opportunities.

Leveraging one's strengths is instrumental in career development. Individuals who focus on building strengths often find themselves in roles that allow them to use their talents. This alignment inevitably increases job satisfaction and overall fulfillment.

A strength-based leadership approach encourages collaboration. Team members often recognize and capitalize on each other's strengths by setting an example. This is the basis for creating a synergistic and high-performing team.

Build Strengths is an initiative-taking strategy for continuous improvement (Keep Growing). By investing time and effort in honing personal talents, you are positioning yourself for long-term success, personal growth, and heightened job satisfaction. Ultimately, building on strengths is the catalyst for realizing one's full potential.

Build Strengths is the third practice of The Inner Game, covered in Chapters 7 and 8.

Keep Growing

Know Thyself, Discover True North, and Build Strengths are practices under the fourth practice: Keep Growing. Growing oneself involves continuous learning, self-improvement, and personal development. It means embracing new experiences, seeking feedback, and acquiring new skills and knowledge to improve ourselves. Keep Growing requires a willingness to step out of one's comfort zone, take prudent risks, and be open to new perspectives and ideas.

Leaders committed to personal growth and development have what Carol Dweck (2008) calls a *growth mindset*.[2] A growth mindset is a belief that one can improve one's skills and abilities through dedication and hard work. Someone with a growth mindset, distinct from a fixed mindset, seeks new opportunities to gain experience. Learning experiences include participating in training programs, seeking feedback from others, reading books, and self-reflection.

Having a growth mindset has multiple benefits. For instance, it encourages leaders to become more self-aware, builds resilience, and improves decision-making. A continuously growing leader adapts quicker in a world of constant and accelerated change. They also inspire their team members to grow and develop.

Keep Growing is The Inner Game's fourth and final practice, covered in Chapters 9 and 10.

Where the Rubber Meets the Road

Overcoming Adversity

Jane is a memorable coaching client. She was a successful corporate executive for 10 years in the building industry. Jane was well respected by her colleagues and had a reputation for being a skilled leader with a strong work ethic. However, her life took a sudden turn when she was diagnosed with a severe medical condition that required extensive treatment and recovery time.

After her diagnosis, Jane faced the challenge of managing her health while maintaining her career and leadership responsibilities. She took a leave of absence from work and underwent several surgeries and months of treatment, which left her physically weak and emotionally drained. Jane also struggled with the fear and uncertainty of not knowing whether she would be able to return to work.

Despite her challenges, Jane showed remarkable self-leadership in overcoming her adversity. She sought support from her family and friends, who provided emotional care and encouragement. Jane collaborated closely with her medical team to develop a treatment plan that would allow her to manage her health while gradually returning to work.

Throughout her recovery, Jane remained focused on her personal and professional goals. It was inspirational for me to watch her recovery. She maintained an optimistic attitude and worked tirelessly to regain strength and stamina. Jane also continued to stay informed about developments in her industry, even while she was away from work. Jane recovered and could return to work thanks to her

> perseverance and determination. She resumed her leadership role with renewed energy and enthusiasm, and her resilience and cheerful outlook inspired her colleagues. This testing experience gave Jane a new perspective on leadership. She began to place a greater emphasis on supporting the well-being of her team members, recognizing that personal challenges can affect anyone at any time.
>
> Jane's experience demonstrates the importance of self-leadership in overcoming adversity. By maintaining a cheerful outlook, seeking support, and staying focused on her goals, she overcame a significant challenge and returned to her career with renewed purpose and passion. Jane's leadership style also evolved as she recognized the importance of supporting the well-being of her team members, and she became an even stronger leader because of her experience.
>
> She is an inspiration to me.

I will now briefly define the three practices of The Outer Game in the self-leadership development framework.

Show Intent

Show Intent involves purposefully communicating and demonstrating one's intentions, values, and objectives. This practice emphasizes transparency, authenticity, and clearly articulating the leader's goals and direction.

One of the primary benefits of Showing Intent is establishing trust and credibility with those they lead. By openly sharing one's intentions and values, the leader demonstrates transparency, which is the basis for building constructive working relationships. Trust and consistency are built when team members understand a leader's motivations and goals.

Clear communication of a direction also contributes to aligning the needs and interests of team members and the leader. In other words, when the team understands the leader's overarching purpose, individual efforts emphasize that purpose—it then becomes a shared purpose. Show Intent promotes collaboration, lessens misunderstandings, and supports a unified approach.

Further, having a clear intention guides the evaluation of options and decision-making. A leader who is explicit about their plans is likelier to make choices consistent with their purpose. Clarity helps to navigate complexity.

Demonstrating intent inspires and motivates others. When a leader communicates their vision and values, it creates a sense of purpose that can galvanize their team. A positive, crystal-clear intention is bound to be inspirational—it engages the hearts and minds of others to contribute their best.

Ultimately, Show Intent builds better working relationships, facilitates alignment, guides decision-making, and inspires others.

Show Intent is the first practice of The Outer Game and is covered in Chapters 11 and 12.

Self-Regulate

Self-regulation involves the conscious management and control of one's emotions, behaviors, and reactions. This practice is about developing emotional intelligence (EQ) and applying strategies to stay composed, focused, and resilient in facing challenges and adversity.

One primary benefit of self-regulation is emotional resilience—individuals who regulate their emotions better manage stress, setbacks, and uncertainties. Staying calm under pressure allows one to think more clearly, make rational decisions, and navigate tricky situations with composure. Self-regulation contributes to well-being and mental health.

Furthermore, self-regulation enriches interpersonal relationships. A leader who can manage their emotional state is less likely to react to team members impulsively or negatively. This builds better working relationships through effective communication and the flexibility to resolve conflict and disagreements. A leader who is more mindful of their feelings and how they respond to stressful situations can facilitate a more harmonious and calmer workplace.

Self-regulation is also integral to other practices in the framework. For instance, being calmer under pressure requires self-awareness (Know Thyself) and helps maintain a consistent approach to setting and achieving goals (Show Intent). The ability to regulate one's emotions and behavior permeates everything we do.

So, the Self-Regulation practice should be taken seriously, as it often is. Leaders who can regulate their emotions inspire confidence and trust in those they work with. They model EQ, create a positive culture, and set the right tone for tackling challenges.

In summary, self-regulation empowers a leader to navigate challenges with emotional resilience, fosters positive relationships, and aids in achieving personal and professional goals. This practice is a cornerstone of effective leadership and individual well-being.

Self-regulation is The Outer Game's second practice, covered in Chapters 13 and 14.

Be Curious

Being curious involves a mindset of exploration, inquiry, and openness to learning. This practice includes seeking knowledge, asking questions, and approaching situations inquiringly. The practice of Be Curious is fundamental for personal and professional growth (Keep Growing), the ability to adapt, and continually improve.

One of the primary benefits of curiosity is that it can stimulate innovation and continuous improvement. Curiousness fuels innovative ideas, perspectives, and solutions. Leaders who approach challenges with a curious mindset are more likely to discover novel approaches that challenge the status quo.

Being curious is also a stimulus for learning (Keep Growing). A leader seeking knowledge and understanding can adapt to volatility, uncertainty, complexity, and ambiguity (VUCA).[3] In short, the leader stays relevant.

A leader's problem-solving capability strengthens through the practice of Being Curious. Curious leaders analyze situations critically, consider alternative viewpoints, and find innovative solutions. Furthermore, a mindset of exploration and inquiry boosts resilience in the face of a challenge (Self-Regulation). In these testing times, the leader is receptive to experimenting, learning from failures, and questioning how things are done conventionally.

The curious leader is more open to hearing and appreciating diverse perspectives within their team. This openness promotes inclusivity and more contributions, building stronger relationships within the team.

In summary, the practice of Being Curious sparks creativity, continuous learning, adaptability, and effective problem-solving. It instills a collective mindset that values exploration and a willingness to look for better answers to the inevitable challenges in the ever-changing workplace.

Be Curious is the framework's third and final practice of The Outer Game, covered in Chapters 15 and 16.

I am sure you recognize some of these traits in yourself and others. consistent with each of these descriptors.

In Part II, we begin with the four practices of The Inner Game, beginning with Know Thyself.

Top 10 Points

1. Seven practices form the self-leadership development framework.
2. The framework offers a manageable action plan for your personal development.
3. Personal practices are defined as methods that originate from inner reflection and self-examination, and interpersonal practices directly impact others.
4. Know Thyself is consciously recognizing and understanding one's thoughts, emotions, strengths, weaknesses, values, and behaviors.
5. Discover True North involves individuals identifying and aligning their core values and personal vision with their thoughts and actions.
6. Build Strengths involves deliberately identifying, developing, and leveraging strengths and talents.
7. Keep Growing involves continuous learning, self-improvement, and personal development.
8. Show Intent involves purposefully communicating and demonstrating one's intentions, values, and objectives.

9. Self-regulation involves the conscious management and control of one's emotions, behaviors, and reactions.
10. Be Curious involves a mindset of exploration, inquiry, and openness to learning.

PART II
The Inner Game

CHAPTER 3

Practice # 1: Know Thyself

The key to self-improvement is doing rather than knowing. However, doing so can be the tricky part.

Two thousand five hundred years ago, someone inscribed "Know thyself" on a column at the Temple of Apollo in Delphi, where the Pythian priestesses famously uttered their prophecies. Socrates, one priestess who claimed to be the wisest man in the world, discussed his maxim with his pupils Xenophon and Plato. Socrates told his students that knowing thyself was a worthy substitute for subordinating oneself to the gods. This formed the foundation for the modern virtues of self-awareness. Today, self-awareness—or metacognition, as psychologists and neuroscientists call it—is just as applicable, especially for leaders (Kinni, 2021).[1]

Most people ponder how well they know themselves at various stages of their lives. Self-awareness is a noticeable trait we all possess, although it is harder to attain than we think. People usually overestimate the extent of their self-awareness. At the end of their Personal Leadership and Change unit, one of my mature MBA students said, "I thought I knew myself pretty well before this course, but I now realize that I still have a lot to learn."

In-depth self-awareness means knowing our deepest thoughts, desires, emotions, character traits, values, what makes us happy, and why we think and do what we believe (Cassam 2014). Is a deep understanding of ourselves necessary to be a good leader? Yes, it is. In this chapter, we explore why it is. The next chapter will look at practical ways to build self-awareness.

As stated in the vignette at the start of the chapter, Socrates created the phrase *know thyself*, which was the beginning of Western philosophy as we know it. Knowing thyself is undoubtedly Socrates' most significant legacy. When Socrates' name is mentioned, this saying immediately comes to mind.

However, the famous movie *The Matrix* prompted Generation X to think about their lives in the context of reality. In *The Matrix*, Morpheus (played by Lawrence Fishburne) is an inspirational leader and influential teacher to people, particularly those in his crew. Morpheus displays some rationality in dangerous situations rather than mindlessly navigating the crisis with a gut feeling. This characterization inspired a generation to consider what is more important: knowing oneself or being oneself. Or is it both?

Socrates's saying, "Know thyself," has echoed through the annals of history. It succinctly captures the essence of self-leadership. These two simple words describe a profound truth about the value of self-awareness and personal growth.

By delving into the voyage of self-discovery and self-mastery, one can unlock one's full potential, make informed decisions, and inspire others to follow their lead. Knowing who one is and what makes one tick enhances the quality of one's life.

Metacognition

Psychologists use the term *metacognition* for self-awareness. Fleming (2021), author of *Know Thyself: The Science of Self-Awareness,* defines metacognition as "our mind's ability to reflect on, think about, and know things about itself, including how it remembers, perceives, decides, thinks, and feels."[2] Metacognition is the ability to think about one's thinking.

Metacognition is based on two distinct and interdependent processes built into our brain's circuitry. One method is unconscious and assesses uncertainty for survival. The other process is conscious and monitoring our internal state and behaviors. Fleming likens these two processes to flying a plane.

The unconscious process is the autopilot system. Moreover, the conscious process is the pilot manually flying the plane. The pilot monitors and adjusts the autopilot's actions. Similarly, our implicit (unconscious) and explicit (conscious) metacognition interact and work together. The difference between flying a plane and human interaction is that metacognition occurs within a single brain.

Even though our brains are equipped and capable of metacognition, we are better at self-awareness than we would like to think we are. Franklin (2018), in the 1750 edition of *Poor Richard's Almanack*, aptly stated, "There are three things extremely hard: steel, a diamond, and to know oneself."[3] Developing deep self-awareness is difficult because we filter our thoughts through numerous cognitive biases.

We humans can entertain approximately 200 cognitive biases. A cognitive bias is a systematic pattern of deviation from rational judgment (Haselton et al. 2005).[4] We create our subjective reality by filtering the input from our five senses. Our construction of reality—not the objective truth—dictates our response and behavior.

For example, I might *see* two people pointing fingers at each other and *hear* their raised voices outside a conference room. I immediately interpreted this as an argument and approached them to be the peacemaker. Subsequently, I discover that they are not fighting. They informed me that they were role-playing an argument from a workshop on dealing with conflict in the conference room. Laughter all around and a dose of embarrassment from me!

These misinterpretations based on cognitive biases occur every day. Sometimes, we become aware of our misinterpretations, like in the example above, but often, we are oblivious to these biases. The problem when we are unaware of these biases is that we assume that we are sensing objective truth. We take our senses for granted—we believe we are experiencing reality. Our misinterpretations—based on cognitive biases—therefore go unchallenged. That is why self-awareness is more complex than we think.

A cognitive bias leads to perceptual distortion, inaccurate judgment, illogical interpretation, and irrationality (Kahneman and Tversky 1972).[5] Nobel Prize winner Kahneman (2011) issues this warning in his book *Thinking, Fast and Slow*: "Our comforting conviction that the world makes sense rests on a secure foundation: our almost unlimited ability to ignore our ignorance."[6]

Studies have connected metacognitive ability and leadership performance (Black 2016).[7] Specifically, metacognition positively stimulates creative problem-solving, decision-making, critical thinking, and learning. Harvard Business School professor Fubini (2020) describes a costly illustration of lacking self-awareness in his book *Hidden Truths: What Leaders Need to Hear but Are Rarely Told*.[8]

CEOs can mistime their departures and subsequently get fired by their boards. We assume that executives who are savvy enough to reach the top of the company pyramid have a very sophisticated and objective understanding of their position and situational awareness. This common assumption about senior executives is a cognitive bias in itself! Fubini states that "the system is far more critical of CEOs than they believe it to be." Why? He points to cognitive blinders such as ego, denial, optimism, and hubristic pride as the reasons CEOs misjudge the timing of their company exit.

Some spend endless hours and thousands of dollars getting to know themselves better. They climb mountains, run marathons, take drugs, meditate, read self-help books, and do courses. Through these and other experiences, people strive to come face-to-face with themselves. Many tests and profiles help people discover their strengths and weaknesses. The excess of personality profiles suggests that we are hungry for self-knowledge. However, how does this knowledge and a more profound self-understanding help?

There is a difference between acquiring more self-understanding and applying that wisdom. What do we do—if anything—with heightened self-awareness? The key to self-improvement is not just *knowing* but *using* it. However, doing is the problematic part.

Where the Rubber Meets the Road

Setting an Intention

In one of the units I teach in the MBA (Personal Leadership and Change), students complete a battery of profiles, assessments, 360° feedback, and diagnostics. The purpose is to help my mature-age

> students know themselves better. Furthermore, this approach enables the students to set an intention. In other words, this voyage of discovery is to help them determine what they want. What is important to them? What do they value? How do they want to show up as a leader? How can they be a better leader? Our intentions should not be confused with what people think they want, what society expects, or what others want from us. What are our values, strengths, and opportunities for growth? Moreover, how can we harness this self-knowledge to be an exceptional leader? These are the questions I challenge my students with.

Being True to Oneself

Knowing oneself is the beginning of *understanding* what one *wants*. Moreover, when you are clear on what you want, you will recognize and attract opportunities to express this intention. However, most live in the shadow of how others expect us to live. More specifically, most people conform in ways they think will please their parents, family, friends, and even people they do not know. Nonetheless, we live in our mind and body from birth to death. It is we whom we must ultimately satisfy.

I think this is worth pondering for a moment.

Please understand what I am saying. I am not suggesting that you and I should be selfish and self-centered, ignoring everyone's opinion of us. We should be aware of others' views and feedback. Listen to it. However, ultimately, we should strive for what Abraham Maslow calls *self-actualization*.[9] Couture and colleagues (2007) define self-actualization as "the psychological process to maximize the use of a person's abilities and resources. This process may vary from one person to another."[10] Ironically, it is only by investing time and energy to know our true essence that we can genuinely serve others.

So, I encourage you to honestly appraise how congruent your life is—with what renowned psychologist and author Boyatzis (2006) calls —your *ideal self*.[11] Just as a champion athlete prepares for competition by visualizing themselves performing at their peak, there is power in you focusing on your perfect state of leadership. Research shows that if people create an image of their ideal self and practice visualizing it, they develop a deep emotional commitment to that state (Boyatzis).[12]

What is your ideal self?

If you start with a clean sheet of paper and design the life you would like, is it congruent with how you live? Clarify your purpose. Set an intent to know yourself at a deeper level. With the development of a razor-sharp purpose, pay attention to what starts to happen. You will undoubtedly be pleasantly surprised. With greater clarity, you see opportunities, ideas, and people that will assist you with your stated purpose. Like Socrates, lead your life your way.

Where do you start this journey of self-discovery?

Knowing oneself has five dimensions:

- self-awareness
- self-improvement
- authenticity
- emotional intelligence (EQ)
- resilience.

Let us briefly consider each dimension.

Self-Awareness

Self-awareness lies at the core of self-knowledge. It recognizes and understands one's thoughts, emotions, strengths, and weaknesses. Self-awareness begins with a genuine and honest look within, acknowledging both the light and dark aspects of one's personality. This can be confronting.

Self-awareness takes contemplation and courage. Deeper self-awareness means having insight into your strengths, weaknesses, values, passions, and purpose. With deeper insight, one is more attuned to one's emotions and motivations and knows why one feels this way. This greater understanding allows one to make deliberate choices that align with one's authentic self.

Self-Improvement

Self-improvement unleashes potential and builds on self-awareness. Self-improvement is about personal growth and development. It enables you to capitalize on your abilities and talents and develop areas of weakness. A leader committed to self-improvement believes in and is open to constructive feedback as an opportunity to gain experience. They view constructive criticism as a vehicle to be a better and more inspiring leader. A leader dedicated to self-improvement is a lifelong learner.

Authenticity

Being open to personal growth and development means being true to oneself. *Authenticity* also builds trust with others. People are comfortable in their skin when they understand themselves and their motivations. Authentic leaders are truthful and honest with themselves and have strong moral principles.

Authenticity means integrity, and this quality fosters real bonds with others. We are drawn to leaders who are transparent, exhibit integrity, and walk the talk. An authentic leader encourages team members to be open and honest, too. In other words, they create a supportive workplace where others feel safe expressing themselves and their ideas.

Emotional Intelligence (EQ)

Authenticity is characteristic of high EQ. An individual with elevated EQ knows themselves and can regulate their emotions. EQ is the ability to understand and manage one's emotional state while being perceptive of the feelings of others. Therefore, a leader with high EQ can better navigate conflict, inspire and motivate others, and nurture a positive work environment. When you are aware of your emotional triggers, you respond rather than react to challenging situations. Responding means making well-informed decisions and observations that combine rationality and empathy.

Resilience

EQ strengthens resilience, which helps with coping with obstacles and overcoming adversity. Resilience is the ability to bounce back from setbacks. A resilient leader faces obstacles and challenges with courage and determination. Resilient leaders respond constructively to unanticipated setbacks and proactively identify and address risks, vulnerabilities, and disruptions. In other words, they develop the ability to navigate uncertainty and change effectively.

To do this, the resilient leader cultivates a culture of flexibility and agility within their team. This attitude enables their team members to respond swiftly to unexpected events and capitalize on emerging opportunities. Briefly, a resilient leader assists their team in thriving in uncertain times.

Socrates' ancient adage of *knowing thyself* holds timeless wisdom and remains just as relevant today. It is a crucial trait of self-leadership. By applying the dimensions of self-awareness, self-improvement, authenticity, emotional intelligence, and resilience, you lay a solid foundation for practicing self-leadership. Developing greater self-understanding empowers you to make conscious decisions, build meaningful relationships, and unlock your true potential. As you traverse the VUCA world, remember the profound significance of Socrates' maxim. For within self-discovery lies the power to lead and inspire others.

In the next chapter, we look at four strategies to develop these five dimensions of knowing oneself.

Top 10 Points

1. In-depth self-awareness means knowing our deepest thoughts, desires, emotions, character traits, values, what makes us happy, and why we think and do what we believe and do.
2. Psychologists use the term metacognition for self-awareness.
3. Many studies have connected metacognitive ability and leadership performance.
4. Knowing oneself is the beginning of knowing what one wants.

5. Knowing oneself has five dimensions: self-awareness, self-improvement, authenticity, emotional intelligence, and resilience.
6. Self-awareness lies at the core of knowing oneself.
7. Self-improvement unleashes potential and builds on self-awareness.
8. Being open to personal growth and development means being authentic.
9. Authenticity is characteristic of high emotional intelligence.
10. Emotional intelligence improves one's resilience.

CHAPTER 4

Four Simple and Proven Ways to Develop Self-Awareness

Self-awareness is a prerequisite for all personal growth.

The aftermath of the World Health Organization (WHO) declaring COVID-19 a pandemic was distressing for humanity. We all will have vivid memories of this pivotal time in history. Against the backdrop of the disease and the economic impact, the world has witnessed racial injustice and natural disasters.

For many people worldwide, it has been challenging to stay emotionally afloat. Even the U.S. Centers for Disease Control and Prevention (CDC) has published guidelines regarding coping, with suggestions ranging from engaging in leisure activities and taking social media breaks to getting sufficient sleep and eating right. One recommendation on the CDC list is journaling (Feldman 2020).[1]

How does one develop deeper self-awareness? Four simple and proven ways are journaling, practicing mindfulness, seeking feedback, and personality profiling. Some may be appealing, others not so. You do not need to do them all to increase your self-awareness, but you should do one or two. All four are valid and effective. We will cover these four reputable approaches in this chapter.

Let us start with the one often overlooked or dismissed strategy: Journaling.

Journaling

Journaling is extensively researched in several fields, including psychology. Studies suggest that the practice of journaling does improve self-awareness (Baikie and Wilhelm 2005).[2] The benefits of journaling are:

- Increased self-reflection;
- An effective way to process negative emotions;
- A technique for unearthing obscure thoughts and beliefs;
- A way to clarify goals and values, monitoring personal growth;
- Reducing stress and enhancing well-being.

Journaling is a tool for self-reflection, which is the beginning of self-awareness. By writing about your thoughts, feelings, and experiences, you can gain valuable insights about yourself and how you think.

For instance, leaders can process and manage their emotional state more effectively by journaling their thoughts and feelings before or after a stressful business meeting. As author Natalie Goldberg puts it, "Whether you're keeping a journal or writing as a meditation, it is the same thing. What's important is you are having a relationship with your mind" (Fain 2017).[3] Dr. Jennifer Williamson says, "Journal writing, when it becomes a ritual for transformation, is not only life-changing but life-expanding" (Heimbigner 2023).[4] By converting your emotions into words, you gain clarity about your feelings, identify patterns or triggers, and develop a more objective understanding of your experiences.

Journaling provides a safe and private space for freely expressing ourselves without fear of judgment. This process can lead to a greater sense of authenticity and self-expression, enabling one to explore and understand one's unique perspectives, values, and desires (Andersen 2023).[5]

Despite these proven benefits, I have discovered that journaling is only for some. However, for others, putting their thoughts down on paper or in a Word document can detach them from thoughts, feelings, or emotions. The journal writer can observe these thoughts through more objective eyes and, therefore, either learn something new or gain greater insight into their thoughts and behaviors. Even if journaling is not your thing, it is a robust process.

How does one begin? If journaling is new to you, start small. Even one journaling session a week can build a valuable habit of self-reflection that will positively impact your life. For example, sit down on Sunday evenings and think about what went well and what went wrong in the past week. What successes should you acknowledge, and what do you want to improve next week? There are no fixed rules about what you write, how you write, or how long you write.

Think about successes and failures. Covering both is essential because journaling is about being honest with oneself. Günel (2018), in her article, *The Power of Journaling*, suggests that apart from reflecting on the week, journaling can be used to express gratitude, learn from daily events, or explore emotions.[6] Once you get used to journaling once a week, you might want to write more frequently.

If you still need to do so, you can try journaling. There is no prescriptive time throughout the day or formula. Just give it a go with an open mind. You might be pleasantly surprised.

> ## Where the Rubber Meets the Road
>
> **Journaling and Immunity**
>
> Research by Pennebaker and Smyth (2016) in their book *Opening Up by Writing it Down: How Expressive Writing Improves Health and Eases Emotional Pain* suggests that writing about emotions and stress can boost immune functioning in patients with illnesses such as HIV/AIDS, asthma, and arthritis. Other research by Pennebaker indicates that suppressing negative, trauma-related thoughts compromises immune functioning and that those who write visit the doctor less often.[7]

Mindfulness

What is mindfulness, and how can it help you become a better leader? Mindfulness intentionally focuses on the present moment while calmly and nonjudgmentally acknowledging and accepting thoughts, feelings, and bodily sensations. Rather than being mindful, we are mindless most of the time!

We often dwell on the past or contemplate the future. However, the past is gone. All we can do constructively with our past is learn from it. Furthermore, the future has yet to arrive. The only practical thing we can do for the future is plan for it. As Tolle (2014), the author of *The Power of Now: A Guide to Spiritual Enlightenment*, says eloquently, "The present moment is all you ever have. There is never a time when your life is not 'this moment.'"[8]

Mindful leadership means being fully present, attentive, open, and purposeful. Learning to be more wholly present allows you to be more aware of your strengths, weaknesses, values, and emotions. A mindful leader recognizes their biases, emotional triggers, and automatic thinking and behavior patterns.

Practicing mindfulness involves developing a nonjudgmental awareness of the present moment. While there are many techniques and exercises for obtaining this state, here are six simple practices that are easy to apply on a busy day. Try one or more of these.

Mindful breathing is an excellent place to start. Before, after, or even during your day, find a quiet and comfortable place to sit or lie down. Close your eyes and bring your attention to your breath. Notice the sensation of the breath as you inhale and exhale. Focus on the physical sensations of breathing, such as the rise and fall of your abdomen or the air passing through your nostrils. When your mind wanders, as it inevitably will, gently brings your attention back to the breath without judgment. This is a straightforward way to center yourself before an important meeting or presentation.

Another helpful exercise is a *body scan*. Lie or sit comfortably and focus on various body parts, from your toes to your head. Notice any sensations, tensions, or relaxation areas without trying to change anything. Observe. The body scan helps us relax and be more present.

You can focus your attention on something external to your body —this is called *mindful observation*. Choose an object in your surroundings, such as a flower, a piece of fruit, or a painting. Please direct your attention to the object, observing its color, shape, texture, and other details. Engage your senses fully, viewing without judgment or interpretation. Allow yourself to be fully present with the object for a few minutes. Mindful observation helps you to be more observant and appreciative of your surroundings.

If you like walking for exercise, try doing it mindfully. Take a walk in a quiet and peaceful environment, preferably in nature. As you walk, pay attention to the sensation of your feet touching the ground, the movement of your body, and the sights and sounds around you. Be fully present in the experience of walking rather than getting lost in thoughts or distractions. *Mindful walking* allows you to practice being more present while you exercise.

What about *mindful eating*? Instead of chopping your food down quickly without appreciating it, observe the food closely, noticing its color, texture, and aroma before eating. Take small bites and chew slowly, savoring each bite mindfully. Notice the taste, the sensations in your mouth, and the act of swallowing. Be fully present and engaged in the experience of eating.

My favorite is *mindfulness meditation*. Set aside a specific time for meditation, starting with a few minutes and gradually increasing its duration. Find a quiet place to sit comfortably and focus on your breath, a specific object, or a meditation phrase (mantra). There are a host of apps and books that can guide you. Whenever your mind wanders, gently bring your attention back to the focal point without judging or criticizing your inevitable drifting.

Think of your mind wandering and bringing it back to the present like a bicep curl repetition. Each rep strengthens your arms, just as bringing your mind back to the present strengthens your ability to be in the moment more often.

Improving your ability to be in the moment is a skill that requires practice and patience. Our minds are averagely prone to wandering during these practices and in daily life. With training, you become more aware of being mindless—without being self-critical—and can gently redirect your attention to the present.

Establish a regular mindfulness practice that starts with short sessions and gradually increases in duration. Additionally, attending mindfulness workshops and courses or seeking guidance from experienced meditation teachers can provide further support and advice. Mindfulness is the ultimate pathway to developing deeper self-awareness.

Seeking Feedback

Another way to improve self-awareness is to observe how others respond to you daily. Seeking feedback is a valuable way to review your communication effectiveness.

Enlist an objective observer or two. Finding observers (your team members) willing to tell you what they see objectively or truthfully can be challenging. Direct reports or colleagues will only sometimes give you candid feedback. Besides, just like you, they have their own cognitive biases. Finding someone who tells it straight—or at least gives you a unique perspective—can be valuable. Alternatively, find a mentor or coach who will be truthful with you. It is beneficial to find a group of trusted advisors. Your spouse or children can sometimes be brutally honest, I have discovered!

In my coaching sessions, I encourage leaders to practice observing their impact on others. How are team members and colleagues behaving? Are they compliant or defiant? Are team members leaning forward or sitting back in meetings? Do they take notes, make eye contact, and listen to what you say? Observing these verbal and nonverbal cues can be insightful. The challenge is to observe without judgment.

Self-awareness is a prerequisite for all personal growth. If you are unaware of how you show up compared to how you intend to, there is no basis for improvement. The risk is that we assume we know how we are coming across to others, only to discover later that it is different from what we intended. For instance, how often have you thought you conveyed a message clearly, only to find out later that others were confused? As Theodore Kinni (2021), in his article, *Leader Know Thyself,* succinctly puts it, "Leaders need to know themselves before they can know anything else."[9]

Personality Profiling

Jacob Engel (2019), in his article, *The Third Commandment of Highly Effective Leadership: Know Thyself and Others,* says that leaders need to know themselves in three dimensions: aptitude, attitude, and altitude (EQ).[10] *Aptitude* is one's ability to do something. To understand your aptitude, complete a reputable personality or behavioral profile if you have not already done so. These tools assist you in becoming more aware of your strengths, weaknesses, and blind spots. Understanding your nature and innate personality type can guide your career development. Making informed decisions about career options and opportunities can save you from frustrations and miscalculations. Apart from navigating career choices, I have found that an aptitude profile can be helpful in your personal life.

Most personality profiles are based on the work of noted psychologist Jung (2016), specifically his updated book *Personality Types.* Although Jung's work was controversial at the time—and still is—understanding behavioral types is beneficial personally and interpersonally.

One well-known assessment tool centered on Jung's original idea of personality type is the Myers–Briggs Types Indicator (MBTI). In 1943, Katharine Cook Briggs and her daughter, Isabel Briggs Myers, interpreted Jung's theory into the MBTI. Aside from understanding oneself better, MBTI can also clarify why one may or may not have the necessary aptitude for a particular line of work. Furthermore, this awareness can explain why a person is happy or miserable in their job. Based on Carl Yung's earlier work, MBTI is only one of many personality profiles and behavior indicators.

We have covered four ways to improve self-awareness: journaling, practicing mindfulness, seeking feedback, and personality profiling.

In Appendix A, I have provided you with a personality profile so you can complete it. It is adapted from the work of Littauer (1983), the bestselling author of more than 40 books.[11]

Top 10 Points

1. Four simple and proven ways to develop deeper self-awareness are journaling, practicing mindfulness, seeking feedback, and personality profiling.
2. Research suggests that the practice of journaling does improve self-awareness.
3. Journaling provides a safe and private space for freely expressing ourselves without fearing judgment.
4. Mindfulness intentionally focuses on the present moment while calmly and nonjudgmentally acknowledging and accepting thoughts, feelings, and bodily sensations.
5. Mindful leadership means being fully present, attentive, open, and purposeful.
6. Another way to improve self-awareness is to observe how others respond to oneself in daily interactions.
7. Another way to seek feedback is to enlist an objective observer or two, another helpful strategy.
8. If you have not already done so, complete a reputable personality or behavioral profile to understand your aptitude.
9. Understanding your nature and innate personality type can guide your career development.
10. Most personality profiles are based on the work of noted psychologist Carl Jung.

CHAPTER 5

Practice # 2: Discover True North

...having a clear purpose helps you to focus and maintain motivation, making it easier to overcome obstacles and stay on track.

President John F. Kennedy delivered one of the most historic speeches early in his presidency. He boldly proclaimed that the United States would lead the new adventure into outer space. However, he was specific. His challenge was to be the first to land a human being on the moon before the 1960s ended.

In his landmark speech, Kennedy acknowledged that the top scientists of that time needed to learn how to execute this mission and that the metal that could endure the journey had not even existed. However, Kennedy stated that the United States would go forth into the darkness of the unknown and pursue this goal. It was an inspirational and visionary speech.

Even after Kennedy's assassination three years later, the "We Choose to Go to the Moon" speech lived on as a goal for the nation to focus on. On July 20, 1969, the U.S. Apollo 11 was the first astronaut mission to land on the moon, fulfilling JFK's vision nine years prior.

The Cambridge Dictionary defines *true north* as "the direction towards the top of the earth along an imaginary line at an angle of 90° to the equator."[*] In a leadership context, true north is your orienting point, your fixed point in a spinning world that helps you to stay on track as a leader. The phrase: *discover your true north* was coined by former Medtronic CEO and Harvard professor George (2015) in his bestselling book.[1] It means a leader's true north is a guiding light—like JFK—that keeps them and those they lead facing in the right direction. It is widely recognized as a quality of inspirational leadership.

---

[*]https://dictionary.cambridge.org/dictionary/english/true-north.

Bill George explains that acting consistent with one's true north is about following one's *internal* compass. Like a fixed compass point, your true north pulls you forward in a specific direction. It guides you on your path to your destination, helping you stay on track.

Clarity is an essential practice of self-leadership. It guides you to navigate situations, circumstances, and decisions with focus. Leaders who know their true north can make consistent decisions, prioritize their time, and lead purposefully. This chapter explores the key benefits of clarity (discover true north) and why it matters. In the next chapter, we will consider some ways to find your true north and how you can craft a meaningful leadership purpose statement.

Determining your purpose is the first step to clarity. The objective is paramount to leading oneself and others. Having a clear purpose helps you focus and maintain motivation, making overcoming obstacles easier and staying on course.

Two Forms of Purpose

For your team to flourish, you must repeatedly communicate a sense of purpose and clarity. Purpose comes in two forms. One form is *strategic purpose*. Strategic purpose involves prioritizing where your team's energy should be directed. Two big questions employees want answers to are:

- Where are we headed?
- Why does it matter?

The strategic purpose is to Show Intent, which is Practice #5 in the Show Intent. We cover this type of purpose in The Outer Game in Part III. However, one must first discover one's true north to show intent.

The second form of purpose is your *reason for being*. What is important to you when leading others? What is the legacy you want to leave? This is the type of purpose in your true north.

Discovering True North and Showing Intent are related practices. However, the first is a practice of The Inner Game, and showing Intent is a practice of The Outer Game.

Great leaders always consider the bigger picture strategically (Show Intent) and personally (Discover True North). Strategically, great leaders keep a bird's-eye view of tasks, activities, and events so they do not lose sight of the bigger purpose. However, they also base this vision on a well-honed philosophy of what leadership means to them.

You then become a guide for your team.

Beyond leading others, finding your purpose in life is an intelligent thing to do, irrespective of what you do or who you are. Making sense of the myriad issues you face in life and work is way more challenging without a true north. Discovering true north is a frame of reference—it is seeing the forest before the trees. Without having a true north is like navigating a jungle without a compass.

Where the Rubber Meets the Road

What Do Others Say About Purpose

> The two most important days in your life are the day you are born and the day you discover why.
> —Mark Twain.

> Your work will fill a large part of your life, and the only way to be truly satisfied is to do what you believe is great work. And the only way to do great work is to love what you do.
> —Steve Jobs.

> The purpose of life is not to be happy. It is to be helpful, honorable, compassionate, and have it make some difference that you have lived and lived well.
> —Ralph Waldo Emerson.

> The greatest glory in living lies not in never falling but rising every time we fall.
> —Nelson Mandela.

> The best way to predict the future is to create it.
> —Peter Drucker.

> The only way to do great work is to love what you do.
> —Warren Buffett.
>
> The purpose of our lives is to be happy.
> —Dalai Lama.
>
> Success is not the key to happiness. Happiness is the key to success. If you love what you are doing, you will be successful.
> —Herman Cain.
>
> The purpose of human life is to serve and to show compassion and the will to help others.
> —Albert Schweitzer.
>
> Your purpose in life is to find your purpose and give your whole heart and soul to it.
> —Gautama Buddha.

Discover True North is a good start, but staying focused on that purpose can be challenging. Continuing the jungle metaphor momentarily, the workplace can be like wading through a thick, dark forest. Apart from a compass, it would be best to have a strong flashlight to stay on track. Navigating through trees, fallen branches, and logs toward your destination is part of the journey. In the modern workplace, perpetual challenges, countless issues, missteps, or obstacles are everywhere. These distractions need the leader's attention and can easily divert them.

The essence of steady and true leadership is effectively dealing with distractions while remaining true to one's core values and beliefs. However, without having a true north, it is easy to get waylaid. This is why Discovering True North is part of the framework.

Purpose-Driven Leadership

Unsurprisingly, over the past decade, there has been an explosion of interest in purpose-driven leadership. Compared with the stable and predictable world of the past, functioning in a warp-speed and unpredictable world requires purpose-driven leadership. In our VUCA environment, business experts make the case that purpose is paramount for exceptional performance, while psychologists describe it as the pathway to greater well-being (Craig and Snook 2014).[2]

Moreover, there is evidence that people with a purpose live longer and are less prone to disease. Hill and Turiano (2014) conducted a longitudinal study of 3,253 participants. After an eight-year follow-up, 24.7 percent of the sample died. The analysis revealed that those with the most vital sense of purpose lowered their risk of death by 15.2 percent compared with people with the slightest sense of purpose.[3] So, apart from navigating the increasing complexity and challenges of a VUCA world, health benefits are associated with living a purposeful life.

Despite its escalating relevance, Craig and Snook (2014) from Harvard found that only 20 percent of leaders have a strong sense of purpose.[4] Even fewer could spontaneously articulate their purpose. A purpose is more than a statement like *Helping others be better*. Although a broad purpose is a valuable starting point, it is better if it is specific and tied to one's values. Most leaders must work to discover their purpose.

Furthermore, Craig and Snook point out that not having a clear purpose limits a leader's potential. They state that clarity of purpose is "the most important developmental task you can undertake as a leader."[5] Although a big statement, I know from my experience as an executive coach that highly effective leaders are always clear about their purpose. I, therefore, spend considerable coaching time helping leaders develop their clarity of purpose.

Here are two questions I pose to leaders and want you to think about:

- What legacy do you want to leave behind when you move on from your current leadership role?

- Why should anyone be led by you?[6]

Although a bit confronting, these two questions focus on the mind. Answering them helps you discover your true north and develop your leadership purpose. I will revisit these questions in the next chapter, but please start thinking about the answers for now.

Leadership Purpose Statement

If a business should have a purpose statement, it should be good enough for a leader to have one, too. However, as we have discussed, most leaders still need a purpose statement or even consider developing one. A leader committed to their personal growth will undoubtedly appreciate the value of having a defined purpose. Moreover, a leader with conviction can answer the two questions I ask.

Even with a purpose statement, it is helpful to revisit it occasionally. As our lives and circumstances change, so does our purpose, so refreshing one's purpose statement makes sense.

As Oliver Wendell Holmes reminds us, "Most of us go to our graves with our music still inside us, unplayed." Holmes's bold statement is both terrifying and motivating.

So, what is in a leadership purpose statement?

Craig and Snook (2014) state, "Your leadership purpose is who you are and what makes you distinctive."[7] A leadership purpose statement is not *what* you do.

A test of the authenticity of a leadership purpose statement is that it resonates with you. When you read it, it rings true. It cuts to the core of who you are. Another test is to run the statement by someone who knows you well. I will provide you with more guidance in the next chapter.

Your leadership purpose stems from your identity—the core of who you are. Your purpose is not your job title, educational qualifications, or skillset. For example, I am a management consultant, author, and executive coach with a doctoral degree. However, my leadership purpose statement does not mention any of this. My purpose statement hanging in my office and staring me in the face as I write this is *To enable leaders worldwide to realize their full potential.*

I express my purpose in many ways—speaking, writing, and coaching—drawing on my experience and qualifications. So, when someone asks me what I do, my response is speaker, writer, and author. However, this is not my purpose—they are the vehicles I use to express my purpose.

Some may be cynical about the value of having a leadership purpose statement. Nevertheless, if it is appropriately crafted, it expresses one's true north.

Your statement should be filled with something other than jargon and buzzwords, as they often are. Clichéd words such as *empower* and *value-add* should not be used. The words you choose are specific and personal—they should, as I say, resonate with you. Your purpose statement is not designed to impress others. The only person it should inspire is you.

Designing an inspirational purpose statement takes a little thought and effort. If it were easy, every leader would have one. As I said earlier, only a small percentage of leaders have a clear purpose that guides their daily thinking and actions. However, we are bombarded with the idea that you *must* have a purpose statement. The assumption is that without a purpose, we are somehow underperforming. This is not necessarily true, but purpose statements are in vogue and can be perceived as a fad. This understandably turns off many leaders. It is the same kind of pressure we feel when we are flooded with images on social media of *perfect* bodies and assume that there is something wrong with us if we have more than 10 percent body fat!

Notwithstanding the negativity and cynicism, my experience is that everything you decide to do and think becomes easier when you have a clear sense of who you are (Discover True North). With a clear purpose, everything we say, think, and do has context and meaning.

If you strive to be an exceptional leader—and you should—you must have a crystal-clear purpose. Discovering your true north has a bearing on The Inner and Outer Games. Our personal choices and decisions can be consistent with our purpose. When interacting with others, your team members will feel psychologically safer knowing they are collaborating with a leader who understands and adheres to their true north.

As I said earlier, our purpose evolves and changes throughout our lives. For example, Jasmine is a leader in a highly regulated workplace who is enthusiastic about quality. She has a clear purpose: *To ensure that all systems, processes, and procedures are continuously improved and adhered to*. However, after the birth of her first child, who was born with a disability—something that can happen to any of us in the lottery of life—Jasmine's purpose changed.

She now realizes that leading people is more purposeful than focusing on systems and processes. Her experience raising a disabled child has made her a more compassionate and empathetic leader. Her priority now is her team's needs and interests. Jasmine's purpose has shifted from *improving* systems to *improving* people.

To recap, a leadership purpose statement captures the value you intend to bring to your leadership role. Your leadership purpose is your True North; it prompts you of the most valuable contribution you make as a leader. Discovering True North also provides you with guidance on how to make decisions and prioritize. True North reminds you of what is essential in a VUCA world.

Next, we look at how to create a leadership purpose statement.

Top 10 Points

1. True North is your orienting point, your fixed point in a spinning world, which helps you stay on track as a leader.
2. Clarity is an essential practice of self-leadership—it guides you to navigate situations, circumstances, and decisions with a focus.
3. Purpose comes in two forms. One form is strategic purpose. The second form of purpose is your raison d'etre, meaning reason for being.
4. The essence of steady and true leadership is effectively dealing with distractions while remaining true to one's core values and beliefs.

5. Over the past decade, there has been an explosion of interest in purpose-driven leadership.
6. Evidence shows that people with a purpose live longer and less disease-prone.
7. At most, 20 percent of leaders have a keen sense of purpose.
8. If a business should have a purpose statement, a leader should also have one.
9. A leadership purpose is not what you do as a job but why you lead.
10. Your leadership purpose stems from your identity—the core of who you are.

CHAPTER 6

Why Should You Lead Anyone?

Discover True North clarifies who you are and what you have to offer.

Sarah Adams began her career as a marketing executive in a multinational corporation. While successful by traditional standards, Sarah felt a persistent void in her professional life. Determined to find deeper meaning and make a positive impact, she embarked on a transformative journey to discover her leadership purpose.

Through introspection, self-assessment, and conversations with mentors, Sarah developed her leadership purpose statement: "To enable individuals and teams to unlock their full potential, fostering a culture of growth, collaboration, and innovation."

Sarah's connection to her leadership purpose profoundly impacted her team. Her commitment to developing a culture of growth led to a noticeable increase in engagement, excellent retention, and commitment to professional development. Collaboration within the team strengthened, resulting in improved problem-solving capabilities and better outcomes. The team experienced a surge in creativity and innovation, leading to the successful launch of new products and services.

The intriguing title of this chapter initially comes from a well-known article written by Goffee and Jones (2000) entitled, *Why Should Anyone Be Led by You?*[1] They reinforce the idea that great leaders have a clear vision. In other words, great leaders can answer the question posed by the title of their article. This chapter is designed to help you create a leadership purpose statement.

Crafting a purpose statement is a valuable way to clarify your leadership intentions. The statement should be clear. In this chapter, I will help you narrow your purpose to a single, meaningful statement.

Your Life Story

Reflecting on your life story is one place to start defining your true north. What are the major trends and themes have occurred so far in your life? What are the things you have valued and enjoyed? What events energized you? We discussed the value of journaling in Chapter 4. This might be an excellent place to start journaling. Here are helpful questions to consider:

1. What activities did I love doing as a child?
2. Why did I love doing those activities?
3. What are two or three life-changing experiences I have had?
4. What did I learn from these experiences?
5. How have these experiences shaped me?
6. What is the one thing I enjoy most about my job?

As children, we are drawn to what we love to do. Later in life, we are conditioned by societal norms to conform. For example, our parents might have told us, "It is nice that you want to be an astronaut, but it might be a good idea to be a bit more realistic." Suspend this conditioning for a moment. Putting aside these filters, what did you enjoy doing when you were young?

Stay calm about whether this childhood love translates to leadership. The link between what you loved to do as a child and how it can guide and inform you as a leader is apparent after a while. In my case, there was an obvious connection. As a young child, I enjoyed pretending to be a teacher. I remember play-acting in front of several teddy bears and bossing them around in my bedroom. Fast forward 20 years, and I have commenced a teaching career. I thoroughly enjoy the experience of standing in front of people, presenting concepts, and facilitating learning experiences. The idea of assisting people to improve the quality of their lives has always been appealing to me. What were your childhood passions?

Consider the third, fourth, and fifth questions. What have been pivotal moments in our life? How have these critical incidents shaped you? Major events could be the unexpected death of a family member, losing one's job suddenly, moving countries, or experiencing a once-in-a-lifetime project or opportunity. If we take the time to reflect, these decisive moments teach us lessons.

Question #6 asks you to consider what brings you the most joy at work. Is it interacting with customers? Is it helping team members grow and develop? Is it coaching? Is it the satisfaction of seeing a project through from start to finish? Is it something else?

Research by Yang and Hu (2023) demonstrates a high correlation between what we enjoy and what we are good at.[2] Matching these two attributes is adopting a *strengths-based approach*.[3] Gallup research (2014) has also indicated that people who regularly use their strengths are more engaged, satisfied, and successful in their personal and professional lives.[4] This is because when we use our natural abilities and talents, we are more likely to experience a sense of accomplishment and fulfillment. So, what part of your current job gives you the most satisfaction?

Let us now consider your values and beliefs.

Values and Beliefs

When leaders communicate their values as actions, they are more consistent for themselves and those they lead. Further, when one leads with open values, one can better navigate complexity, make value-based decisions when appropriate, and reduce anxiety. Value-based leadership offers a charter to take appropriate action, make more precise choices, and act consistently and confidently. A value-based leader is transparent. This clarity resonates with those working beside the leader.

Leading with values has two benefits. First, when you are clear about your values, they offer a solid foundation for acting, making decisions, and prioritizing your work. This reference point steers you during tough times when we are being tested and essential decisions must be made. Second, leading with values means you act with integrity. Moreover, being driven by values gives you the strength to change direction when your principles and circumstances are misaligned. Our values inspire us to stay true to who we are and how we appear.

In Appendix B, you will find Brown and Kelly's (1996) *Life Values Inventory*.[5] I strongly urge you to complete this. The inventory will affirm the values that resonate with you.

Our core values tend to be stable throughout our lives, but they are not cast in stone. Values can evolve and change. Living by our values brings greater fulfillment and happiness. However, as I am sure you realize—it is not always possible to behave consistently with one's values.

For example, Ivan embraces the values of fairness and equity. He delegates a job to Tom, one of his busiest team members, knowing he can be relied upon to complete the task. However, in the back of his mind, he knows this is unfair to Tom, who is overworked. Although our values can be compromised occasionally—either by us or others—they provide us with a solid foundation.

There will be people and situations where we must compromise or fight to uphold our values. Knowing your values—even when you cannot maintain them—helps with situational awareness. Knowing and acting according to your core values means being true to yourself. Moreover, when life's big decisions come calling, you can rely upon them to steer you.

Crafting a Purpose Statement

It is time to craft your leadership purpose statement. A purpose statement should contain the following characteristics:

- Short: One sentence at most.
- Inspirational: It needs to be uplifting and motivating for you.
- Rings true: It should capture who you are.
- Focused: It needs to focus on your team and the value you add.

Here are some examples of leadership purpose statements that meet these criteria. You might find them helpful.

> ## Where the Rubber Meets the Road
>
> **Leadership Purpose Statements**
>
> - To inspire those around me to achieve important things.
> - I treat everyone I meet with respect and compassion.
> - I want to focus my energy on helping as many people as possible.
> - To be kind to myself and everyone I meet.
> - To help as many people as possible throughout my life.
> - I want to improve the lives of everyone I meet.
> - To equip others with the tools and resources they need to live their best lives.
> - Always support other people's goals and help them achieve them.
> - I want to put other people's needs before my own wherever possible.
> - I want to use my skills to impact people's lives positively.
> - I want to work to improve opportunities in my field for those who come after me.[*]

As tempting as it is, please do not copy one of the preceding statements; make it your own. Instead, could you use these statements as inspiration for crafting your leadership purpose? Your leadership purpose is unique to you and nobody else. Moreover, your purpose sums up your legacy as a leader.

The first step should be to complete the Life Values Inventory in Appendix B. What were your top three values? How do these values relate to leading yourself and others? For example, if *achievement* is the #1 value on your list, what does this mean for you, and how do you lead? It could mean striving to get the best from yourself and those you work closely with. A significant value might be *creativity*. This value

---

[*]https://au.indeed.com/career-advice/career-development/examples-of-personal-mission-statements.

should inspire you to lead an innovative and continually improving culture. What are your top three values?

Once you have finished the inventory, could you reflect on the results? I have prompted this reflection with some questions in Appendix B. Complete this exercise, too.

These exercises provide awareness and inspiration to create a meaningful statement. However, if it is still challenging, consider your passions. If you are passionate about something, it energizes you—you are likely to follow through. What are you passionate about?

For example, you might be enthusiastic about discussing big ideas. In other words, you are idealistic and love talking about ideas with others. A leadership statement reflecting this passion could engage those *I continually work with others to generate a better work setting*. Considering your passions is another pointer.

If that does not work for you, think about your talents. What is the one thing you enjoy most about the work you do? Is it collaborating with customers? Is it problem-solving? Is it coaching and mentoring others? As I said earlier, research indicates that there is a strong relationship between what one enjoys and what one excels in. This is based on the three *P* principles: we *practice* and become *proficient* in what we *prefer*.[†] We explore this idea when discussing practice #3: Build Strengths in Chapter 7. What you enjoy doing can be another hint to crafting a purpose statement.

What is it that you offer others? Please look at your leadership skills and talents that can be used more frequently. How can these skills be expressed in your purpose statement? For instance, if you are a good listener who can get others to feel comfortable sharing, how can you build this into a leadership purpose? Here is an example: *I listen to understand and engage my team in our projects*. Using your talents does two things: First, it makes you more effective. And second, you will enjoy yourself more—more about this idea in Chapter 7.

Another strategy for crafting your statement is to think of your talents and then compare these with your top values. Is there any

---

[†] www.performancepotential.com.au/blog/what-you-practise-you-become.

apparent relationship between your innate talents and values? Often, there is.

Considering these strategies, you will have everything required to craft your leadership purpose statement. Use all the lists you have created to write an inspirational, authentic, and clear statement in one sentence. Remember: Your leadership purpose statement reflects your overall leadership aspirations—it is not about the details of how you do this. The leadership purpose statement is a bird's eye view of what true north looks like.

Could you start playing around with your statement? Could you revise it several times? Something different may pop out to you on a second or third viewing you had not noticed before. Could you invite someone you trust to read your statement and make a comment?

Three More Tips

Primarily, be honest with yourself. Your statement is about you and nobody else. Writing a purpose statement that does not align with your core beliefs or talents will be useless.

Second, seek feedback. They may be able to provide insights you might have yet to consider.

Third, could you adjust your statement when you need to? Although a statement reflects your overall leadership aspirations now, your purpose will change several times. Could you revise your statement from time to time? Circumstances change, and so can your leadership purpose. So, the statement needs updating. If it is no longer relevant, be prepared to change it.

In conclusion, thinking about your leadership purpose builds EQ. EQ is a mindset and skillset that allows you to understand and manage your feelings and those you lead. Discovering True North clarifies who you are and what you have to offer.

Boosting your understanding builds confidence and conviction. This journey empowers you to be true to yourself and express your authenticity.

The most significant benefit of discovering true north is finding the unique value you offer as a leader. This clarity will shine through in your workplace like a beacon. Through the prism of your purpose, you can then seek out tools, actions, choices, and priorities that amplify this light.

If you still need to do so, complete the Life Values Inventory in Appendix B.

Top 10 Points

1. Crafting a purpose statement is a valuable way to clarify your leadership intentions.
2. Reflecting on your life story is one place to start defining your true north.
3. When leaders' values are apparent in their thinking and actions, we are more explicit about ourselves and those we lead.
4. Leading with values has several benefits.
5. Our values are stable throughout our lives, but they are not fixed.
6. Knowing our values—even when we cannot live and behave in alignment with them—helps us become more self-aware.
7. The purpose statement is short, inspirational, captivating, and focused on the end-user.
8. Your leadership purpose statement reflects your overall leadership aspirations—it is not supposed to cover the details of how you lead.
9. Discovering your true North is gaining clarity and understanding of who you are and what you have to offer as a leader.
10. Your purpose statement is unique to you.

CHAPTER 7
Practice # 3: Build Strengths

Developing a talent rather than overcoming a weakness allows us to learn faster, gain greater traction, and be more efficient and effective.

Emma enters Sandra's office with trepidation, knowing she is about to be appraised for her performance after six months on the job. Sandra is an accountant in a professional services firm specializing in small businesses. Since Emma started, she has received no feedback; she is apprehensive about Sandra's appraisal of her work.

Sandra begins by asking, "Now that you have been in this job for six months, what tasks do you enjoy most, Emma?"

Emma was blindsided—she was not expecting this kind of question. She paused and thought carefully for a moment.

"I guess I usually like dealing with our clients."

"Approximately how much of your day is taken up with clients?"

"Not too much, maybe one in eight hours."

"What about the client contact that you enjoy, Emma?"

"I enjoy providing solutions to their problems. It energizes me, and I feel useful."

"Yes, I agree this is one of your strengths, Emma; I get great feedback regularly from some of our clients."

"How can we work together to allow you to do more of this? Could I delegate more of the routine accounting work to one of the administrative assistants in the office and move you into a client liaison role? Perhaps we could make you the first point of contact for client requests, which may entail you being out on the road more. That will not happen overnight, but we can work towards this."

"That would be great, Sandra; I would appreciate that opportunity!"[1]

The workplace, reflecting society at large, is obsessed with spotting and overcoming people's weaknesses. As Rath (2007) puts it in his famous book, *Strength Finder 2.0*, "Society's relentless focus on people's shortcomings has turned into a global obsession."[2] Nevertheless, ironically, we always get a better return on the investment of time and effort in developing a capability instead of trying to perfect a weakness.

All things being equal, spending an hour developing a talent—assuming that hour is well spent—is a far better use of one's time than correcting a weakness. We learn faster, gain excellent traction, and are more efficient and effective by developing a talent than overcoming a weakness.

Nevertheless, our obsession with overcoming weakness is deeply rooted in our psyche.

Societal Conditioning

At school, we are told to lift our grades on subjects we struggle with while maintaining the good grades we get in subjects that become easier for us. This focus on weaknesses is reinforced when we enter the workforce. The performance appraisal devotes a disproportionate amount of time to errors, weaknesses, and deficiencies. Little, if any, time is spent on what we do well. With all this conditioning, it is little wonder that we are consumed with our weaknesses and take for granted our talents.

Think back to your school days. You come home with your report card. What is the first thing your parents comment on? It is the relatively lower grades. Your parents emphasized your need to lift your game in these subjects. However, they may skirt over the subjects where you performed well.

Gallup (2007) surveyed over 10 million people worldwide since the 1990s on employee engagement and how positive and productive people are at work.[3] Only a third of those surveyed consistently *strongly agreed* with this survey statement: *I can do what I do best every day at work*. However, two-thirds regularly either *strongly disagreed* or *disagreed* with that statement. In other words, most employees believe that their manager does not focus on what they do best. Furthermore, they also do not feel engaged at work.

The message seems clear: If you want to engage people's hearts and minds at work, you must allow them to exercise their talents there. What about you as the leader? Does this apply to you, too? Do you concentrate on building your capabilities?

To illustrate the point further, Rath's (2007) research indicates that people who utilize their strengths at work are six times as likely to be engaged in their jobs and more than three times as likely to report having an excellent quality of life.[4] Engaged employees can excel in what they naturally do best.

Let's face it: much of what we do at work is drudgery. Looking for ways to exercise one's strengths makes sense. Giving yourself and those you lead more scope to exercise innate talents benefits everyone. For example, Harry is naturally risk-averse—for him, most things in life are viewed as half-empty glass rather than half-full. His teammates perceive Harry as pessimistic. Nonetheless, he can quickly spot the pitfalls in an argument, plan, or project. Margaret, Harry's boss, invites him to critique her plan to implement a new customer contact procedure. Harry immediately spots a legitimate flaw in Margaret's plan—a risk Margaret did not consider. Building the strengths of others—which, if not exercised, may be perceived as a weakness—helps you, your team, and the business.

Obsession With Overcoming Weaknesses

I am not implying that we should disregard our and others' weaknesses. We should be aware of our limitations and see them as opportunities for growth. My point is this: We are better served—despite our conditioning—by putting our time and energy into turning our talents into strengths. This does not mean ignoring or neglecting our shortcomings. At the very least, we should insist on meeting a minimum performance standard in these weak areas.

For example, Hugo is not a natural public speaker. Nevertheless, he acknowledges he should make some effort to improve. Because speaking in public is part of leadership, Hugo understands it is unavoidable.

Hugo joins Toastmasters International* and practices to meet an acceptable standard. However, he understands that any discretionary effort—beyond addressing his limitations—is best spent on the things he is naturally good at—in his case, data analysis. Hugo grasps that he can more likely convert this data analysis talent into a strength.

As I explained earlier, we have been accustomed from an early age to concentrate on conquering our flaws and taking for granted our innate talents. I want you to know that you will do well to redress this disparity.

This fixation with identifying weaknesses extends to the way we manage performance. Traditional performance appraisal systems are weighted heavily toward detecting deficiencies. Once identified, resources are directed toward remediating these limitations. Most learning and development programs are designed to rectify poor performance rather than exercise talent. As Rath (2007) puts it, these training programs "help us to become who we are not."[5]

For instance, if one needs to improve with numbers and budgets, they are earmarked for a course to develop accounting skills. Alternatively, if people appraise people as poor, they are sent on a course to enhance their EQ. Of course, remediation always has value. However, our whole lives seem programmed to find and overcome inadequacies. There needs to be more room for emphasis on developing talent.

Contributing to this focus is the tendency to look up to those who have overcome massive obstacles. For instance, people who excel despite a physical disability or triumph over barriers such as age, discrimination, and economic circumstances are understandably admired. Our lives are filled with narratives about these exceptional people in film, the media, and books. These stories are undeniably inspirational. They teach us that we, too, can overcome obstacles on the journey to success. However, these accounts also teach us that overcoming a disability is more virtuous than capitalizing on our innate talents.

---

*Toastmasters International is a nonprofit educational organization that teaches public speaking and leadership skills through a worldwide network of clubs. www.toastmasters.org/About.

We can sometimes be dismissive—even envious—of those who succeed with a natural advantage. For instance, we dismiss as good luck a person gifted with a stunning singing voice or born with great beauty. We take for granted the arduous work someone with natural talent puts into turning this advantage into a strength. In other words, at the very least, we are indifferent to their effort to exploit their talent fully. We do not see—or want to see—the dedication to developing a natural advantage.

Where the Rubber Meets the Road

I Must at Least Try...

In June 1985, two British mountaineers, Joe Simpson and Simon Yates, made the first-ever climb of the West Face of the 21,000-foot snow-covered Siula Grande mountain in Peru. It was a callous assault—but nothing compared to what was coming. Early in the descent, Simpson fell and smashed his right knee. Yates could have abandoned him but managed to find a way of lowering him down the mountain in a series of difficult drops blinded by snow and cold. Then Simpson fell into a crevasse, and Yates eventually had no choice but to cut the rope, utterly convinced that his friend was now dead.

In his subsequent book on the climb entitled *Touching the Void*, Simpson (1988) wrote:

As I gazed at the distant moraines, I knew that I must at least try. I would die out there amid those boulders. The thought did not alarm me. It seemed reasonable, a matter of fact. That was how it was. I could aim for something. If I died, well, that was not so surprising, but I would not have just waited for it to happen. The horror of dying no longer affected me as it had in the crevasse. I now had the chance to confront it and struggle against it. It was not a bleak, dark terror any more, just fact, like my broken leg and frostbitten fingers, and I could not be afraid of things like that. My leg would hurt when I fell, and if I could not get up, I would die.

> *The survival of Yates himself was extraordinary. That Simpson somehow found a way of climbing out of the crevasse after 12 hours and then literally crawled and dragged himself six miles back to camp, going 3 days and nights without food or drink, losing three stone, and contracting ketoacidosis in the process, would be the stuff of heroic fiction if it was not so confirmed. Indeed, six operations and 2 years later, he was back climbing. All because, against all the odds, he tried ....*[6]

Inspirational stories such as the one aforementioned perpetuate a powerful myth. Overcoming shortcomings is romanticized to such an extent that it is considered an essential element of our culture. Movies, books, TV series, and the like are filled with the underdog beating the odds. This leads us to idolize those people who succeed despite their natural abilities. We need more room to celebrate individuals who use their innate talents for achievement.

Therefore, we emulate or support the underdog. We believe that the way ahead is to conquer our shortcomings. Capitalizing on our gifts is a secondary consideration. Unfortunately, overcoming our weaknesses instead of building on our strengths is the path of most resistance.

Turning Talents Into Strengths

A talent can evolve into a strength if it is nurtured. Campbell (2021), a leadership coach, argues in his article, *Strength-based Development Requires a Growth Mindset*, that strength-based development is about investing in one's talent to create strength.[7] So, skill and strength are not the same. Campbell explains:

> Talents are naturally recurring patterns of thought, feeling, and behavior that can be productively applied. On the other hand, a strength is the ability to deliver consistent, near-perfect performance on a given task.[8]

A commitment to developing a talent so that it becomes a strength requires a growth mindset.

Moreover, a growth mindset is a precondition for transforming talent into strength. With a growth mindset, one is ready to practice applying one's talent before it becomes a sustainable strength.

As I stated in Chapter 2, a growth mindset is the belief that one's ability to achieve any outcome can only be achieved through dedication and hard work. We embrace a fixed mindset if we take our innate talent for granted. A fixed mindset is the belief that one's characteristics, qualities, and ability to achieve results are predetermined—they are cast in stone. Whether developing talent or overcoming limitations, a growth mindset is necessary.

Even when we apply what comes naturally, we will fail occasionally. Perseverance is a characteristic of a growth mindset. Harnessing a growth mindset means bouncing back from inevitable failures. With a fixed mindset, there is a tendency to either avoid opportunities for growth or throw the towel in at the first sign of failure.

Louis (2009) of Azusa Pacific University studies mindsets in action.[9] Louis is interested in the connection between mindsets and building strengths. Part of her research looked at the distinction between talent identification programs and strength development programs. Louis discovered that talent and strength-based programs are predicated on different mindsets. Talent programs typically identify and confirm participants' natural talents and tendencies. These programs assume that talent is an attribute one has or does not have. You either have it or you have not. Talent programs focus more on identifying ability than how it is nurtured. Louis concludes that these programs foster a fixed rather than a growth mindset to one's natural abilities.

On the other hand, strength-based development programs are based on a growth mindset. These learning experiences focus on helping participants view their talents as assets that can be strengthened through intentional development. Strength-based development programs stress the importance of deploying a variety of ways of converting ability into strength.

Louis (2009) concluded that talent identification programs promote a fixed mindset, and strengths development programs promote a growth mindset.[10]

In practice, what this means is that it is not enough to discover one's talents merely. Without investing time, effort, and energy, one will not inevitably transform talent into a strength—at least not sustainably.

For instance, we witness many talented athletes rise to the top in their sport based purely on potential. However, athletes who do not apply their talent with commitment and obsessive practice often experience a short-lived career and fall by the wayside. Just knowing your abilities and doing nothing with them is embracing a fixed mindset.

Strength is a product of talent and application. In *StrengthsFinder 2.0*, Rath (2007) offers this formula:

Talent × Investment = Strength.[11]

Investment is based on a growth mindset. Although a growth mindset assumes that one can develop any personal attribute, it does not accept that we do not have innate talents. In other words, a growth mindset supposes everyone has certain gifts that can be developed and maximized through intentional investment, hard work, and learning.

According to Campbell (2021), we can adopt a growth mindset toward overcoming our limitations but have a fixed mindset about our talents.[12] When people know they can do something, they often take this gift for granted and rest on their laurels. Briefly, they stop investing and, therefore, stop growing. However—while taking their gifts for granted—they switch from developing their predisposed talent to investing in areas they perceive as weaknesses. This, too, is not uncommon.

Those who rise to the top in their vocation are unlikely to take their natural gifts for granted. Individuals who practice a growth mindset about their talents strive for excellence. They understand that it is not just about being born with certain aptitudes that make one successful. Furthermore, they work on their innate capabilities, investing time and energy in turning their talents into strengths.

So, assuming a growth mindset about one's talents is the basis for the practice of building strengths.

In summary, you need to do three things for strength-based development to flourish. First, please keep in mind your talents. However, you'll need more than to recognize your talents. Knowing your abilities is only the beginning of the journey. Second, invest in those talents—grow and develop your abilities to become strengths. Third, never assume that you have *arrived*. Building strength is not a destination. Strengths are continually honed and applied in different contexts and situations.

Next, we look at the *Digital Leadership Strengths Model*, which provides more tangible areas for building strengths in modern living and working.

Top 10 Points

1. The workplace, reflecting society at large, is obsessed with spotting and overcoming employees' weaknesses.
2. All things being equal—spending an hour developing a talent—assuming that hour is well spent—is a far better use of one's time than correcting a weakness.
3. This fixation with identifying weaknesses extends to how we manage performance.
4. Overcoming shortcomings is romanticized to such an extent that it is considered an essential element of our culture.
5. A talent can evolve into a strength if it is nurtured.
6. A growth mindset is a precondition to transforming talent into a strength.
7. A growth mindset is the belief that one's ability to achieve any outcome can only be achieved through dedication and hard work.
8. Talent programs typically identify and confirm participants' natural talents and tendencies.
9. Strength-based development programs are based on a growth mindset.
10. Strength is a product of talent and application.

CHAPTER 8

Leading in a Digital World

The ability to negotiate effectively becomes even more crucial as virtual interactions continue to increase in the world of work.

What defines outstanding leadership in the digital economy? A report from MIT Sloan senior lecturer Ready (2020) states that it combines emerging and enduring behaviors. Recognizing these attributes is only the start. According to Ready, the real challenge is confronting cultural inertia and making new organizational behaviors the norm.[1] Build strengths in a digital world means identifying these burgeoning attributes, identifying one's talents, and turning them into strengths.

My key message from the previous chapter is to focus on your talents and develop them into strengths. This chapter defines 10 attributes necessary for leading in the digital age. In Appendix C, you can assess yourself against these attributes. Your digital leadership profile will help you confirm your talents. With practical guidance, I encourage you to apply these talents so that they become leadership strengths in a world of rapid technological advancements.

Where the Rubber Meets the Road

Is Not a Digital Leader Just a Leader?
Many of the attributes of a digital leader are the same as those of a traditional leader. For example, digital leaders need to have a vision—they need to be able to communicate that vision through their words and actions to inspire their team to deliver the energy required to make digital transformation projects happen. A digital leader, for the most part, is still a people leader.

> They also need to be good listeners and collaborators. Leaders today need to be able to listen to experts in their team (often younger than they are) or collaborate across departments and external providers to ensure they are getting the best digital solutions for the future.
>
> All seven self-leadership practices apply and are as important as the *digital* component.
>
> Research by Westerman, Bonnet, and McAfee (2014) in their book *Leading Digital: Turning Technology into Business Transformation* indicates that only 20 percent of digital transformation projects are successful. What is clear is that when these projects fail, the damage is caused by the people and processes rather than the technology.
>
> Nonetheless, digital leaders need a level of fluency with technology. Outsourcing everything wholesale to a vendor or an IT team is not possible. The modern leader needs to be comfortable personally with what best practice looks like and understand the potential for technology within their organization.
>
> Digital leadership attributes enable the leader to speak the language, be more effective persuaders, and be respected by their teams and digital providers. Furthermore, they must be able to design solutions that are future fit for their organization's requirements, rather than just following the trend or crowd.[2]

Figure 8.1 shows the digital leadership strength model. My model has been adapted from Guzmán (2020) and her colleagues' research, cited in their conference paper, *Characteristics and Skills of Leadership in the Context of Industry*. From the extensive literature study, they identified 10 attributes vital for leading in a digital world. These attributes have been organized into the following model.

Broadly, three types of leadership are required for digital or any kind of leadership illustrated in the inner circle: *Cognitive, interpersonal,* and *strategic*. In the outer layer of the model are 10 corresponding attributes. These three types of leadership and their attributes have some overlay. For instance, the attribute of *influencing* (interpersonal) does require the attribute of *active listening* (cognitive) and vice versa. Nevertheless, in

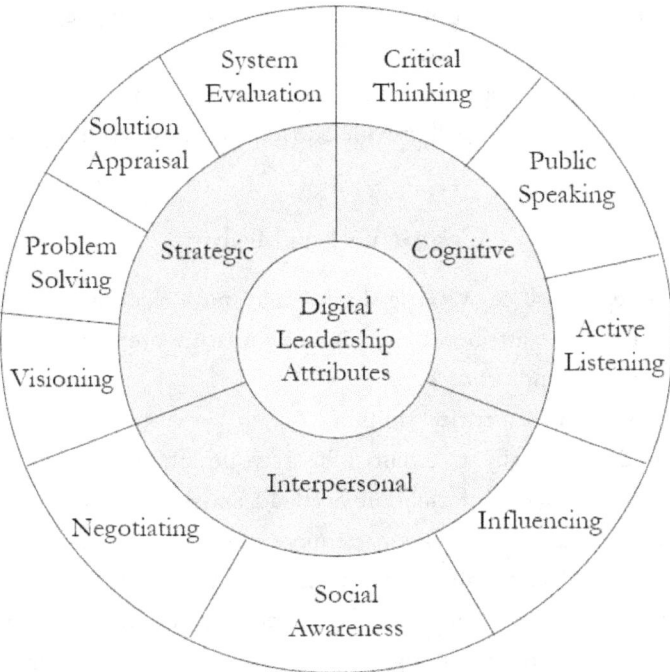

Figure 8.1 Digital leadership strengths model

the interests of clarity, we will be able to define each of the 10 attributes in the model separately.

The Digital Leadership Strengths Profile I have designed in Appendix C is based on this model. The profile is a self-assessment tool. However, I am developing a 360° assessment tool to give leaders several perspectives for more validity.* The profile in Appendix C is designed to assist you in identifying the attributes that come relatively easy to you (talents) and which are more challenging. Having completed the profile, I will provide five practical suggestions for developing each attribute. Although all 10 characteristics in the model are relevant for leading in the digital age, the focus for you in the practice of build strengths should be on the highest-scoring attributes. By doing so, you are converting talents into strengths.

---

*Contact Dr Tim Baker tim@winnersatwork.com.au for more information on the Digital Leadership Strengths Profile 360-degree assessment tool.

Focusing your efforts on nurturing talent yields a higher return on the time and energy you dedicate.

The following is a brief definition of each attribute in the model. After the explanation, I will provide a workplace illustration for context.

Cognitive Leadership

We will begin with cognitive leadership and move clockwise around the model. The three attributes cited in the literature are *critical thinking*, *public speaking*, and *active listening*.

Let us begin with critical thinking.

Thinking critically is essential in a world of rapid technological advancements. With information overload and swift decision-making, objective analysis and evaluation are more important than ever. In other words, where data are abundant but not always reliable, a leader must decipher and assess information accurately. Critical thinking lets you discern credible sources, recognize your biases, and separate fact from fiction. These cognitive skills ensure that decisions are grounded in evidence rather than speculation.

> Yasmin is the chief information officer (CIO) facing a decision to adopt a new cloud computing solution for her company's data storage needs. One of Yasmin's strengths is critical thinking. She attempts, wherever possible, to understand the potential benefits and risks associated with a solution before implementing it. Yasmin meticulously evaluates data security, scalability, cost-effectiveness, and compatibility with existing systems. As the CIO, she ensures that the chosen solution aligns with the company's long-term IT strategy and supports its digital transformation goals. Yasmin's approach means she makes a well-informed decision that optimizes the company's digital infrastructure, enhances operational efficiency, and positions it competitively in the ever-evolving technological landscape.

The ability to speak in public, whether online or face-to-face, remains relevant for leaders. Speaking skills enable leaders to articulate their vision and strategic objectives with clarity and conviction. Distilling complex concepts into coherent verbal messages is an asset in a digital environment characterized by information overload. Leaders must continue to inspire and guide their teams, albeit increasingly through virtual channels.

> Consider Ted, the CEO of a tech company. He regularly communicates virtually with his globally dispersed team. Ted's practical speaking skills are indispensable. He must continually communicate the company's evolving strategic direction and emphasize the need for cross-functional collaboration. Ted has a talent for speaking articulately and compellingly. This is his superpower, especially when capturing his team in a virtual setting. Ted's strength is inspiring team members to embrace the changes ahead.

The third attribute of cognitive leadership is active listening. The value of active listening is more pronounced in this era of virtual interactions. Now, face-to-face communication is being replaced by screens and messages. Digital interactions can easily lead to misunderstandings and misinterpretations, as nonverbal cues diminish. However, leaders with strength in listening actively transcend this limitation by noticing the subtleties of spoken words.

> Margot leads a remote team of software developers collaborating on complex projects through virtual meetings and messaging platforms. In this digital setting, Margot actively listens to her team members. She hears their insights, concerns, and suggestions. Margot practices active listening by paraphrasing, following up with relevant questions, and acknowledging different viewpoints. Through this strength, she has promoted an inclusive and engaging virtual environment. Margot is also adept at better understanding her team's dynamics. This ability to listen actively enables Margot to offer targeted guidance, address potential roadblocks, and cultivate a cohesive team culture that transcends the limitations of virtual interactions.

Let us now turn to interpersonal leadership and its three underpinning attributes: influence, social awareness, and negotiation.

Interpersonal Leadership

Influencing in the digital era differs from persuading in the traditional workplace. What has changed, however, is the tools used to exert influence. Influence is a pivotal attribute for leaders operating in a digital landscape. Where face-to-face interactions are limited, exerting positive influence is crucial for driving change, inspiring collaboration, and achieving business goals.

> Toni is a leader working for a digital marketing agency that aims to secure a high-profile contract with a global brand. Her ability to influence is invaluable. Toni's role is to craft compelling online content, thought leadership articles, and engaging social media campaigns. These tools showcase the agency's expertise and innovative strategies. She can sway the brand's decision-makers in her favor. Toni wins the big contract.

Social awareness—a substantial chunk of EQ—enables a leader to read the room. It is an indispensable quality for effective leadership when navigating virtual interactions and remote collaborations. Social awareness is valuable for comprehending the nuances of online communication, building rapport, and fostering genuine connections with others.

> Jacob is a project manager overseeing a virtual team of members from various cultures and backgrounds brought together on a product launch campaign. Despite the challenges, he builds an inclusive atmosphere where everyone in his team feels valued and understood. Jacob actively recognizes and respects his cross-functional and globally dispersed team's diverse perspectives, work styles, and time zones. However, his heightened social awareness and ability to read the room in a virtual room mitigate potential misunderstandings caused by virtual interactions. Jacob also

cultivates a sense of belonging, trust, and cohesiveness among team members, resulting in a successful and harmonious product launch in the digital space.

A strength in negotiating assists a leader in navigating complex relationships, compromising disparate views, and achieving mutually beneficial outcomes. The ability to negotiate effectively takes on even greater significance as virtual interactions continue to increase in the world of work. Without face-to-face interactions, they negotiate online, which demands a lot of communication acumen. Digital platforms facilitate a rapid exchange of information, often needing the ability to make swift decisions. Negotiation skills enable leaders to analyze scenarios, prioritize objectives, and craft solutions adeptly, often under time constraints.

ZenithTech Labs is a multinational corporation seeking a strategic partnership with a tech startup. The SME wants to integrate its advanced AI algorithms into the corporation's existing product line. Rebecca has the task of a virtual negotiation with ZenithTech to define terms around intellectual property rights, revenue-sharing models, and data privacy considerations. Effective negotiation results in her facilitating a mutually beneficial arrangement that aligns the goals of both entities. Through skillful negotiation, Rebecca ensures a successful partnership that leverages cutting-edge technology, enhances product offerings, and positions the corporation competitively in the digital market.

Strategic Leadership

Finally, we consider the four attributes supporting strategic leadership: visioning, problem-solving, solution appraisal, and system evaluation.

In Chapter 5, I pointed out that great leaders adopt two types of vision: strategic (Show Intent) and personal (Discover True North). Visioning in the context of digital leadership is strategic, although personal visioning plays a part. A well-defined and convincing vision is a guiding light in a rapidly evolving technological landscape. More specifically, aligning teams, fostering innovation, and steering organizations toward meaningful objectives in this dynamic environment is easier with a compelling strategic vision. The practice of Show Intent, which we will cover later as part of the outer game (Chapter 11), provides stability and direction amidst uncertainty. Leaders who articulate a compelling vision create a sense of purpose, transcending virtual barriers and motivating teams to pursue shared goals with enthusiasm and determination.

QuantumLeap Innovations is a startup poised to disrupt the e-commerce industry through innovative technology solutions. Mark is the CEO who understands the power of visioning. He is constantly articulating a clear and inspiring vision of the future. Mark's vision is for customers to experience seamless shopping across online platforms, virtual reality showrooms, and personalized AI-driven recommendations. This vision guides the development of cutting-edge technologies. Mark galvanizes his team toward a culture of innovation and collaboration. This visionary narrative enables *QuantumLeap Innovations* to remain at the forefront of the dynamic e-commerce market.

The need to solve problems is a daily occurrence with increased complexity and a barrage of information from all directions. The ability to discern the root causes of challenges and opportunities is crucial for effective decision-making. Digital landscapes often present multifaceted issues that the sheer volume of available data can obscure. The leader who excels in problem-solving can peel back layers of complexity, revealing the underlying factors that create the problem.

Joanne heads a software development team grappling with a recurring issue of missed project deadlines despite her team's considerable expertise. The effective identification of the root causes is pivotal to improving on-time performance. Joanne delves below the surface symptoms and uncovers the core reason for the frequent delays. She analyzes the development process, communication flows, and potential technical obstacles. Joanne discerns the two primary contributors to the delays: Substandard communication tools and unclear task allocation. Armed with this insight, she implements new project management software. This program dramatically improves coordination of information and task visibility, effectively addressing the root causes of the problem—the result is significantly better on-time project delivery.

The ability to critically assess and select the most suitable solutions is essential for driving innovation, efficiency, and effective decision-making. As I said, negotiation in a digital setting without face-to-face interactions demands heightened communication acumen. Digital environments often present multifaceted problems that require creative and strategic solutions. Rapid technological advancements and complexity can be challenging in a landscape.

The leader who excels in solution appraisal can weigh various options, evaluate their feasibility, assess them against organizational goals, and gauge their potential for positive impact. This strength supports informed choices that resolve immediate issues and position the team and the company for long-term success.

Meg is a leader who is strong in solution appraisal. She works at *Pinnacle CodeWorks*, a technology company facing challenges in optimizing its customer support processes. Meg's team presents her with various potential solutions. The three options are AI-powered chatbots, expanding the remote support team, or adopting new CRM software. Meg thoroughly appraises each of these possible solutions. She evaluates each option's pros and cons based on cost, scalability, customer impact, and alignment with the company's long-term goals. By critically evaluating these solutions, Meg makes an informed decision to expand the remote support team. This appraisal positions the company to adapt to future changes and effectively serve its customers in the ever-evolving digital landscape.

Finally, let us define the attributes of systems evaluation.

Assessing and optimizing systems is paramount for achieving efficiency, innovating, and sustaining ever-evolving processes in a landscape of rapid technological advancements. Digital environments are built upon sophisticated networks of interconnected systems, tools, and methods. So, a leader who prioritizes system evaluation can detect inefficiencies or bottlenecks within these structures. System evaluation is about streamlining operations, allocating resources effectively, and enhancing productivity.

Cloud Land Systems is a multinational corporation specializing in implementing cloud-based collaboration systems across global teams. System evaluation is critical to assessing the compatibility of the new platform with the existing IT infrastructure. This evaluation ensures data security and compliance with various regulations and determines the platform's scalability to accommodate future growth. *Cloud Land Systems* has project managers who evaluate systems and empower their teams to do regular software and tool assessments. By thoroughly evaluating the system, they can identify potential integration challenges, cybersecurity risks, and performance bottlenecks. This allows them to decide whether to proceed with the implementation, select a different system, or invest in necessary upgrades.

If you have not already done so, complete the Digital Leadership Development Profile in Appendix C. This will give you a perspective on where your strengths lie.

Top 10 Points

1. Thinking critically is essential in a world of rapid technological advancements.
2. The ability to speak in public, whether online or face-to-face, remains relevant for leaders.
3. The value of active listening is more pronounced in this era of virtual interactions.

4. The ability to influence in the digital era is no different from persuading in the traditional workplace.
5. Social awareness—a substantial chunk of EQ—enables a leader to read the room.
6. A strength in negotiating assists a leader in navigating complex relationships, compromising disparate views, and achieving mutually beneficial outcomes.
7. A well-defined and compelling vision is a guiding light in a rapidly evolving technological landscape.
8. The need to solve problems is a daily occurrence with a rapid flow of information and increased complexity.
9. The ability to critically assess and select the most suitable solutions is essential for driving innovation, efficiency, and effective decision-making.
10. Assessing and optimizing systems is paramount for achieving efficiency, innovation, and sustainable growth in a landscape characterized by rapid technological advancements and ever-evolving processes.

CHAPTER 9

Practice # 4: Keep Growing

...learn to be comfortable outside your comfort zone.

The distraction industry is a growth industry for good reason. We spend vast amounts of our precious time on things that numb us to the realities of life—such as mindlessly scrolling the Internet and social media for hours or watching Netflix to the point of restlessness. We understandably want to escape from the pressures of life.

Entertainment is fun—and necessary—but how much time do we spend on personal growth? How often do we set aside time for self-development, where we can learn and grow in a way that defines our destiny? Probably not enough time.

As Ernest Hemingway reminds us, "There is nothing noble in being superior to your fellow man; true nobility is being superior to your former self."[*]

Personal growth is not optional but essential for thriving and prospering as a leader in today's warp-speed world. Continuous personal development exponentially impacts one's private and professional effectiveness. In this chapter, I explore the significance of personal growth for leadership and introduce a practical framework.

Personal growth is fundamental to leadership success. Constantly developing one's knowledge, capabilities, and mindset builds deeper self-awareness and more excellent capability. Leaders must prioritize personal growth in their busy lives to adapt to a VUCA world and its unavoidable trials and tribulations.

Leaders who are dedicated to their growth inspire others to do the same. A growth-oriented leader actively seeks feedback from others,

---

[*]www.goodreads.com/quotes/76281-there-is-nothing-noble-in-being-superior-to-your-fellow.

engages in self-reflection, and embraces lifelong learning, setting an impressive example for those they lead.

In Part II, we discussed the relevance of self-awareness and personal growth. The first three practices, Know Thyself, Discover True North, and Build Strengths, are all based on greater self-understanding. What is the connection between self-awareness and continuous growth? Aren't they the same?

While self-awareness and personal growth are inexorably linked, continuous development is based on the belief that one has never arrived; there is always more to learn—the practice of keeping growing means embarking on a lifelong development journey.

Also, throughout *Successful Self-Leadership: An Inside-Out Approach in Seven Steps,* we have discussed the growth mindset as it applies to The Inner Game. As I stated in Chapter 2, Stanford professor Carol Dweck wrote about it in her book *Mindset: The New Psychology of Success*.[1] Having a growth mindset means being on an endless path of self-discovery.

In this chapter, we will thoroughly discuss the value of adopting a growth mindset, distinct from a *fixed mindset*, and how this mindset applies to the practice of keeping Growing.

Emotional Intelligence (EQ)

Being self-aware is a precondition of high EQ. As stated several times, EQ plays a pivotal role in leadership success. Leaders with high EQ can navigate complex interpersonal dynamics, understand and manage their own emotions, and more capably empathize with others. Emotions drive behavior, and behavior impacts people, either constructively or destructively.

Managing one's emotional state is necessary for dealing with everyday pressures. Consider these ordinary potentially stressful circumstances, for example:

- Giving and receiving negative feedback
- Meeting tight deadlines

- Dealing with a challenging relationship
- I need more resources to do the job
- Navigating change
- Working through setbacks and failure

Leaders face countless emotionally charged situations every day.

Two researchers, Salavoy and Mayer (1990), coined *emotional intelligence* in their article *Emotional Intelligence*.[2] EQ was later popularized by Goleman (1995) in his book *Emotional Intelligence: Why it Can Matter More than IQ*.[3]

According to Goleman, unlike IQ, EQ can be developed with practice. He contends that one's IQ level remains stable throughout one's life. However, whether one's EQ can be enhanced is contestable. Developmental psychologists have mixed views about this.[4] Nonetheless, Goleman claims we can significantly improve our EQ with sufficient awareness and practice.[5]

Leaders with well-developed EQ are adept at fostering positive work environments, resolving conflicts, and motivating individuals to achieve their full potential. Further, leaders with high EQ create psychologically safe workplaces where team members feel valued, heard, and empowered.

So, developing one's EQ—a dimension of the practice of Keep Growing—is possible by embracing constant learning and its application. Successful leaders appreciate that the world is constantly changing and strive to stay ahead by working on their personal and people skills. This lifelong learning commitment entails embracing innovative ideas, challenging limiting assumptions, and seeking diverse perspectives.

As I said in Chapter 1, top leaders promote a culture of learning within their teams by their example. A team that embraces continuous learning supports innovation, bolsters resilience, and stimulates agility. These are the preconditions for flourishing during uncertainty.

Undoubtedly, successful leaders inspire and empower those they lead by their example. Walking the talk is often underestimated. Through dedication to personal development, these leaders serve as positive role models. Moreover, a leader devoted to their growth also understands the value of investing in their team members' development.

Companies must consider new ways of developing the necessary knowledge, skills, and abilities to survive and thrive in a VUCA world. Firms now recognize that to remain competitive, they must rely on their leaders to engage in self-directed learning. Formal training programs still have their place in the milieu of learning and development. However, traditional classroom learning is not only expensive and time-consuming, but it is also somewhat disconnected from the current complexity and dynamism of the workplace. One inescapable and effective alternative is placing more and more emphasis on self-paced development.

For decades, we have known that leaders who commit to their continuous development are likely to be more productive and successful. Because today's leaders will work across multiple companies during their careers, taking charge of their development is increasingly a personal responsibility.[6]

Growth Mindset

The practice of keep growing begins with a growth mindset. As I flagged earlier, Carol Dweck pioneered studying fixed versus growth mindsets. Dweck argues that predicting success in all occupations has more to do with one's mindset than innate talent. What matters more than born traits, in other words, is self-belief.

More specifically, a fixed mindset assumes that abilities and talents are God-given and unchanging. It makes sense that if one thinks their talent—or lack of talent—is inherent, they will also believe their capacity to improve is limited. However, if a person feels that they were born with set traits, both positive and negative, then these assets and liabilities are fixed throughout life.

So, someone harboring a fixed mindset is less inclined to commit to a path of personal growth. With the belief that we have inherent characteristics, one assumes that learning opportunities—no matter how effective—will not make much difference. Like *Popeye the Sailor Man*, the fictional cartoon character, a person with a fixed mindset may rationalize that *I am what I am, and that is all I am.*†

This does not mean someone with a fixed mindset completely dismisses training and education. Instead, they are fixated on the idea that. A fixed mindset: they believe they (and everybody else) have a restricted aptitude for personal change while studying and attending education programs.

What about someone with a growth mindset?

A person with a growth mindset believes that with the proper training and development, they can grow and develop new skills and capabilities. With the belief that talent is malleable and not fixed, one is motivated to explore opportunities to improve, expand, and hone one's abilities. Besides capitalizing on their strengths, a person with a growth mindset is prepared to improve in areas they have less aptitude for. They see these areas as opportunities to gain experience rather than *weaknesses*.

Where the Rubber Meets the Road

The Value of a Growth Mindset

To paraphrase Whitener (2021) in her article, *The Value of a Growth Mindset and How to Develop One*, those of us with a growth mindset can, with time, effort, and practice, acquire and improve skills and abilities to accomplish things previously thought impossible. With a fundamental growth mindset, you do not just believe this; you live it.[7]

Henry Ford, the 20th-century industrialist and exemplar of a growth mindset, famously said, "Whether you believe you can do a thing or not, you are right."‡ Ford recognized that nothing holds one back as much as believing one cannot do something. He did not call it a fixed mindset, but he certainly could have had that term been around back then.

---

†www.goodreads.com/quotes/677938-i-am-what-i-am-and-that-s-all-that-i.
‡https://quoteinvestigator.com/2015/02/03/you-can/.

I hope you are now connecting the dots between your outlook and the practice of Keeping Growing. It would be best to adopt a growth mindset to sustain a commitment to keep growing. It is deceptively easy to assume one has a growth mindset, just as it is to think one has a great attitude when others think otherwise! And you can undoubtedly comprehend the psychological restrictions a fixed mindset imposes on one's growth and development.

Let me introduce you to Trish and Cliff.

Trish is a leader with a growth mindset. She embraces most challenges as an opportunity to learn. She is receptive to constructive feedback. If it is practical advice, she will act on it. Trish also endeavors to learn from her mistakes. She mostly enjoys learning new things, even if they are challenging. Trish is persistent in solving problems at work. She usually finds a way. Her growth mindset makes Trish thinks laterally and creatively to solve thorny challenges.

A fundamental distinction between a growth and a fixed mindset is developing rather than protecting oneself. Someone like Trish, with a growth mindset, is likely to feel safe from the success of others. Instead, she will be inclined to find inspiration from the success of others and consequently remain open to learning from them. Meanwhile, someone with a fixed mindset protects their ego, and they feel vulnerable when they make inevitable comparisons with others they perceive as more successful.

In contrast to Trish, Cliff has a fixed mindset that restricts his growth and development as a leader. It threatens his ego when his boss asks him to attend a leadership development program. Our ego's sole purpose is to protect us. With a fixed mindset, rather than seeing this learning experience as an opportunity for growth, Cliff views it as an admission of failure by his manager. From Cliff's perspective, attending this leadership workshop is less about learning and more about comparing himself with others. During the seminar, Cliff talks himself up to protect his ego and feelings of inadequacy.

A person with a growth mindset has more scope to realize their full potential. Trish is not held back by limiting beliefs; she is eager to improve. With her openness to learning new things, she believes everything is possible. Trish is ready to learn, courageous, and motivated. Her method is usually: try, fail, and try again.

Leaders who embrace continuous growth believe that they can change not only their own lives but also the lives of others. Developing oneself is considered an opportunity rather than a risk. Cultivating a growth mindset makes it easier for a leader to embrace this practice of Keep Growing.

Where do we learn these mindsets?

Our beliefs are formed from various sources. Mindsets are shaped by our experiences, observations, interpretations of those observations, and education. They are not cast in stone. With awareness and practice, we can change our limiting beliefs.

You and I are a mix of growth and fixed mindsets. For example, Manny is a leader in an IT startup. He has a growth mindset about learning new technical capabilities. However, Manny thinks he was not born to be a leader. He has a fixed mindset about his leadership potential. This attitude holds Manny back from growing his leadership capabilities.

Please look for a moment where you have a fixed mindset. How is this limiting your growth?

Cultivating a Growth Mindset

Let us finish the chapter by considering eight ways to foster a growth mindset.

The first thing is to believe you can change—that you are not stuck with an innate predisposition. Challenge the idea that your talents, strengths, and weaknesses are static. Look around you; there is overwhelming anecdotal evidence—not to mention neuroplasticity research[8]—that people can overcome their perceived limitations. I am sure you have met people after years of absence, such as at a school reunion, and been surprised how they have changed for the better (or worse!).

Second, take responsibility for your growth. It is easy (and convenient) to blame circumstances or others for one's shortcomings. We are all responsible for our future—to make the most of our God-given talents and abilities. For a person with a fixed mindset about their capabilities and limitations, it is easier to shun looking in the mirror. Instead, look in the mirror and take charge of your development.

Third, be curious—it is integral to self-awareness and growth. Instead of clinging to what we know, marvel at how much we do not know. What we know is infinitesimal compared with what we do not know. Be inquisitive. Ask questions and seek answers. Be Curious (Practice #7) is covered in more detail in Chapters 15 and 16.

Fourth, permit yourself to fail. As uncomfortable as it is, challenge yourself—failing is unescapable from time to time. Even when playing it safe, this can lead to letdowns. So, we might as well have a crack. With an attitude of continuous improvement, we position ourselves to prosper from setbacks rather than wallow in them.

Numerous illustrations of people have failed wretchedly and gone on to a magnificent triumph. An often-quoted example is Thomas Edison, the inventor of the carbon telephone transmitter, light bulb, and phonograph. When questioned about his setbacks in inventing the light bulb, Edison responded: "I have not failed 10,000 times—I have successfully found 10,000 ways that will not work."[9] That is a growth mindset in action!

Fifth, learn to be comfortable outside your comfort zone. Your comfort zone should not be a refuge—a place to go and be free from life's trials. As Whitener (2021) puts it: "Being free from challenges means being free from growth."[10] Stretching yourself. Try new things. Have a go.

Sixth, could you recognize your efforts? Being too fixated on outcomes can be disheartening. Results do count in the end. However, it is essential to acknowledge the journey along the way. Recognizing our bold steps to reaching our goals can sustain us over the long haul. When times get tough, please focus on the process.

Seventh, try not to compare yourself with others obsessively. When we are too preoccupied with how we stack up against others, it inevitably breeds jealousy and envy. When observing someone's success, it is more constructive to ask: *What can I learn from their triumph to help me on my journey?* Admire other's achievements, but do not be envious of them.

And finally, do not let your ego get in the way. Your ego is your protection mechanism—with a fear of failure—it can prevent you from trying new things. Having a growth mindset pushes you into spaces where you feel less comfortable, less accomplished, and more uncertain. These realms are not appealing to one's ego. Nevertheless, letting your ego control you is the pathway to mediocrity. If you want a whole and prosperous life—and you should—you must moderate your ego and face your limiting beliefs.

Next, we look at the Leadership Growth Framework. This framework will guide you on the path to the practice of keeping growing.

Top 10 Points

1. Personal growth is not optional; it is essential for thriving as a leader in today's warp-speed world.
2. Besides strengthening us, leaders dedicated to their growth inspire others to do the same.
3. Being self-aware is a precondition of high EQ.
4. Reviewing one's emotional state is a plus when dealing with everyday pressures.
5. According to Goleman, EQ can be developed with practice, unlike IQ.
6. Leaders with well-developed EQ are adept at fostering positive work environments, resolving conflicts, and motivating individuals to achieve their full potential.
7. The practice of keep Growing begins with a growth mindset.
8. Someone harboring a fixed mindset is less inclined to commit to a path of personal growth.
9. A person with a growth mindset believes that with the proper training and development, they can grow and develop new skills and capabilities.
10. A person with a growth mindset has more scope to realize their full potential.

CHAPTER 10

Leadership Growth Framework

Leadership is an interpersonal vocation.

In an interview for the Guardian, Polman (2011), former CEO of Unilever, says this about being a leader:

As a leader, you must consider developing yourself to make some of these crucial decisions for the future. First, you need to feel comfortable about who you are. A good leader is a good human being in the first place. Too often, we are being programmed by our environment to behave differently. However, true leaders are authentic and feel good about who they are. I don't have a problem crying when I need to cry. There's nothing wrong with showing that you care because it's the same in any organization; if you show that you care, others will care for you 100 percent.[1]

Keep Growing is what separates exceptional from ordinary leaders. Since the pandemic, the world has been facing social, psychological, and financial upheaval, civil and political unrest, and economic uncertainty. We're being tested with personal and professional dilemmas and opportunities we've never encountered in human history. This VUCA world is challenging us never to stop growing.

So, where does a leader start on the journey of personal development? Apart from leading oneself, leaders lead others. Leadership is an interpersonal vocation. A leader's success is determined by their ability to work with and through other people to get the work done. The *Leadership Growth Framework* identifies four elements of interpersonal

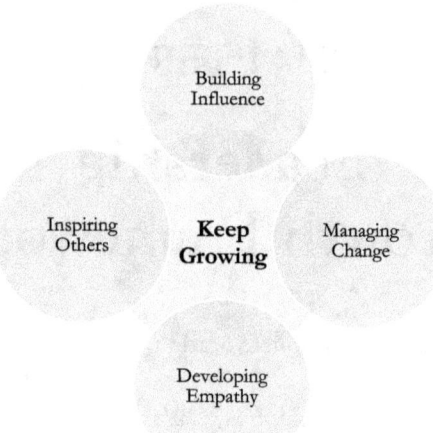

Figure 10.1 Leadership growth framework

efficacy. This framework is designed to give you a starting point for practicing Keep Growing.

The framework is illustrated in Figure 10.1.

Why these four elements? These elements are essential for any leader. Building Influence gives you leverage with those you need to interact with. Leading people through changes is the new normal. Empathy is the currency of interpersonal engagement. Moreover, inspiring and uplifting people is like gold dust in an unpredictable world. These four elements make up the Leadership Growth Framework.

I will describe the relevance of each element in this chapter, starting with building Influence.

Building Influence

In my book *The New Influencing Toolkit: Capabilities for Communicating with Influence*, I define influence as "the power to make other people agree with your opinions or get them to do what you want willingly and ethically."[2] Positive influence is persuading others to think and act in ways that benefit themselves, the business, and the customer. Influence in this context is not about manipulation or trickery.

I wrote *The New Influencing Toolkit* because most managers I coach struggle with exerting influence. The days of command and control—where you direct subordinates to do what you want—are over, or should be! Traditional power bases are breaking down. For example, teachers no longer have the traditional authority they once had in the classroom. Alternatively, police officers can no longer rely on their uniform to command compliance. Moreover, managers cannot always return to hierarchy to get things done. The new currency of persuading has mostly replaced commanding.

Today, influence is more potent than relying on one's position. It would be best to be persuasive when you want your team, peers, or boss to adopt your approach or idea. As management guru Ken Blanchard reminds us, "The key to successful leadership today is influence, not authority" (Cohen and Bradford, 2011). Titles mean little, except perhaps for the person who owns them.

Following is my *Influencing Capabilities Framework*. This framework illustrates four strategies to influence (Baker, 2015) (Figure 10.2)[3].

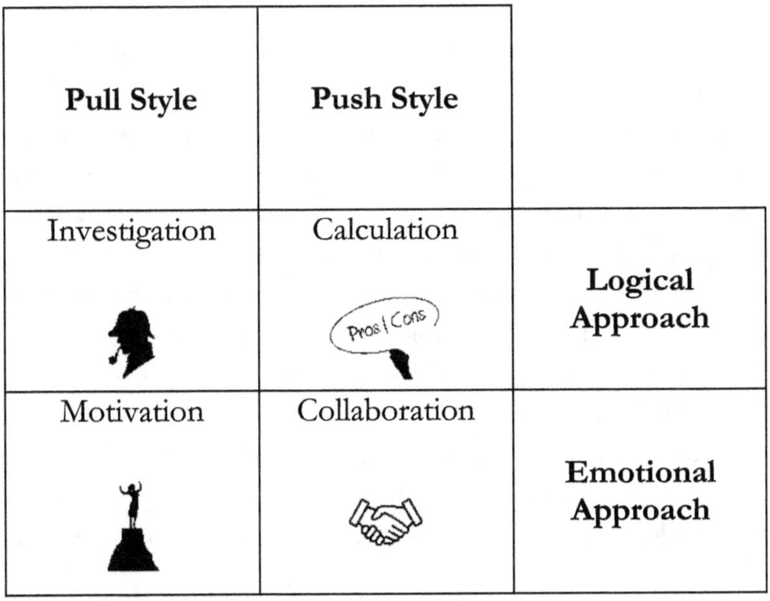

Pull Style	**Push Style**	
Investigation	Calculation	**Logical Approach**
Motivation	Collaboration	**Emotional Approach**

Figure 10.2 Influencing capabilities framework

Investigation, *Calculation*, *Motivation*, and *Collaboration* are the four influencing strategies. We usually favor one of these when we try to persuade others or are persuaded. The temptation is to overuse one strategy when you have four.

For example, Genevieve, who leads a team in the finance department, favors using facts, figures, processes, and logic (Investigation) when framing her argument. She finds that Investigation works well with a team of accountants who favor logical arguments. However, Genevieve needs help convincing her boss, Gary, who is values-based (Collaboration). For her to persuade Gary, Genevieve needs to pivot to building rapport and cooperation.

To magnify your scope and span of influence, be flexible and adaptable in how you frame your thoughts, arguments, and opinions. This means applying all four strategies, depending on the situation and the person(s) you are trying to influence.

In any influencing scenario, three variables are at play:

1. Your preferred influencing strategy.
2. The recipient's preferred influencing strategy.
3. The situation or circumstances you face.

If your strategy (1) is misaligned with (2) and (3), you will likely not get your way.

For example, Tom is an accountant appealing to James, a salesperson, about the need to cut expenses in the business. Tom uses a spreadsheet to make his point (Investigation). He likes numbers. James is a big-picture thinker (Motivation). James does not buy what Tom is selling; he identifies an expense from the spreadsheet that's not in the budget. Tom's preference is outcome-driven, not process-driven.

Knowing your preferred influencing style and approach is the first step to being more adaptable. In Appendix D, you can complete a shortened version of the *Influencing Capabilities Framework*.[*] The profile will give you an insight into your preferred influencing strategy. You can then consciously broaden your influencing tactics to be more effective.

---

[*] Contact me at tim@winnersatwork.com.au if you'd like to complete the electronic copy of the Influencing Capabilities Profile.

Managing Change

Improving change leadership is about leading your team capably through change. Managing change is challenging, with 70 percent failing change programs (Ewenstein, Smith, and Sologar 2015). Most change falters due to poor execution. Workplace change can be anything from putting up a noticeboard in the kitchenette to merging two companies. Change is ubiquitous.

Managing change is necessary to drive better business outcomes. Even if it is done capably, change is disruptive. However, when it is poorly executed, morale and productivity plummet. So, managing change is in the framework because change is omnipotent, and when handled poorly, it can be disastrous. Navigating change is an inescapable part of leading.

Typically, there is no or scant regard for supporting employees through change. The focus is often on the change process: devotion to the systemic rationale. Besides, the mistaken assumption is that people will eventually get on board. It is, therefore, unsurprising that most change initiatives fail.

Scott and Jaffe (1988) *Change Grid*[4] is one of the most valuable models for understanding the emotional states people predictably experience during change. The Change Grid focuses on the people going through change, not the change process. What is unusual about the Change Grid is its emphasis on the typical psychosocial ride an individual either experienced or will experience in any change.

The Change Grid is based on the work of renowned psychologist Elisabeth Kübler-Ross. Kübler-Ross (1969) pioneered identifying the stages of grief, from death to dying.[5] The Scott and Jaffe model adapted Kübler-Ross's grief stages to the workplace.

I adapted Scott and Jaffe's work to create the *Workplace Rollercoaster Model*.[6] I have changed the name and relabeled the four emotional states. Each state predicts how people will react during a workplace rollercoaster ride. By forecasting how team members will respond at different stages of a change project, the leader can facilitate a smoother transition from start to finish. The Workplace Rollercoaster Model assists a leader in altering their style to accommodate the dominant emotional state of the change.

> ### Where the Rubber Meets the Road
> **Life Is a Rollercoaster Ride**
> The attraction of rollercoasters is the gut sensation of fear, much like watching a horror movie. Physical signs of anxiety, such as a pounding heart, faster breathing, and an energy boost caused by the release of glucose, are known collectively as the *fight or flight* response. We know that a rollercoaster ride is likely to trigger this response.
>
> Researchers measured the heart rates of riders on the double-corkscrew Coca-Cola Roller in 1980s Glasgow. Heartbeats per minute more than doubled from an average of 70 beforehand to 153 shortly after the ride had begun. Some older riders got uncomfortably close to what would be deemed medically unsafe for their age (Stephens 2018).[7]

Figure 10.3 an illustration of the workplace rollercoaster model.

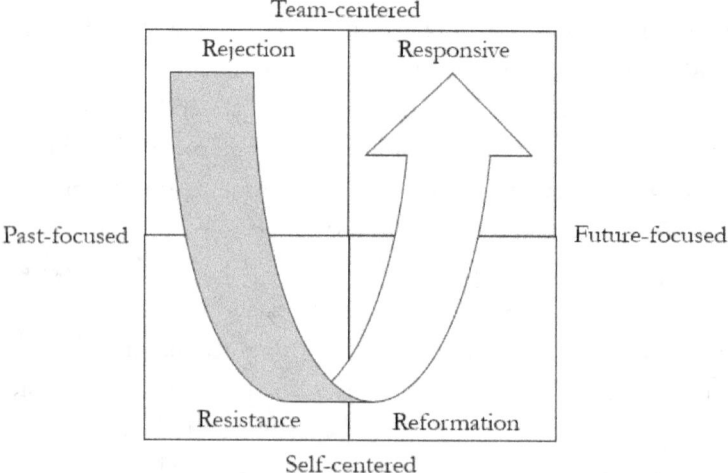

Figure 10.3 Workplace rollercoaster model[8]

The four dominant stages of change are *Rejection, Resistance, Reformation,* and *Responsiveness.* Before rolling out any change process, you can plan for these inevitability phases. Once the change is underway, observe people's behavior. Communicate compatible with each state.

It is natural for people to reject change at the outset (Rejection). Provide adequate information at the commencement of a change initiative. Apart from responding to why the change is being made, communicate how the change will impact your team. Too often, managers concentrate on the benefits for the business. Instead, communicate the benefits for team members if there are any! How will the change affect their work? Your team would like to know this when you start a change program.

With this targeted information, people shift quicker from rejecting or denying the change to resisting it. People will understandably feel threatened if they know the change is real (Resistance). During resistance, you need to listen to their concerns.

If people know you are listening and considering their concerns, they will begin to explore change (Reformation). Although they are more open to change, their ability to master change is limited because they are trying something new. Your response: Support your team members with encouragement, training, coaching, and capacity building.

Finally, with familiarity and growing capability, team members will be receptive to the change (Responsiveness). A feeling of ease and commitment prevails. Energy and productivity are high. This is the stage to review progress and celebrate success.

My book, *Mastering Change: A Practical Guide for Better Leadership Conversations,* provides more about this model and its application.[9]

Developing Empathy

Empathy is a characteristic of all successful leaders. Most people are capable of empathy, psychopaths excluded! Empathy is the compassion and understanding one gives to another person. On the other hand, sympathy is a feeling of pity for another person and relief in not having the same problem or situation!

Connecting with others has multiple benefits. Empathy is the foundation for building a meaningful working relationship or any relationship. Developing empathy can also inspire others, boost engagement, and help give constructive feedback that's listened to. Consistently showing empathy goes beyond displaying compassion for someone.

Presidential historian Goodwin (2018), in her book *Leadership: In Turbulent Times*,[10] identifies empathy as one of the top six qualities of outstanding American presidents. Great leaders are empathetic.

There are three qualities of empathy:

- Actively listening
- Being non-judgmental
- Being impartial and objective

While these qualities working together in one person are the exception, they are essential for deepening human connection.

I will briefly explain the value of each quality.

A good listener is attentive. When someone speaks, a good listener offers them their full and undivided attention. An active listener makes eye contact and removes distractions (like e-mail or phone calls) to allow that person to express themselves without distraction and interruption.

Empathetic listeners suspend their judgment. Empathy is not about agreeing or disagreeing—it is about understanding. They are nonjudgmental, meaning I understand their point of view entirely *without judging it as right or wrong, good or bad*.

Being nonjudgmental means listening unconditionally. Being impartial and objective means stepping back from your and their emotions and observing what is said reasonably. This further encourages the other person to be authentic and open. They can be confident that you are not appraising; they feel free to speak your mind.

Halpern (2023), professor of bioethics at the University of California Berkeley, offers several constructive suggestions for developing empathy.[11] Empathy is not a handholding and heartfelt conversation.

You do not have to be emotionally involved to empathize. You can better understand their feelings and position by asking open-ended questions (beginning with *Why, What, Where, When, Which, and How*). Halpern calls this *empathetic curiosity*.[12]

Being empathetic is not about taking on a burden. Showing empathy does not need to be time-consuming or energy-sapping. Empathy is only taxing when one takes on the emotions of others as their own. You can be empathetic with minimal effort without being drained. As Halpern (2023) explains: "Instead of viewing empathy as a way to feel things *for* other people, just focus on being curious about their lives and willing to listen and find out more about them."[13]

The simplest way to display empathy is to ask open-ended questions. Empathy is understanding the perspective of the person with whom you are interacting. How can one appreciate another person's point of view if they have not taken the opportunity to understand it? Without mind-reading powers, the only way to understand is to ask them questions. I like to refer to this as being *respectfully curious*.[14]

Listen to understand. As discussed in Chapter 3, we all bring our cognitive biases to conversations. Our experiences and beliefs shape our biases. Nevertheless, try to hear another person's words from *their* perspective, not *yours*. The *golden rule* is treating others as *you* want to be treated. Better still, apply the *platinum rule*: treat people as *they* want to be treated.

Inspiring Others

A leader's primary role is to get the absolute best from the people they lead. On energy and engagement at work, if you rated your team members on a scale of 1 to 10 (10 is high and 1 is low), how would they rate? Your ratings will fluctuate depending on how the person feels, what is happening in their life, and what challenges they face at work. It is unrealistic to expect all team members to score 10 out of 10 all the time or even some of the time.

A worthy aim is to improve the engagement levels of all team members by 10 percent. For example, if Jonah rates 6 out of 10, it is realistic for him to reach a 7 with some inspiration. Across a team, a 10 percent individual improvement will make a significant difference.

Multiple survey results from Gallup (2021) indicate that engagement levels are low worldwide.[15] Some surveys suggest that disengagement could be as high as 70 percent. More disturbing is that *active* disengagement could be as high as 20 percent. So, there is significant room to boost work engagement across all industries.

Since the pandemic, many people are reconsidering their career choices. On the surface, this is healthy contemplation. However, reviewing one's career is often predicated on low job dissatisfaction. There is evidence from Dogru's (2023) research findings that staff turnover levels are rising across all industries, ranging from 14 to 49 percent in the United States.[16] Higher attrition rates contribute to talent shortages in many companies. Anthony Klotz (2023) of Texas A&M University termed it the *Great Resignation*.[17] There is also evidence that productivity has plummeted sharply since 1947 (Telford 2022).[18] The term *quiet quitting*—popularized on TikTok in 2022[†]—describes this phenomenon.

This bleak landscape justifies inspiring others as an element in the Leadership Growth Framework. As Linda Holbeche reminds us in her article, *How Good Leaders Inspire and Motivate Others*, "To perform at their best in an ever-changing world, employees need the best from their leaders."[19] Apart from this being a growth opportunity for leaders, having the ability to inspire and motivate is imperative in today's workplace.

Boosting engagement is more than formulating a strategy. While it is ultimately up to the individual to be engaged, a good leader accepts that they, too, have a role to play in their daily interactions.

Here are three practical considerations to inspire others.

First, a leader must provide direction, especially in uncertain and rapid change. In Chapters 11 and 12, we cover Show Intent, the first practice of The Outer Game. Team members want to know *where* the business is heading and *what* their role is in its future. Without communicating intent, navigating a growth strategy for a business today

---

[†]www.personio.com/hr-lexicon/quiet-quitting/.

is arduous and unpredictable. The uncertainty we face in a VUCA world fuels the need for clarity from the leader.

With heightened ambiguity, Grint (2005) argues in his paper, *Problems, Problems: The Social Construction of Leadership*, that the solution is not necessarily top-down leadership.[20] One leader cannot resolve complex or wicked problems, A leader is better served sharing the leadership baton by engaging their team to work together to solve work problems.

Second, be genuinely interested in the well-being of team members. Since the pandemic, we have witnessed a dramatic escalation of workers working from home. Hybrid working arrangements are not the latest HR fad. Working from home is now the new norm for many. It is one of the most significant workplace changes since the Industrial Revolution. However, disengagement and insecurity can result from physical isolation. Therefore, mental health, psychological safety, and workplace well-being should be top-of-mind for today's leaders.

Qualtrics' (2024) *Employee Experience Trends Report* found that having a sense of belonging to their organization was the number one factor impacting employee engagement during the pandemic.[21] Forging connections—both in person and virtually—is fundamental to engagement. A priority should be building an engaging vibe with several well-used and meaningful communication channels.

Third, an effective leader successfully juggles tasks and interpersonal responsibilities. Getting this equilibrium right is the basis for cultivating a psychologically safer work setting. A workplace that supports jobholders in doing their jobs is safer for everyone. This means setting unmistakable and reasonable outcomes, establishing clear-cut standards, and collaborating on solving problems.

Support for removing organizational roadblocks can also relieve anguish. These barriers often result from excessive bureaucracy and confusion about team members' roles and responsibilities. Eliminating roadblocks can clear the line of sight between an individual's task and the company's purpose.

Good leaders are often good coaches. The best coaches create space for people to develop and grow. Coaches energize others by capitalizing on their strengths. The leader-coach—wherever practical—matches one's strength with the work needed.

In summary, the Leadership Growth Framework covers the interpersonal elements of building influence, managing change, developing empathy, and inspiring others. It provides a pathway for your growth. With a growth mindset and some dedicated practice, you can master them all.

Please go to Appendix D to complete your Influencing Capability Profile.

Top 10 Points

1. The Leadership Growth Framework identifies four elements of interpersonal efficacy.
2. Positive influence is persuading others to think and act in ways that benefit themselves, the business, and the customer.
3. Investigation, Calculation, Motivation, and Collaboration are the four influencing strategies.
4. Improving change leadership is about leading your team capably through change.
5. To improve your change leadership capability, focus on these four emotional states: Rejection, Resistance, Reformation, and Responsiveness.
6. Empathy is the compassion and understanding one gives to another person.
7. Empathy has three qualities: active listening, nonjudgment, impartiality, and objectivity.
8. The primary role of a leader is to get the very best from the people they lead.
9. Aim to improve the engagement levels of all team members by 10 percent.
10. The Leadership Growth Framework is designed to provide you with a pathway for your growth.

PART III
The Outer Game

CHAPTER 11

Practice # 5: Show Intent

Employees in a command-and-control regime leave their brains at the company gate, expecting the leader to spoon-feed them.

In her search for material on being a better leader, Michelle found a surplus of articles, books, podcasts, and training. One topic repeatedly piqued her interest—intentional-based leadership. Michelle had never thought much about intentional-based leadership before, but she began reading and thinking about how it applied to her. She was attracted to being clear about the why and allowing others to figure out the how.

In Part III, we look at the three remaining practices of self-leadership that I classify as The Outer Game. Although these three practices originate from within, with the proper mindset, their execution directly affects the tone of a work setting. We consider Show Intent, Self-Regulate, and Be Curious in Part III. Show intent is the first cab off the rank.

What is the difference between Practice #1: Discover True North and Practice #5: Show Intent? Discover True North, as covered in Chapters 5 and 6, defines your leadership purpose. True north addresses the question: *Why should you lead anyone?* Show Intent focuses on communicating the strategic direction. Another distinction is that Discover True North is an internally generated personal leadership philosophy, and Show Intent is an external focus on business goals. Discover True North and Show Intent have different foci.

In this chapter, I define the practice of Show Intent and its benefits. The next chapter offers you practical suggestions to Show Intent.

To Show Intent, the leader communicates their goals and aspirations with clarity and conviction. This practice embodies Covey (2020), first two habits in his book, *The 7 Habits of Highly Effective People: Be Proactive and Begin with the End in Mind.*[1] A leader shows intent, explaining the what and why, and lets their team figure out the how.

What direction do we need to take? Furthermore, why it is essential? These are two questions that support the practice of showing intent.

In other words, intent-based leadership involves expressing a strategic vision and explaining its relevance. Articulating a clear direction allows team members to align their thinking and behavior with the leader's vision.

To Show Intent, a leader continually communicates their vision to the team. The intention is expressed compellingly, ensuring the team understands and embraces the leader's direction. Leaders who Show Intent are inspirational and motivating, positioning the team's effort with a common purpose.

By expressing your intention in words and actions, you are authentic. Consistency in words and behavior demonstrates your integrity and commitment to the strategic direction. Being true to your intention inspires confidence and builds trust. This commitment encourages unity and shared responsibility. People get on board when you display passion and dedication to a direction.

Furthermore, by showing intent, you empower your team to make informed decisions and take ownership of their role. With an unwavering commitment to a compelling vision, team members are guided rather than managed. To Show Intent creates a team culture where individuals aspire to achieve collective success. Showing intent is a practice that separates the leader from the manager.

Given these advantages, it is no wonder that intent-based leadership remains a widely discussed concept, often falling short in its application. Purpose-driven leadership is more relevant now in a topsy-turvy world. In any case, impressive results can occur when team members are sold on their leader's direction and supported to work toward it. By being encouraged to exercise their strengths, team members stretch, grow, and become a better version of themselves. When team members feel valued and empowered, they become motivated and productive.

Servant Leadership

Servant leadership and the Show Intent practices are harmonious despite originating from distinct perspectives. Intentional leadership and servant leadership are based on the principles of shared purpose and people's well-being. The term *servant leadership* was coined by Greenleaf (1970) in his essay, *The Servant as Leader*. Greenleaf states that:

> The servant-leader is servant first .... It begins with the natural feeling that one wants to serve first. Then, conscious choice brings one to aspire to lead. That person is sharply different from a leader first, perhaps because of the need to assuage an unusual power drive or acquire material possessions .... The leader-first and the servant-first are two extreme types.[2]

The philosophy of the servant-leader is to support their team. Support entails prioritizing the development of team members and cultivating conditions that empower them to thrive. In prioritizing team members, a servant-leader engages in active listening, demonstrates empathy, fosters collaborative relationships, and harnesses talent effectively. The overarching goal of a servant-leader is to facilitate the success and well-being of those under their guidance.

Leading with intent is inherently purpose-driven, entailing communicating a vision that offers direction. Leaders adopting this approach establish objectives, formulate strategic decisions, and synchronize their and their team's efforts toward a desired outcome. This leadership style necessitates effective communication of the vision and inspiring and motivating others to collaborate toward a shared goal.

While a servant-leader fosters a supportive work environment, an intent-based leader offers clear direction to steer the actions of team members. Demonstrating intent, a leader communicates the desired outcome. Utilizing a vision, the intent-based leader aligns the needs and interests of individuals with those of the organization. Showing Intent and servant leadership mutually reinforce each other's approaches, enhancing overall effectiveness.

Leading with intent provides strategic guidance, whereas servant leadership promotes a positive and empowering work environment. By skillfully merging these approaches, a leader can nurture a collaborative culture that evolves and matures while striving toward strategic objectives.

Studies show that when leadership intent and servant leadership work together, it promotes innovation and elevates productivity. Sipe and Frick (2015), in their book *Seven Pillars of Servant Leadership: Practicing the Wisdom of Leading by Serving*, discuss this research. One study compared profits in *good to great* firms—practicing servant leadership with clear intent—with general S&P 500 companies.[3] The findings showed significantly higher earnings in servant-led companies with clear purpose by a profit margin of 24 percent compared with 10 percent profitability in the general S&P 500.

> ## Where the Rubber Meets the Road
>
> **Servant Leadership and Intent-Based Leadership Are Not New Ideas**
>
> The concepts of servant leadership and intent-based leadership have been around for centuries. For example, Lucius Quinctius Cincinnatus,[*] a military leader in fifth-century Rome, was twice granted supreme power and relinquished his position not a day longer than necessary. Furthermore, he stepped down despite the power and wealth a dictatorship would provide him with. Cincinnatus consistently demonstrated great honor and integrity. He was beloved and admired for his selfless service. Cincinnatus is cited as a role model for servant leadership.
>
> Similarly, George Washington was appointed Commanding General of the Continental Army before being elected the first president of the United States from 1789 to 1797. He led American and allied forces to a decisive victory over the British during the

---

[*]www.mountvernon.org/library/digitalhistory/digital-encyclopedia/article/cincinnatus/.

> Revolutionary War at the siege of Yorktown in 1781. Washington's leadership paved the way for American independence. Having led the United States to independence, he subsequently resigned from office. Like Cincinnatus, Washington was trusted and admired for his character and clear intentions. These two men were influential leaders because they demonstrated significant strength of character and dedication to serving ideals that were more excellent than themselves (Stazesky 2000).[4]

Responsibility-Based Leadership Approaches

Leading with intent and servant leadership are responsibility-based approaches. Responsibility-based leadership is different from a reward-based approach. With a responsibility-based approach, the leader believes leading others is a privilege rather than a burden. Furthermore, this leader feels obligated to improve the lives of those they lead.

Reward-based leadership assumes that one has earned the right to lead others. Having *arrived*, the leader feels entitled to enjoy the trappings and status of the leadership title (Petkovic 2020).[5] There are no prizes for guessing which of these two approaches is more inspiring to those they lead!

What is more, Lencioni (2020), in his book *The Motive: Why So Many Leaders Abdicate Their Most Important Responsibilities*, points out that reward-based leadership is ineffective.[6] If leaders think they have earned the right to lead others, they feel authorized to use extrinsic rewards to motivate their team. By dispensing rewards (and punishment), the reward-based leader does not see the value in building connections and inspiring those they lead. Using extrinsic rewards to motivate is still commonplace in the workplace. Nevertheless, as Pink (2018) claims from studies in his book *Drive: The Surprising Truth About What Motivates Us*, reward and punishment regimes can demotivate knowledge workers, resulting in underperformance.[7]

Servant leadership is not simply about pleasing employees by giving them what they want. Leading to please leads to disorder. Intent-based leadership is not a euphemism for micromanagement; it is the opposite. People want and need a vision they can aim for and believe in. With an overarching vision, people have the foresight to express themselves. Additionally, they have the freedom and scope to exercise their autonomy—to make judgments and decisions that align with the leader's intent (Eubanks 2020).[8]

Characteristics of Intent-Based Leaders

Intent-based leaders share three broad characteristics. In the next chapter, I will explore these characteristics more deeply.

First, an effective intent-based leader is clear on why they lead. We covered this in Chapters 5 and 6 when discussing the second practice of self-leadership: Discover True North. Before people can feel valued and take pride in accomplishing something bigger than themselves, the leader must have a mature understanding of their true north. Without this insight, it is easier to be sucked into the vortex of day-to-day *busyness* and not take a step back to see a more significant cause.

Besides, people feel disempowered when their leader hovers over their shoulders, checks up too frequently and meddles in minutia. A leader's focus should be on setting and communicating the big picture.

Second, intent-based leaders feel comfortable letting go and enabling others. The practice of Show Intent is the antithesis of being a control freak! It is challenging for many leaders to surrender and allow team members to deliver on a designated outcome. If you expect your team members to deliver results—as I am sure you do—set the direction and get out of the way.

Once your team understands the direction, please support them in performing. For instance, support could mean stripping away unnecessary red tape and bureaucracy or helping the team navigate it. Support does not mean meddling in operational matters.

Third, intent-based leaders value the expertise and diversity of team members. Most people will express their perspectives, thoughts, and ideas, given the opportunity and a psychologically safe workplace. Harnessing your team's energy is the fuel that drives innovation and continuous improvement. Intent-based leaders welcome original thoughts, encourage diverse opinions, and encourage prudent independent judgment.

Nonetheless, the workplace has several barriers that inhibit original thought. One prevalent obstacle is hierarchy. Hierarchical decision-making frameworks can fuel a culture of blame, while vertical reporting structures stifle individual autonomy. Nevertheless, in navigating the complexities of a VUCA world, companies increasingly embrace innovation—leveraging insights from all members rather than solely relying on leadership.

Delegating control and decision making beyond a select few leaders at the helm of the organizational hierarchy supports agility. Improved cross-functional communication and increased autonomy in decision making permit more excellent responsiveness in a dynamic marketplace.

When all the power resides with management, employees are more inclined to play it safe for fear of making errors. Intent-based leadership typically involves a team whose members are expected and supported to use their judgment to pursue a goal. Instead of being reactive, team members are primarily proactive when their leader lets go of their ego, sets a destination, and trusts their team to reach it.

Intent-based leadership requires a little discomfort for it to prosper. Employees unaccustomed to thinking for themselves may hesitate to exercise independent judgment. However, being overly cautious and too reliant on the leader's input is not feasible in a marketplace of change and uncertainty. Besides, a zero-mistake work zone is impossible and inhibits the scope to grow and develop from mistakes.

Your team may initially feel uncomfortable when they are not instructed on *how* to work toward a specific goal. With a clear outcome and a hands-off approach, intent-based leadership challenges team members to take on more responsibility and ownership. With a compelling *why*, the team is challenged to figure out the *how*. You are stretching the team beyond their comfort zone to take more accountability, which benefits you, your team, and the business.

The practice of Show Intent is communicating in an overarching direction and supporting others to work toward that goal. With practice, most team members will be receptive to this approach—they will seek out solutions without relying on you for answers. Instead of tightly controlling people's day-to-day activity, the team has a more significant stake in arriving at the outcome you want. Let go and trust your team to find the solutions.

Giving up control is not easy. Letting go of making decisions might seem counterintuitive. Intent-based leadership is opposite to the centuries-old traditional command-and-control mindset. Paradoxically, putting your faith in others to deliver on a strategic vision enhances—not diminishes—your influence.

Enabling, rather than instructing team members unlocks their potential. Changing the leader–follower dynamic can take time. Be patient. Persevere. With conviction from the leader, most team members respond positively to this practice. They will gradually take ownership and drive the business in the direction you want them to head (McCracken 2020).[9]

What is the alternative? With the traditional command-and-control mentality, people apportion blame, become disengaged, and take little or no responsibility for their work. Employees in a command-and-control regime leave their brains at the company gate, expecting the leader to spoon-feed them. So, Show Intent!

Next, we look at some practical ways you can Show Intent.

Top 10 Points

1. To Show Intent, the leader communicates their goals and aspirations with clarity and conviction.
2. To Show Intent, a leader continually communicates their vision to the team.
3. Intent-based leadership is well documented, if not well practiced.
4. Servant leadership and Show Intent are compatible.
5. The philosophy of the servant-leader is to commit to serving team members and put their needs first.
6. While a servant leader commits to creating a supportive environment, an intent-based leader provides direction to guide the actions of team members.

7. Studies show that when leadership intent and servant leadership work together, they promote innovation and productivity.
8. Leading with intent and servant leadership are responsibility-based approaches.
9. Intent-based leaders have three attributes: They are clear on why they lead, feel comfortable letting go and enabling others, and value the expertise and diversity of others.
10. Your team may initially feel uncomfortable when they are not instructed on how to work toward a specific goal.

CHAPTER 12

Eight Characteristics of Intentional Leaders

How you show up has a significant bearing on your effectiveness.

Providing context is underrated. Leaders need to communicate the why of decisions daily. Ironically, employees ask themselves why they work for their manager every day. You probably ask yourself regularly why you work for your boss. People mostly come to work wanting to perform. Beyond a paycheck, employees want to do meaningful work.

Now that you better understand what the practice of Show Intent means and its benefits, we will consider some practical ways to lead with more intention in this chapter. Craig (2019), founder and president of WebFX, identifies eight characteristics necessary to lead with intention:

- Become a better communicator.
- Focus on the future.
- Build on people's strengths.
- Develop emotional intelligence.
- Give constructive feedback.
- Actively listen.
- Define responsibilities.
- Please encourage others to be their best and healthiest selves.[1]

All these eight characteristics are covered in *Successful Self-Leadership: An Inside-Out Approach in Seven Steps*. We build on how one shows intent from Day 1. In the next chapter, we allow you to reflect on these characteristics and consider how to apply them.

First Impressions Count

Will Rogers, an American vaudeville performer and actor, said: "You never get a second chance to make a good first impression." Stepping into a leadership role as a seasoned executive or a novice supervisor is daunting and exciting. How you show up has a significant bearing on your effectiveness. Studies suggest that developing a 90-day plan, with 30-day and 60-day milestones, improves your odds of success (Manzoni and Barsoux 2009).[2] Although a plan helps, your new team members assess who you are and what you bring to the table from Day one.

Goman (2015), in her article: *Why First Impressions Stick: And What You Can Do About It* says,

> Two seconds—30 seconds, tops—that's all the time it takes to assess your confidence, competence, status, likeability, warmth, and trustworthiness. That's how much time you have to make a first impression.[3]

Goman calls this first impression a "sticky" evaluation. This judgment begins with the very first conversation a team member has with their new leader. So, having a Day-1 plan helps to make an excellent first impression.[4]

How does a leader create an excellent first impression?

Could you share a little about yourself? Please do not overdo it. Communicate enough about yourself to build rapport. We know from research that when a leader and team member have a positive connection, it usually translates to better performance (Sluss et al. 2012).[5] A broader definition of performance includes the following four traits:

- Exercising one's independent judgment.
- Thinking creatively about solving problems.
- Collaborating with colleagues.
- Displaying energy and enthusiasm.

Kouzes and Posner (2011), in their book *Credibility: How Leaders Gain and Lose It, Why People Demand It*, state that "leadership is a relationship."⁶ A new leader can build a constructive working relationship from their first conversation with a team member.

People who work with a new leader naturally want to know something about them. Team members want to understand what makes their new leader tick. This does not mean you should bear your soul! Your colleagues will already know you if you have been promoted from within the team. Be mindful that you are now in a different role—you are now their leader, not their teammate.

If you are hired from outside the company, share what drives you, what you value, and your priorities. As mentioned, team members have already assessed these things from their first conversation with you. In addition to comprehending what a new leader stands for, people who work closely with you will mostly want to develop a bond. Be relatable without telling everyone you meet your life story. I think it's the foundation for building rapport.

Besides disclosing a little about yourself, people want to know about your work experience. This means a rundown of only some of the companies you have worked for and your positions. Team members are broadly interested in your background and its relevance to this new leadership role. Sharing some of your stories instills confidence in your leadership capability. Your new team members particularly want to understand how your experience will shape your expectations of them (Sluss 2020).⁷ Could you share our story, not your resume?

Your story should be one or two pivotal moments offering insight into your value. What stories can you share that illustrate your identity and what is important to you? These should be true stories! We have been conditioned from childhood to listen and learn from stories. What are some interesting episodes in your life that help others know you? Could you start with what motivated you to apply for the new role?

Communicate Your Intentions

Apart from what drives you, people want to know our intentions. What is your vision for the role? How will this vision impact them? Your vision should connect with your story. For instance, if you value personal growth and development, your life story should reflect that.

In the early days, I'd like you to explain an intention that builds upon what is already in place within the team and company. People get anxious if you disregard everything that's happened previously, particularly those things that work well within the team. Your goal is to intentionally assist the team in building on its foundations.

Communicate how you see your team playing a critical role in your vision. Sluss (2020), in his article, *Stepping into a Leadership Role? Be Ready to Tell Your Story* reminds us that,

> ...everybody likes to be part of a story—especially a success story. And if, as a new leader, you put some thought into making an excellent first impression on your reports and winning their support, you can help them be part of yours.[8]

Being a good communicator is about more than just making grand announcements. How leaders converse in their informal interactions is often underestimated. Corridor conversations affect perceptions and performance. Poor communication or a lack of information is a demotivator. I want you to know that leading with intent means reminding people of your vision in most of your interactions, albeit briefly.

Vision provides context. I think explaining why you made your decisions should be consistent with your future focus. Crosby (2018), in his article, *How Great Leaders Get Employees Motivated by Explaining Intent*, says that providing context is the essence of intent-based leadership.[9]

A study by Korn Ferry found that 73 percent of employees say their primary motivator for their work is its purpose and meaning (Crosby 2018).[10] Furthermore, 82 percent of employees work for their company for other reasons than pay. We also know from Frederick Herzberg's research that money, beyond a certain threshold, is not a motivating factor (Ewen, Smith, and Hulin 1966).[11]

This does not suggest that a salary does not have any motivating effect. It means that pay increases beyond a certain level—although undoubtedly welcomed by the recipient—will not necessarily boost one's performance in the long term. Moreover, if an employee does not feel valued, there is a limit to what they are willing to accept. This is why constantly communicating the meaning and relevance of the work team members is effective.

Providing context and clear intention is not only inspiring; it also affects the bottom line. For example, the Manufacturers' Alliance for Productivity and Innovation (MAPI) identified that employees spend an average of 20 hours per year meeting with leaders. However, it was reported that a third of these employees leave these meetings confused about what their manager wants and where the company is heading (Crosby 2018).[12] Moreover, the MAPI estimates that companies with 5,000 employees lose an average of U.S.$770,000 annually in lost productivity from misaligned goals and unclear expectations.

A leader's responsibility goes beyond achieving sales targets and hitting key performance indicators. Even though an employee is responsible for whether they are engaged at work, it is the leader's job to establish a favorable setting for commitment to prosper. Communicating with purpose and intention is the basis for team members to realize that their work is valuable if they do not already know it.

Where the Rubber Meets the Road

Giving Rather Than Taking Control
Captain David Marquet, a former submariner, turned around the fortunes of the U.S. Navy's worst-performing nuclear submarine by refusing to give orders.[*] Marquet adopted an intent-based leadership approach instead of taking control of operations. He treated his crew as leaders. Marquet rationalized that his crew were highly trained specialists. Rather than assuming command, he gave his crew autonomy and control. In other words, he empowered the experts, who in turn empowered their team of experts. Performance improved dramatically.

---

[*]https://davidmarquet.com/my-story/

Beyond hitting targets, take a step back and consider the value of your team's work. Ask yourself these three questions:

- *How* does the work my team does have influence?
- *Who* benefits?
- *How* do they benefit?

Not only can intent-based leaders answer these questions—but they also look for daily opportunities to communicate the relevance of the team's work.

The Why of Work

Even mundane and tedious tasks can have a higher purpose. For example, John, the production supervisor, asks Tom at the end of his long shift to sweep the floor of the production area. This will take approximately 20 minutes to complete. John explains why he wants this done:

> I know you are tired at the end of your shift, Tom, but can you please sweep the floor in the production area? We have a significant potential customer visiting us in the morning, and they want to see how we operate before placing a large order. A tidy workplace will create a good first impression, which could mean the difference between placing a large order or not. Thank you.

It is unlikely that Tom will be bouncing off the walls with excitement after hearing this message from his supervisor—he is tired and wants to go home and get some sleep. Tom at least understands John's reason for this request.

Too often, managers think that employees understand the value and purpose of what they do. This is an incorrect assumption—team members frequently do not know or have lost sight of the task's purpose. Briefly, we often cannot see the forest for the trees.

An intent-based leader ensures that jobholders understand the purpose of their jobs. If the leader does not know the project's intention, they should seek clarification from their boss. Intentional leadership starts with realizing the more significant reason for the tasks, activities, and projects in their sphere of influence.

Sinek (2011) wrote an international bestseller, *Start with Why: How Great Leaders Inspire Everyone to Take Action.*[13] Sinek poses two questions: *Why are some people and organizations more inventive, pioneering, and successful than others?* And, *why are they able to repeat their success again and again?* Sinek states that *what* employees do in business is less relevant than the *why* behind it. Successful individuals and companies understand the purpose of the work they do.

Michels (2017), director of Bain & Company, shares a story about a new CEO who rolled out several changes in his article *Because I Said So: Lessons in Parenting and Change Management.* These initiatives got zero traction. Employees pushed back because they did not see the value in making these changes. They stuck to their old routines. Michels explains that executives were impatient in implementing the CEO's initiatives. They incorrectly assumed that employees would understand the rationale for these changes. This misunderstanding was costly.

The executives unintentionally slowed down the time these changes took hold because they did not engage the workforce. Michels claims that forcing decisions without a sufficient explanation of their intention is a key reason 88 percent of change programs do not work as planned.

Defining your intent and taking the time to explain this to your team saves you time overall.

Engaging Others in the How

You involve others in the *how*, closely aligning with the *why*. Facilitating open and honest dialogue about implementing the change enables others to be engaged in the solution. Yes, it does take time. And yes, you have a great plan, but … not including your team in a conversation at the start of a new project will eventually be frustrating and take more time.

Initiating dialogue at the outset of a project is like investing money. It can be painful at first—departing with your hard-earned cash.

Nevertheless, assuming the stock or property appreciates, you will be grateful for investing and engaging in dialogue about how it pays off later.

Start collaborating when times are calm and stable. Do not wait for an emergency when you are forced to down tools and discuss fixing a crisis. Besides, it is expected to apportion blame and find excuses when things go off the rails. You will have more trust and influence working together with your team before cracks appear in a new project plan. If you are wondering whether to communicate something openly with your team, that is probably an indicator that you should do so.

Lai (2017) reminds us in her article, *Motivating Employees Is Not About Carrots or Sticks*,[14] that talking with your team about the relevance of their work is sound practice. She says, "Put away the carrots and sticks (rewards and punishment) and have meaningful conversations instead."

But I have a great plan; why should I bother consulting my team about it? you may be thinking. Even with a lot of thought and thorough planning, your perspective is limited to one perspective—yours. Could there be a better way? Have I assessed *all* the risks? You might discover enhancements or find risks you had not considered by discussing the plan with the team. You are relying on your team to execute the project successfully. Give your team time and space to discuss the plan at the start of a project.

Nevogt (2022), cofounder of Hubstaff, succinctly sums up the importance of collaboration:

> If you are the only one who knows all the essential information, you're the only person in your company who can make good decisions. That's not an efficient way to work.[15]

A clear and open intention encourages your team to be engaged and focused on the future.

Look to the Future

Finally, the second characteristic of leading with intention listed at the beginning of this chapter is to *Look to the future*. Crosby (2018) explains how open dialogue about your intent with your team shifts the focus from the past to the future:

> It is natural for your team members to dwell on past problems or the good old days; however, leaders focus on the future. When employees are excited about what is to come and feel like the future is bright, their work efforts will reflect their hopes and drive for the company's success.[16]

We started this chapter by identifying eight characteristics of showing intention. I have covered all of these in this and other chapters. Practice putting Show Intent into effect by applying these characteristics.

Next, we look at practice # 6: Self-Regulation.

Top 10 Points

1. You never get a second chance to make an excellent first impression.
2. People who work with a new leader naturally want to know something about them.
3. If you are hired from outside the company, share what drives you, what you value, and your priorities.
4. Apart from what drives you, people wanted to know our intentions.
5. Vision provides context. I think explaining why you made your decisions should be consistent with your future focus.
6. Providing context and clear intention is not only inspiring; it also affects the bottom line.
7. Beyond hitting targets, take a step back and consider the value of your team's work.
8. Even mundane and tedious tasks can have a higher purpose.

9. Too often, managers think that employees understand the value and purpose of what they do.
10. An intent-based leader ensures that jobholders understand their job's purpose.

CHAPTER 13

Practice # 6: Self-Regulate

The ability to self-regulate is managing our thoughts, emotions, and behaviors.

Biological impulses drive our emotions. These biological impulses are beyond our control, but the resulting emotions are not. When emotions are running high, they certainly cannot be ignored but can be carefully managed. This is called self-regulation, and the quality of emotional intelligence liberates us from living like hostages to our impulses (Goleman, 2015).[1]

Although self-regulation commences within us, how we regulate our actions affects those around us. This is the reason self-regulation is a practice of the Outer Game. In this chapter, we unpack self-regulation; in the following chapter, we look at strategies to improve self-regulation.

What Is Self-Regulation?

Self-regulation is a facet of EQ. It is valuable at any time, but particularly in stressful circumstances. The ability to self-regulate is managing our thoughts, emotions, and behaviors. Self-regulation means not being derailed, adhering to one's values, maintaining focus, and sustaining effective working relationships. Managing emotions can assist a leader in being more rational and adaptable when dealing with problems and issues.

Leadership writer and consultant Wallbridge (2023) breaks self-regulation into four factors.[2] First, there is *attentional control*. This factor is the ability to focus on a specific task and filter out distractions. Second, there is *emotional regulation*. This is the capacity to manage emotional responses to minimize destructive emotions. Third, there is *impulse control*. This is the ability to resist acting on urges and impulses, even when dealing with difficult people and frustrating situations. And finally, there is *goal setting*. Avoiding waylaid with clear objectives and a manageable action plan. In concert with the practice of Show Intent, Self-regulation can be helpful in not getting ambushed and taken off course.

Terry is facing a challenging situation. He has tight deadlines for a major project. Terry has a choice. He can Show Intent, step back, and work with his team to analyze the objectives and the most effective route forward. This is the path of self-regulation. Alternatively, Terry can panic and make rushed and erratic decisions to do the job. This is the path of self-deregulation. To his and his team's benefit, Terry chooses the path of self-regulation.

So, Terry focuses on the task at hand (attention control). He remains calm and manages his emotional state (emotional regulation). Terry tempered his impulses (impulse control). He also has a goal and plan (goal setting). Terry's team trusts his cool head and benefits from his level-headedness. His choice to self-regulate contributes to a successful and calmer approach.

Responding or Reacting

So, self-regulation is a choice. It is no different from choosing a hot or cold breakfast each morning. Furthermore, self-regulation is a choice between *responding* or *reacting*. Reacting stems from an unconscious automatic process in the brain. In other words, reacting is an impulsive reply to stimuli. A reaction takes a second or less—it is instant. Choosing to respond, on the other hand, is deliberate and considered. Of the two choices, reacting is easier and quicker than responding.

As discussed in Chapter 3, our actions are driven mainly by unconscious patterns in the brain. Our thoughts and feelings often trigger our behavior. For instance, an unpleasant memory of an experience elicits a strong emotional response. These unregulated emotions can lead to irrational behavior.

For example, Christine remembers being embarrassed and humiliated by her boss in a meeting years ago. Even though this horrible and demeaning putdown occurred a decade ago, Christine is occasionally triggered by fear and apprehension when she attends meetings.

Frequently, we are not aware of these triggers. Even with a lack of consciousness, the subconscious patterns in the brain are present. These triggers can lead to a thoughtless, impulsive reaction without considering the consequences.

Habitual behavior patterns can be impulsive reactions, especially in high-stress situations. To throw another spanner in the works, a poor workplace culture can reinforce negative behavior patterns. Social norms and peer pressure can contribute to and support destructive, reckless actions.

For instance, if aggressive outbursts are commonplace in a business, a new hire—already challenged by aggressive triggers—may think it is okay to let off some steam occasionally. If aggressive behavior is standard practice, the new employee is socialized to communicate without filters, bolstering an already hostile work culture.

Responding, unlike reacting, requires a conscious decision to slow down, assess the situation, consider multiple perspectives, and choose an appropriate course of action. Knowing one's potential triggers is a good start. Self-awareness helps one be alert to potential trigger points and better manage one's emotional response.

Learning to Self-Regulate

We can curb unproductive or harmful outbursts with greater personal insight (the practice of Knowing Oneself). Awareness of your hot buttons also helps you develop empathy when someone reacts poorly to you. By understanding another person's impulsive reaction, such as making a sarcastic comment, you can prevent yourself from retorting badly. Empathizing with their outburst does not mean you agree or accept what they say and how they act. It means understanding why they reacted that way and choosing to respond rather than react.

Self-regulation is a critical success factor in life. Emotional regulation can be developed and improved with practice. By improving intentional control, practicing emotional regulation, applying impulse control, and setting goals, you improve your ability to self-regulate. This contributes to your well-being, relationships, and success.

A longitudinal field experiment by Yeow and Martin (2013) examined the impact of self-regulation on teams engaged in a university program.[3] Half the leaders were randomly allocated to learn self-regulation tactics from a professional coach. The other half did not have any coaching on regulating their behavior. There was a dramatic and measurable improvement in the leaders' success who applied the skills they learned during pressure situations. More specifically, the leaders who learned to self-regulate had higher ratings on leadership effectiveness from their team, performed better, and received superior grades compared with the control group.

Researchers Latham and Locke (1991) observed that people are *natural* self-regulators but not all are *effective* self-regulators.[5] Further, they suggest that self-regulation is promoted as a personality trait rather than a capability to be mastered. This assumption leads to a fixed mindset about self-regulation. You may recall that we defined growth and a fixed mindset in Chapter 9. In other words, *you either have it, or you have not*. A person harboring this fixed mindset will believe that learning to control their emotional reactions is futile.

However, self-regulation is a skill that needs to be developed. It is a learned behavior. It is not a gift that you are born with. How many babies have you seen practicing self-regulation? Being calm is often challenging but can be developed with practice.

Leaders are pressured to make many decisions spontaneously, so they have plenty of daily opportunities and choices to respond or react. How do I manage an unexpected traffic jam on the way to work when I am late for a meeting with a client? How do I deal with a colleague yelling at me in a meeting? How do I answer someone blaming me for a mistake that was not my fault? We are tested every day on how we manage our emotions.

One way to think about self-regulation is by comparing it with a shaken bottle of Coca-Cola and a shaken bottle of tap water. When you open a shaken bottle of Coke, the contents spew all over the place and ruin everything. That is like reacting rather than responding. Our unregulated emotions have no filter and have a negative impact. Relationships can be damaged, sometimes permanently.

By contrast, self-regulation is like opening an agitated bottle of water. No matter how much the bottle of water is dropped or shaken, it does not spew like a carbonated beverage when opened. The water remains tranquil. We can respond like a water bottle, but one must consciously decide. The temptation under duress is often to react and yell out our raw feelings and emotions. Unfortunately, as simple as responding is, there is usually a costly price afterward.

Goleman (2015), the emotional intelligence guru, states that self-regulation is a core leadership skill. "In my experience, I've never seen the tendency toward radical outbursts to surface as an indicator of strong leadership."[4] Most good leaders are calm and considered when under pressure.

Despite being a hallmark of good leadership, self-regulation is often underrated and misunderstood. Others can perceive people who demonstrate great control over their emotions as cold, aloof, or dispassionate. On the other hand, we tend to lionize, or at least forgive, the leader who occasionally blows their top. There is *fire in the belly* of that leader. Or we might mistake this behavior as characteristic of a *straight shooter*. However, as Goleman rightly points out, radical outbursts are not a sign of a strong leader, even occasionally. It is a sign of a leader needing emotional self-regulation practice.

Benefits for Leaders

Here are four reasons why developing self-regulation is imperative for a leader. First, a leader who controls their emotions is reasonable to work with. They sustain a safe and fair workplace.

Second, self-regulation can positively influence others. Who wants to be a fiery rabble-rouser when their boss is calm and even-handed? When the leader is composed and measured, their team tends to follow suit.

Third, self-regulation is a competitive advantage. In an organization where things are constantly chopping and changing, remaining calm and in control is an asset. Technology is continually evolving. Companies divide and merge regularly. Competition is fierce. In a stressful and high-pressured marketplace, people need and benefit from calm, measured leadership.

Fourth, self-regulation boosts one's integrity. Most disasters we read about in the corporate world result from impulsive behavior or a lack of self-regulation. Examples include abuses of power, jeopardized workers, exaggerated profit reporting, and embezzlement. Leaders who can self-regulate think twice before committing to what might end up being a disastrous course of action.

Where the Rubber Meets the Road

What Others Say About Self-Regulation

> Mastering others is strength. Mastering yourself is true power.
>
> —Lao Tze.

> Self-leadership … is about influencing ourselves, creating the self-motivation and self-direction we need to accomplish our goals.
>
> —Charles C. Manz.

> All human beings are self-leaders; however, not all self-leaders are effective at self-leading.
>
> —Charles C. Manz.

> Being a self-leader is to serve as chief, captain, president, or CEO of one's own life.
>
> —Peter Drucker.

> The first and best victory is to conquer self.
>
> —Plato.

> The one thing you can't take away from me is how I respond to what you do to me.
>
> —Viktor E. Frankl.

> First, be a leader of yourself. Only then can you grow to lead others.
> —David Taylor-Klaus.
>
> Leadership's First Commandment: Know Thyself … No tool can help a leader who lacks self-knowledge.
> —Harvard Business Review Editorial.

The scientific studies of self-control started about 40 years ago in criminology and psychology. Since then, hundreds of studies have shown the positive effects of self-discipline. For instance, people with higher levels of self-control eat healthier, are less likely to engage in substance abuse, perform better at school, and build high-quality friendships (De Ridder, Lensvelt-Mulders, and Baumeister 2011).[6] At work, leaders with higher levels of self-control display more effective leadership styles (Yam et al., 2016).[7] These leaders with self-control are more likely to inspire and intellectually challenge their followers instead of being abusive or micromanaging (Byrne et al. 2014).[8]

With these benefits, why do people lack self-control at work?

Yam and his colleagues (2016) conducted a comprehensive review of research findings on employee self-control.[9] Analyzing more than 120 management papers, they found that there are three main reasons why people occasionally lose self-control:

- Self-control is a finite cognitive resource.
- Diverse types of self-control tap the same pool of self-control resources.
- Exerting self-control can negatively affect future self-control if it is not replenished.

Self-control is like developing muscle strength. Our physical strength is limited, like self-control. Physical activities like football, basketball, and walking deplete our strength reserves. Continued exertion can negatively affect future physical strength if it is not restored.

For example, employees in the retail and hospitality industries trained to force a smile in their interactions with customers cannot sustain this happy veneer forever. Moreover, being trained to put on a friendly face with customers is an exercise in self-control that suppresses one's true feelings. However, later, when dealing with their colleagues, these superficially happy employees are less likely to be able to regulate their interactions (Yam et al., 2016).[10]

Some research findings illustrate some surprisingly costly consequences of having lower self-control at work. For instance, poor self-regulation can lead to unethical and deviant behavior. A study by Grissinger (2017) found that nurses are more likely to be rude to patients when self-control resources are low.[11] Tax accountants without self-control are likelier to commit fraud (Yam, Chen, and Reynolds 2014).[12] Employees with poor self-regulation engage in unethical behavior, such as lying to their supervisors and stealing office supplies (Barnes et al. 2011).[13]

As I stated in the introduction of this book, Frankl (2013) describes in *Man's Search for Meaning* that he was able to survive the Holocaust and three years of incarceration in a Nazi concentration camp when most did not.[14] Despite the immense hardships he experienced, Frankl was able to survive. Moreover, throughout his traumatic experience, he demonstrated many of the seven self-leadership practices covered in *Successful Self-Leadership: An Inside-Out Approach in Seven Steps*.

Frankl understood that he could not change what was happening to him or his fellow prisoners. However, he could choose how to respond to it. More specifically, he talks about the importance of living by a set of values. Frankl had a strong awareness of his values and lived them. Moreover, Frankl found meaning and purpose in his otherwise terrifying surroundings by doing so. He applied constructive thought strategies and contributed not only to his well-being but also to the well-being of his fellow inmates. Through heightened self-regulation, Frankl persevered, not only throughout the entire period of incarceration but also afterward. His is a truly inspirational story.

Next, we look at practical ways to self-regulate.

Top 10 Points

1. Although self-regulation commences within us, how we regulate our actions affects those around us.
2. Self-regulation is a facet of EQ.
3. Self-regulation can be broken down into four factors: attentional control, emotional regulation, impulse control, and goal setting.
4. Self-regulation is a choice between responding or reacting.
5. Our actions are driven chiefly by unconscious patterns in the brain.
6. Responding, unlike reacting, requires a conscious decision to slow down, assess the situation, consider multiple perspectives, and choose an appropriate course of action.
7. Greater personal insight (the practice of Knowing Oneself) can curb unproductive or harmful outbursts.
8. Self-regulation is a critical success factor in life.
9. Self-regulation is a skill to be developed.
10. There are many benefits for leaders in developing self-regulation skills.

CHAPTER 14

13 Proven Ways to Boost Emotional Self-Regulation

Good leaders do not react; they respond.

Taking breaks is beneficial for relieving stress and improving one's performance (Meijman and Mulder 2019). *Recovering from work stress restores energy, replenishes mental resources, diminishes fatigue, improves sleep, and safeguards against cardiovascular disease* (Geurts and Sonnentag, 2006). *Why is taking a break often frowned upon?*

Now, it is time to explore 13 simple and practical ideas for practicing self-regulation. I hope you will see that improving self-regulation is a worthwhile endeavor. Nevertheless, like most things in life, it needs practice. Developing self-regulation entails an awareness of bridging the gap between our thoughts and emotions and how we want to show up. With heightened self-awareness, one can recognize a mismatch between what is intended and what happens.

Self-Care

Emotional self-regulation is not only about caring for others but also about self-care. Moreover, a leader's emotional state sets the tone for their team. How you react or respond to situations teaches others what is appropriate. So, another benefit of emotional self-regulation is the example you set for others. Your team will not only appreciate your ability to stay calm under pressure, but they will also most likely follow suit.

Being kind to oneself takes several forms. It is beneficial to practice self-compassion and forgiveness when you are struggling. Instead of being down on yourself when you fail at something, ask: *What was there to learn? How can this learning be applied next time?* These questions exhibit a growth mindset. Another way to be kind to yourself is to celebrate small wins or when you achieve a goal. Shifting from self-cruelty to self-kindness involves training oneself to ask different questions.

Proper Sleep

Research shows proper sleep is vital for self-control (Yam et al. 2017).[1] Good sleep does not guarantee emotional restraint, but it is a great start. Sleep has a fantastic restorative effect on self-control. One study examined leaders and their sleep patterns (Yam et al. 2017).[2] The conclusion was that leaders who slept well at night (defined as having minimal interruptions to sleep) were much more likely to exercise self-control. The study also showed that these leaders—compared with their counterparts who did not sleep well—refrained from being abusive, such as yelling and being argumentative.

All the other strategies in this chapter will have negligible effect if you do not sleep enough.

Companies often expect employees to work beyond traditional office hours. However, excessive overwork can be counterproductive. A sleep-deprived employee can experience emotional volatility at work and home, and a lack of sleep weakens self-control.

Managers should be more aware that long work hours impact employees' behavior and well-being. For example, Google has installed sleep pods at the office to allow employees to nap and be reenergized (Yam et al. 2017).[3] You do not need to go that far. Working overtime occasionally is perfectly reasonable. However, leaders are responsible for monitoring work hours and their team members' well-being.

Being in Touch With Your Emotions

Another neglected part of workplace wellness is providing safe opportunities for people to tap into their emotions. In the last chapter, you will recall that I discussed the nauseating *service with a smile* concept and its detrimental effects on self-control, a finite resource.

Service-oriented companies often compel employees to smile in front of customers. While *smile training* might please—or at least appease—customers in the short term, it can drain the customer's self-control. Abandoning smiling in face-to-face customer interactions is not my point. A better approach is training employees in customer-facing roles to feel the positive emotions behind a genuine smile. Tapping into one's feelings is a more authentic and effective form of smile training.

Another study on physicians and bedside manners reinforces this impact of being in touch with one's emotions (Larson and Yao 2005).[4] The research illustrates the psychological benefits of doctors trained to empathize with patients. These doctors reported greater self-control. Meanwhile, the doctors in the study who were told to fake empathy later reported more symptoms of burnout. Furthermore, they reported lower job satisfaction. Service-oriented employees benefit from engaging fully with their clients, customers, and patients rather than faking their feelings.

Get Physical

Physical exercise increases the release of endorphins, which boost your mood and help counter stress. Moreover, regular exercise helps concentration, giving you control over your body and life. Exercise can also improve sleep, which I have just discussed. Take a few moments to step away from work, stretch, walk, and reset your mind. You will undoubtedly find yourself in a better mood and more refreshed when you return to work.

Where the Rubber Meets the Road

Closing the Gap

Self-leadership's early definition was based on three central theories: self-control, social-cognitive theory, and self-determination (Neuhaus 2020).[5] Self-control is synonymous with self-management and self-regulation. It describes the iterative process of determining a desired end state, comparing that to the current state, and subse-

> quently taking action to close the gap between the two (Miller 2020).⁶

Be Aware of the Red Mist

Here are some techniques to catch your thoughts and feelings before it is too late. One way is to recognize the physiological cues. Please take a look at your heart rate. Is it increasing? Are you perspiring or sweating? Do you feel tension in your muscles? Are your breathing patterns becoming shallower? Nonverbally, are you closing yourself off? Are your shoulders hunched? Is your eye contact diminishing? These are the tell-tale signs of anxiety and the potential loss of control.

Awareness of these physiological signals can help regulate emotions and impulses.

Be aware of the red mist! The red mist is a state of momentary, intense anger and frustration—our judgment is suspended. The red mist is a cue that, unless arrested, will lead to a brief loss of self-control and failure to think sensibly in the face of strong negative feelings. The red mist can also result in an onslaught of impulsive, irrational, and potentially career-limiting behavior. You have probably experienced the red mist unless you are a Buddhist monk!

What are your hot buttons? A hot button is a trigger for being vulnerable and overreaching emotionally. Without sufficient awareness, a hot button elicits a strong reaction. For example, Jasper believes wholeheartedly in fairness and equity. He observes Jen taking credit for an idea proposed by one of the quieter team members. Jasper explodes and criticizes Jen. Like Jasper, we can act impulsively when our hot buttons are tested without a moment's thought. By being aware of these sensitive topics, you are in a better position to bypass emotional impulsivity.

Knowing is half the battle. The other half is finding alternative and more constructive ways to deal with your triggers. Ask yourself preemptively: *How am I going to manage this when I am triggered?*

Breathing and Pausing

My favorite way to create a momentary space is to focus on breathing. Much empirical research shows a causal link between mindfulness and emotional regulation (Hülsheger et al. 2013).[7] This is especially true when dealing with interpersonal conflict. A key component of mindfulness is breathwork (Arch and Craske 2015).[8] This involves concentrating on deliberate breathing for self-regulation purposes.

When you feel the blood flushing to your head and the urge to either shut down or blow up (red mist), focus on your breath. Concentrating on your breathing assists in mitigating a poor response and being mindful.

Here is the bottom line: Good leaders do not react; they respond. Knowing how to respond constructively is a big part of self-regulation.

Creating momentary time and space to respond is imperative in stopping an instantaneous reaction. For instance, firing off an e-mail angrily is not a wise move. Pause. Sleep on it. Moreover, please send it in the morning. By pausing, you will inevitably view the situation in a calmer and more objective light. Take the time to process your feelings and emotions—it usually pays off. Go home and think about what happened during a difficult meeting. Write your thoughts down. Alternatively, talk about them with someone you trust.

Apply the 24-hour rule. Instead of sending that scathing e-mail or speaking to *that* person when you are upset, step back and take a day to absorb what happened. Venting your anger might make you feel better in the short term, but there will inevitably be a price to pay. Moreover, reacting in the moment will prolong and amplify your anger. You may also feel guilty about the words you used. You will see things more lucidly by taking time to think.

So, before blowing your stack and doing something you will probably regret, such as throwing a temper tantrum for all to see, learn to pause. I'd like you to please practice until you find yourself in total control.

Self-control starts by being more aware of your emotions and how you react to them. Know Thyself (another of the seven self-leadership practices) allows you to make better decisions. For example, it could be as simple as knowing you are cranky in the afternoon because you slept in and missed an important conference call. Recognizing your emotions, why you are feeling them, and how you are helping temper your emotional impulses helps.

One helpful tactic to buy time in a heated encounter is actively listening. Ask questions instead of instantly defending yourself. As I discussed in Chapter 10, be respectfully curious. Respond to a provocative comment by asking a question. *Why do you think that? Can you give me an example?* These open-ended questions provide breathing space to think and process what is being said. Active listening is a powerful and underrated tool.

Adapt to your environment. Please don't allow an inflammatory comment to dictate your unhelpful emotional reaction. Shift your mindset by asking *yourself* open-ended questions. For example, *What is the most important thing I can do right now?* is a better response than *How dare they say that!*

Recalibrating one's emotional state is challenging. That is why it is essential to pause, even momentarily.

Mindfulness Meditation

I briefly extolled the virtues of mindfulness meditation in Chapter 4. Meditation trains you to reflect quietly and gain more controlover your thoughts. Any amount of meditation, whether daily or a five-minute session here and there, positively affects one's ability to self-regulate. Schedule a time each day to sit in a quiet space, clear your mind, and focus on breathing. This practice will help develop a sense of calm when negative thoughts arise. This, in turn, assists you to control your emotions and behavior by being more practiced at being in the moment.

Emotional Display Rule

I would like you to commit to staying calm. It sounds too basic. However, it is less likely to happen if you do not make this pledge, or you will drop the ball at the first sign of agitation. This promise to oneself is what Gosserand and Diefendorff (2005) refer to as an *emotional display rule*. Research supports having *emotional display rules* as an antidote for poor self-control.[9]

For example, a rule might be: *No matter what happens, I stay calm. I do not react emotionally.* Alternatively, *I speak calmly and respectfully. I do not raise my voice.* Once you have established the rule, live by your rule. Make this a personal code of conduct. Fight the urge, at every moment, to break your code. Live by this rule like a professional athlete lives by their training regime. Furthermore, do not beat up on yourself when you slip up—as you surely will. Breaking your emotional display rule is bound to happen from time to time. Nevertheless, having a rule in the first place will temper many more destructive emotional outbursts.

Engage in positive self-talk. We typically feel great when something exciting happens, like a promotion at work. When mistakes happen, self-talk is primarily negative. Thoughts produce feelings.

Please repeat a mantra to yourself. When you feel defensive and are urged to react emotionally, you can repeat a simple directive to yourself. For example, your mantra might be to *stay calm and not react*. Please repeat this to yourself as long as possible to fight the urge to erupt. Again, research supports the power of positive self-talk to regulate one's emotions in stressful situations (Kross et al. 2014).[10]

Create a written reminder of your mantra. Place it where you will see it every day. For example, have your mantra on your desk. This will be a visual cue to stick with your emotional rule when under pressure. I have the following words written above my desk:

Calm, Caring, and Curious.

Make the mantra short so it is read and internalized in two seconds. These words set the tone for you and anyone entering your workspace or office. According to a study by Bargh and Williams (2007), these visual aids foster an unconscious link between the setting (your office) and the occupant's emotional state.[11]

The Power of Journaling

Could you keep a journal? You may recall that in Chapter 4, I explained that journaling helps clear your mind. Writing allows one to self-soothe—you can process your day, whether good or bad. A journal can also document your progress in developing more self-regulation or any other self-leadership practice. You can then look back and reflect on your journey.

People often need to get the right idea about journaling. However, in my experience, when people try it—even if they are skeptical at the outset—they inevitably become converts.

Seek Feedback

It is easier to look at yourself objectively with some external feedback. As I said in Chapter 3, seeking input from a trusted colleague can be beneficial in improving your self-awareness. Feedback is helpful to monitor one's self-control. Receiving critical feedback can leave you vulnerable, but it is also one of the most effective ways to gain insight into how others perceive you.

When leaders take responsibility for their goals (Show Intent), they will likely control their actions. Showing intent makes you accountable. Invite a coworker to be your accountability partner. An accountability partner supports others in committing to or maintaining progress toward a desired goal.*

Researchers interviewed recovering drug addicts at a rehabilitation center for 10 months. The pattern they uncovered was how influential accountability was for one's recovery. Individuals who took responsibility for their recovery had a reciprocal sense of responsibility, both to and for each other. In other words, recuperating people with an addiction felt responsible for providing and receiving support. The researchers speculated that accountability enhances addicts' recovery (Lewis, Hopper, and Healion 2012).[12]

Who can you trust to check your self-regulation progress each day? When you hold yourself accountable and take steps to have others do

---

*https://en.wikipedia.org/wiki/Accountability_partner.

the same, you strengthen how you act and react in challenging situations and circumstances.

Educate Yourself

Read books and educational journals, listen to podcasts, or take an online course. As you learn more, you will become more observant, not just of yourself, but of the people and world around you. You will recognize trends, habits, and triggers more readily to avoid negatively reacting to certain situations. Educating yourself boosts your overall EQ.

Like the other six self-leadership practices, Self-regulation requires commitment, self-reflection, and training. Building this capability, as with the different practices, is ongoing. Learning should never end. Modify your thoughts and actions as you practice monitoring them to suit the occasion. Practice some of these techniques to thoughtfully choose a constructive response rather than an impulsive reaction under duress.

In Appendix F, you can take a look at your current level of emotional self-regulation.

Top 10 Points

1. Emotional self-regulation is not only about caring for others but also about self-care.
2. Proper sleep is vital for self-control.
3. Physical exercise increases the release of endorphins, which boost your mood and help counter stress.
4. Please keep in mind your hot buttons.
5. Good leaders do not react; they respond.
6. Mindful meditation trains you to reflect quietly and gain more control over your thoughts.
7. Engage in positive self-talk.
8. I would like you to commit to staying calm.
9. Could you keep a journal?
10. Educating yourself boosts your overall EQ.

CHAPTER 15

Practice # 7: Be Curious

Leaders should be in the business of asking questions rather than answering them.

A survey of 520 chief learning and talent officers found that senior leaders often shy away from encouraging curiosity. Leaders usually assume that letting employees follow their curiosity will lead to chaos. Furthermore, they believed the company would be more challenging to manage if people could explore their interests. Those surveyed thought allowing others to follow their curiosity would lead to more disagreements. Also, encouraging curiosity would slow down decision-making and increase business costs.

Although most leaders aspire to be creative and innovative, they frequently reject original ideas when presented with them. Being curious often involves questioning the status quo, which only sometimes produces a better result. So, why leaders avoid entertaining curiosity is understandable (Gino 2018).[1]

Be Curious is the last but by no means the least essential practice in the Self-Leadership Development Framework. A growing body of research stresses the value of curiosity as a leadership trait (Gino 2018). In this chapter, we explore the concept of curiosity and how it significantly augments leadership capability. In the subsequent chapter, I share several practical tools for being inquisitive without being too intrusive.

Curiosity is an intrinsic human trait. Early hunters and gatherers needed to be interested in survival. Curiosity drives exploration, learning, and understanding. It is the spark that ignites creativity and innovation. A curious leader is inclined to question the status quo, seek new information, and encourage diverse perspectives.

The Curious Leader

Being curious, however, is about more than seeking answers. It is also about embracing uncertainty and ambiguity. Although initially a survival trait in the savanna, curiosity is an asset in today's fast-paced, ever-changing business landscape.

In a rapidly evolving business environment, innovation is critical to staying ahead of the curve. Innovators are intrinsically curious—they are constantly looking for better ways to do things, are prepared to challenge assumptions, and are willing to explore novel ideas. A leader with a curious mind also inspires their team to think outside the box. Later in the chapter, I will return to the underrated value of leading by example.

A curious leader promotes divergent thinking and inclusive decision-making. Wherever appropriate, an inquisitive leader encourages experimentation and trial and error. To them, failure is accepted as a stepping-stone to success. Team members, therefore, feel empowered to take prudent risks, knowing that their curiosity and creativity are valued. A prime example is Google's famous *20 percent-time* policy, allowing employees to spend a fifth of their workweek on projects of their choosing (Gersch 2013).[2] The 20 percent-time policy illustrates that curiosity can be institutionalized to drive innovation.

Instead of dismissing various opinions, a leader practicing curiosity seeks diverse perspectives. They recognize that innovation thrives in workplaces where disparate ideas converge. By pushing for inclusive decision-making, the curious leader ensures that the solutions and strategies developed are robust and reflect diverse viewpoints.

Leading others involves navigating through complex challenges and solving complicated problems. Being curious equips a leader to approach issues from various angles, consider alternative solutions, and adapt to changing circumstances.

Cultivating one's curiosity helps stay current, builds connections, and elevates EQ. Be Curious is a practice that can be learned like the other six self-leadership practices.

Curiosity and a Growth Mindset

While curiosity is a human trait, some people are more naturally curious than others, and not everyone is curious about the same things. The good news is that you can learn to become more interested, which benefits you and your team.

Being curious and open to learning new things makes a leader more informed and well-rounded. As mentioned, it increases EQ, creativity, and problem-solving abilities. Staying current, connected, and innovative are a few of the payoffs for being curious.

Alternatively, a leader who is apathetic and closed-minded will need help to relate to their team members. When leaders do not learn from or express interest in others, their growth and development are stifled. Team members will inevitably perceive this leader as uninterested, disconnected, and out of touch.

Having a fixed mindset—which I have said throughout *Successful Self-Leadership: An Inside-Out Approach in Seven Steps*—is fraught with danger. A fixed mindset takes hold when leaders think they have all the answers. The leader with a fixed mindset is driven by their ego. Not seeking or dismissing new perspectives, ideas, and opinions is characteristic of an ego-driven leader. The leader entertaining a fixed mindset feels threatened by the counterviews of others.

Being curious is based on a growth mindset, the opposite of a fixed mindset.

In *The Business Case for Curiosity*, Harvard Business School's Gino (2018) wrote,

> Curiosity allows leaders to gain more respect from their followers and inspires employees to develop more trusting and collaborative relationships with colleagues.[3]

Gino's perspective accords with Gallup's 2023 *Guide to Engaging and Retaining Employees*. Gallup's findings found that employees want motivating leaders who care about them as people, focus on their well-being, and communicate with them clearly and consistently.[*]

The Benefits of a Curious Mind

Let us probe deeper into the benefits of developing one's curiosity.

People who practice curiosity look beyond existing information, are open to expanding their understanding, and ask many questions. This inclination, when put into practice, broadens one's self-awareness. The first practice of self-leadership is Know Thyself. When we are inquisitive, we look within and self-reflect. We also desire to understand the perspectives of others. In other words, cultivating curiosity means being open to learning, willing to listen, and ready to entertain alternative ways of thinking.

By being curious, you seek to understand yourself and the world better. Being in a perpetual state of curiosity prevents you from becoming outdated and obsolete. As our world changes rapidly, today's leader needs to pivot rapidly. Being mindful and agile helps to respond to the ever-changing needs of the workplace and marketplace. A successful leader today must be curious and relationship-driven, prioritizing open communication. If leaders are indifferent to learning new things, unwilling to reflect on their behavior occasionally, and closed to other opinions, they will be left behind.

Inquisitiveness expands one's thinking, fosters creativity, and enhances problem-solving capabilities. In other words, if you are open to new ideas and opinions, you will widen your perspective and be able to find a solution to even the most challenging problem. Gaining new knowledge boosts brain power.

Another benefit of curiosity is that it builds connections and improves relationships. Human connections thrive when there is two-way communication and a nonjudgmental interest in the thoughts and opinions of others. Whether taking interest in someone's work, inquiring about someone's happiness, or listening to an alternative point of view, authentic curiosity builds engagement—a deeper and more fulfilling relationship.

When we are curious, dopamine immediately floods our brains. Dopamine, a feel-good pleasure hormone and neurotransmitter, is

---

*www.gallup.com/workplace/349484/state-of-the-global-workplace-2022-report.aspx.

released in the brain, reinforcing the excellent feeling curiosity brings. Being curious produces a positive state of mind. Apart from this physiological reaction, psychological curiosity opens the mind. Curiosity fuels more curiosity.

In summary, curiosity heightens self-awareness, builds better connections and relationships, and keeps you in a state of mindfulness. Staying curious assists in all aspects of life.

Intentional Curiosity

While some are naturally curious, others must be more intentional about developing their curiosity. Being curious intentionally reaps many benefits. It develops EQ, teaches you new things, and builds better connections. You become a more effective leader. Others prosper under the leadership of a curious leader. It is never too late to be curious-minded—it can be developed intentionally.

You can begin by asking more questions and giving fewer answers. Leaders should be in the business of asking questions rather than answering them. You open your curiosity by asking an open-ended question—whether of yourself or another person. For example, ask yourself these questions:

- What else must I know about this topic, individual, or problem?
- What information or opinion would add to my understanding?
- What do I need to include?
- Who can give me another perspective or more information?

When you ask someone a question, please be there and actively listen to their response. This builds a connection. No one wants to communicate with a know-it-all who is dismissive or indifferent to hearing their thoughts. I'd like you to approach your interactions from a relational perspective, seeking to bond and understand the other person. When you are in the moment and genuinely interested in what someone has to say, you create a psychologically safe place to interact. The conversation is more likely to be positive and productive for you both.

When you ask another person a question, you shift from monologue to dialogue. A question starts a conversation, and asking a question shows respect for the person and their circumstances. Stay within the bounds of asking prying, judging, or interrogating questions. When you ask overly intrusive questions, the other person will interpret your curiosity as an intrusion rather than a connection.

We have all heard the phrase: *curiosity killed the cat.* The implication is that curiosity about other people's affairs may get you into trouble. That is why leaders are often reluctant to ask questions and be curious. Nonetheless, being respectfully curious, vulnerable, and authentic are three priceless leadership traits.

Albert Einstein reminds us,

> The important thing is not to stop questioning. Curiosity has its reason for existing. One cannot help but be in awe when he contemplates the mysteries of eternity, life, and the marvelous structure of reality. It is enough if one tries merely to comprehend a small amount of this mystery every day (Miller 1955).[4]

We must always listen and seek to comprehend. We must never stop being curious.

As I have said several times, curiosity builds better engagement, heightens motivation, and produces results. Like most things, improving curiosity takes practice, but it is worth it.

Where the Rubber Meets the Road

The Power of Curiosity

Harry went into a one-on-one meeting with Jason and practiced being curious. Specifically, this meant being willing to admit he was wrong when he was instead of clinging stubbornly to his need to be correct. Harry actively listened to Jason's opinion, which was different from his. He acknowledged what Jason said in his own words and let Jason know he heard him. Harry finished by asking if

> there was anything else Jason wanted to say—he was present in the conversation.
>
> The result?
>
> Jason observed that Harry became more relaxed. He went from a posture of defense to one of openness and receptivity. Because Harry was not focused on being right and immediately defending his position, he offered a different perspective than the one he prepared. He could take in the information and pivot it into something better. The conversation was productive and not combative. From then on, Harry and Jason's working relationship improved.
>
> This is the power of curiosity (Bashar 2023).[5]

Bashar (2023), in her article, *How the Art of Curiosity Transforms Leadership* defines curiosity this way:

> Curiosity is about letting go of being right. It means being actively curious and open in every discussion, strategy meeting, or tough conversation. It means listening and understanding before responding. If you do it right, the result of this approach will be immediately felt. There will be a positive shift in the room's dynamic towards greater openness and buy-in.[6]

Barriers to Curiosity

What gets in the way of preventing a leader from expressing their curiosity?

For starters, centuries of conditioning around the outdated notion that the leader has *all* the answers inhibits the response: *I don't know*. With this misguided belief, a leader feels pressure to be the bastion of all knowledge and wisdom. This social conditioning—although invisible—manifests in behaviors such as giving a *decisive* answer rather than asking a question, such as *How can we find out?* This outdated notion of leadership is not the stimulus for curiosity to blossom. It is probably still the #1 impediment for a leader to cultivate a curious mind at work.

Having all the answers—or at least pretending to—is ineffective. It will not engage, motivate, encourage creative thinking, or produce. By asking questions and being open to learning, the leader adds more value than simply conveying the impression that they know best.

Another barrier to curiosity is distraction. Distractions are everywhere. With relentless pings, rings, and notifications on our desktops, cellphones, and smartwatches, the modern human being's ability to be present is tested countless times daily. "Distraction is the new normal," says Goleman (2013).[7]

Being curious begins with being present. This means not being in our heads during a conversation, actively listening, and reflecting before responding. We know we are supposed to do these things, but we only do them sometimes, which can be challenging.

Is there anything you can do to remind yourself to be in the here and now when you feel like being elsewhere mentally?

Another big obstacle to expressing curiosity is the virtual work environment. Video meetings are less conducive to openness and vulnerability than in-person meetings. Nonetheless, we must get better at communicating in online meetings. Practice having more casual, curious conversations, particularly with remote team members.

Leading by Example

I promised earlier to return to the undervalued impact of the leader's example. To nurture curiosity in one's team, leaders must show the way. Leaders need to be good listeners. A good listener listens to understand instead of listening to respond. They ask open-ended questions. By paraphrasing their key messages, they let team members know they have been heard. With regular practice, these listening skills will mirror the behavior you seek in others.

Good listening does not mean agreeing with someone's point of view. Leaders who listen well acknowledge what has been said and ensure there is nothing else team members need to say. Showing interest, asking questions, and paraphrasing others' responses set the tone. If leaders do this consistently, they form the foundation for an open and receptive workplace where ideas are discussed and trusting relationships are built. Acknowledging one's contribution without necessarily agreeing with one's viewpoint is the essence of respect.

Being Curious is a simple concept that's challenging to apply, given the barriers I have covered. I keep a sticky note on my computer reminding me to stay curious when I inevitably forget. The note reminds me to pause after listening to the person I am talking to and ask two questions before I respond. I do not allow myself to say anything unless I have come up with at least two questions. When I remember to be curious, I am more present; the dialogue is more dynamic, and often the conversation shifts in new and unexpected directions. Try it, and you will see for yourself.

Next, we look at ways to apply the practice of Be Curious.

Top 10 Points

1. Curiosity is an intrinsic human trait. Early hunters and gatherers needed to be curious to survive.
2. A curious leader promotes divergent thinking and inclusive decision-making.
3. While curiosity is a human trait, some people are more naturally curious than others, and not everyone is curious about the same things.
4. Being curious is based on a growth mindset, the opposite of a fixed mindset.
5. People who practice curiosity look beyond existing information, are open to expanding their understanding, and ask many questions.
6. Inquisitiveness expands one's thinking, fosters creativity, and enhances problem-solving capabilities.
7. Another benefit of curiosity is that it builds connections and improves relationships.

8. While some are naturally curious, others must be more intentional about developing their curiosity.
9. You can begin by asking more questions and giving fewer answers.
10. When you ask another person a question, you shift from monologue to dialogue.

CHAPTER 16

Unleashing the Power of Inquisitiveness

Despite what some may think, asking lots of questions does not make you sound dumb—it makes you intelligent and competent.

Much of an executive's workday is spent asking others for information—requesting status updates from a team leader, for example, or questioning a counterpart in a tense negotiation. However, unlike professionals such as litigators, journalists, and doctors, who are taught how to ask questions as an essential part of their training, few executives think of questioning as a skill that can be honed—or consider how their answers to questions could make conversations more productive (John 2018).[1]

Now that we have considered the benefits of Being Curious in the previous chapter, we look at ways to develop this practice in this chapter. Here are five ways of bolstering curiosity at work. We will explore these approaches and illustrate their use in several companies.

Hiring for Curiosity

In 2004, an anonymous billboard appeared on Highway 101, in the heart of Silicon Valley, posing this puzzle:

{first 10-digit prime found in consecutive digits of e}.com.[*]

This puzzle led curious passersby online, where they found another equation to solve. The handful of people who solved the second problem were invited to submit their résumé to Google. The company took this

---

[*]The answer: 7427466391.com.

unusual approach to find curious candidates. As Eric Schmidt, former Google CEO, said, "We run this company on questions, not answers."[†]

Google also identifies naturally curious employees with a line of interview questions like:

1. Have you ever been unable to stop learning something you have never encountered?
2. Why?
3. What kept you persistent?

IDEO, the design and consulting company, seeks to hire *T-shaped* employees. The vertical stroke of the T represents good, specialized knowledge and skills. The horizontal stroke of the T is a desire and ability to make connections across different disciplines, a quality requiring empathy and curiosity (Wale n.d.).[2] IDEO appreciates that empathy and curiosity are related.

Empathy lets an employee listen thoughtfully and see problems and decisions from another person's perspective. Companies like Google and IDEO understand that people perform at their best, not just because they are specialists. Their incredible skill is accompanied by an intellectual curiosity that leads them to ask questions, explore, and collaborate.

IDEO pays attention to how candidates discuss past projects to assess potential T-shaped employees. Someone who talks only about their contributions may not appreciate the value of collaboration. T-shaped candidates are more likely to talk about how they succeeded with the help of others. This emphasis may indicate a willingness to work cooperatively on future projects as an IDEO employee.

When hiring, ask candidates about their interests outside work. Reading books unrelated to one's field and exploring questions just for discovery are indicators of a curious mindset. You can also use an increasing array of reputable diagnostics that assess one's curiosity. These tools fundamentally measure people's interest in exploring unfamiliar areas. For instance, evaluating one's curiosity includes a willingness to analyze data to expose innovative ideas, reading widely beyond one's

---

[†]www.destination-innovation.com/lead-and-create-by-asking-questions/.

field, having diverse interests outside work, and relishing new learning experiences.

Pay attention to the questions the candidate asks in the job interview. Recognize that the answers they provide and the type of questions they ask can signal curiosity. For instance, a curious candidate may want to know about aspects of the organization that are not directly related to the job they are applying for.

Interview for curiosity, like everything else you typically assess in a job applicant. Getting it right at the hiring stage can save you much grief later.

Model Inquisitiveness

In the last chapter, I discussed the importance of walking the talk. Modeling curiosity should not be underestimated. If you are trying to inspire your team's curiosity, be inquisitive. Gina (2018), in her article, *The Business Case for Curiosity*, tells a remarkable story about modeling inquisitiveness:

> In 2000, when Greg Dyke had been named director general of the BBC but had not yet assumed the position, he spent five months visiting the BBC's central locations, assembling the staff at each stop. Employees expected a long presentation but got two simple questions: "What is the one thing I should do to make things better for you?" Dyke would listen carefully and then ask, "What is the one thing I should do to make things better for our viewers and listeners?"
>
> The BBC's employees respected their new boss for taking the time to ask questions and listen. Dyke used their responses to inform his thinking about the changes needed to solve problems facing the BBC and to identify what to work on first. After officially taking the reins, he gave a speech to the staff that reflected on his learning and showed employees that he had been genuinely interested in what they said.[3]

By asking these two questions and genuinely listening to the responses, Dyke modeled inquisitiveness. His approach showed that when exploring new terrain, listening is more important than talking: Actively listening plugs the gaps in our knowledge and leads to more informed questions.

Even so, why are we reluctant to ask questions? We fear we will be judged incompetent, indecisive, or unintelligent. Also, time is precious, and we want to avoid bothering people. The hesitancy to ask questions is exacerbated as people climb the organizational ladder. Senior managers may assume that they have less to learn. As I said in the previous chapter, there is still a belief that leaders are expected to talk and provide answers rather than listen and ask questions.

> ## Where the Rubber Meets the Road
>
> **Socialized to Answer Questions**
> We have been socializing since we can talk to answer questions. For example, as a child, we visited our grandparents. Our grandmother asked us a question, and we ignored it. What happens? We get a little clip behind the ear and get told by one of our parents, Always answer grandmother when she asks you a question. Then we get to school, and the teacher asks us a question just as we stare out the window, daydreaming. The teacher criticizes you for not being able to answer the question. In our early careers, we also got into trouble for not answering our boss when they asked us a question. We become conditioned to answering questions.

Be Open to Learning

The good news is that if you ask questions, team members (or anyone else) will respond with an answer. It might not be the answer we want, but it is an answer, nonetheless. Despite what some may think, asking lots of questions does not make you sound dumb—it makes you intelligent and competent.

Gina's (2018) research findings indicate that when we demonstrate curiosity about others by asking questions, people like us more and view us as more competent.[4] This builds trust and better working relationships. In other words, by asking questions, we create meaningful connections and promote creative outcomes.

Another way leaders can model curiosity is by acknowledging when they do not know the answer—that makes it clear that it is okay to be guided by curiosity. I vividly recall working with a world-class orchestra in Australia several years ago. I had arranged a meeting with the section principals, 18 in this orchestra. Principals are the heads of their section of the orchestra. The head violinist is referred to as the concertmaster. They are the leader of the orchestra and the conduit between the conductor and the rest of the orchestra.

When I was in the fourth grade, an insensitive teacher told me that I was tone-deaf. This memory compounded my anxiety in preparation for this meeting. I feared the orchestra would disrespect me because I was not a musician.

So, I started with a question:

"How are you playing as an orchestra?" After an awkward silence, the concertmaster responded:
"We aren't playing well at the moment."
"Why?" I asked inquisitively.
"We do not respect our conductor," another principal bravely volunteered.
"What can you do about that?"
"We could all play tightly together and follow my lead," said the concertmaster. He continued,
"I can take the lead, and everyone can follow."

Orchestras are the ultimate copycat—everyone follows the lead from the person sitting before them.

The energy in the room lifted. There was hope and positivity in the room.

"Do you have tickets for tonight's concert, Dr. Tim," one asked.
"No, I don't, but I would like to attend out of curiosity!"

That evening, I was sitting in the front row of the packed theater and thoroughly enjoyed the concert. At the concert's end, the orchestra received three standing ovations from the audience. The conductor dutifully bowed each time. He thought it was his genius conducting! Or did he know that the orchestra was taking matters into his own hands?

In either case, the remarkable performance began during the meeting with the principals. I posed several questions driven by curiosity, initiating an empowering dialogue with the orchestra's leaders. Together, we devised a solution to address an awkward issue and reached a consensus on a course of action in what initially appeared to be an impossible situation.

Hugo, a coaching client, was appointed CEO of an engineering firm, even though he was not a trained engineer. He told me he met with his senior engineers on Day 1. These senior engineers were skeptical of Hugo's value to the role. Right off the bat, one asked the newly appointed CEO, "What do you know about engineering?" Without hesitation, Hugo made a zero with his fingers. "This is how much I know about engineering. However, I do know how to run a business, and I hope you can teach me what I need to know about your world."

When leaders concede that they do not know something, they display humility and openness. This attitude inspires others to do the same. Be prepared to ask questions and listen to your teammates.

New hires at the successful animated studios of Pixar are understandably hesitant to question the status quo, given the company's record of hit movies and brilliant work over the years. To combat this reluctance to question the current situation, the cofounder and president Catmull (2008) discussed times when Pixar made terrible choices. He explained that Pixar is imperfect and needs fresh eyes to spot improvement opportunities like other companies.[5] This way, Catmull gives recruits license to question existing practices. Recognizing the limits of our knowledge and skills sends a powerful signal to others that we are open to learning.

Demonstrating one's *intellectual humility* is the essence of modeling inquisitiveness. Porter and colleagues (2022) define intellectual humility as:

> ...recognizing that there are gaps in one's knowledge and that one's beliefs might be incorrect. For instance, someone might think it is raining but acknowledge that they have not looked outside to check and that the sun might be shining. Research on intellectual humility offers an intriguing avenue to safeguard against human errors and biases. Although it cannot eliminate them, recognizing the knowledge limitations might help buffer people from some of their more authoritarian, dogmatic, and biased proclivities.[6]

Porter et al.'s research validates the power of intellectual humility. Intellectually humble people do better in school and at work. Why? When we accept that our knowledge is finite, we appreciate that we have lots to learn.

Intellectual curiosity and continuous learning go together. I recently read the inspirational autobiography by Captain Sully Sullenberger, one of the most captivating American heroes of our time. You may recall that he was the pilot who miraculously landed a crippled U.S. Airways Flight 1549 in New York's Hudson River, saving the lives of all 155 passengers and crew (Sullenberger and Zaslow 2009).[7]

On January 15, 2009, the world witnessed a remarkable emergency landing when Sullenberger skillfully glided U.S. Airways Flight 1549 onto the Hudson River. His cool actions averted tragedy and made him a hero and an inspiration worldwide. Sullenberger's story is now a major motion picture from director and producer Clint Eastwood, starring Tom Hanks, Laura Linney, and Aaron Eckhart.

Sullenberger described his passion for continuous learning when asked how he landed a commercial aircraft safely in the Hudson River. Although commercial flights are never routine, every time his plane pushed back from the gate, he would remind himself that he needed to be prepared for the unexpected. *What can I learn?* Sullenberger would think. This question reminded him that he needed to be ready for the unforeseen whenever he flew. When the unexpected happened, on a cold January day in 2009, Sullenberger was able to ask himself what he *could* do, given the available options. He produced a creative option to land the plane on water rather than land.

Sullenberger successfully fought the tendency to grasp the most obvious option of landing at the nearest airport. Significantly, when under pressure, we immediately focus on the obvious answer. However, those enthusiastic about continuous learning have the mindset to contemplate various options and perspectives. As the accident report shows, Sullenberger carefully considered several alternatives. There were 208 seconds between his discovery that the aircraft's engines lacked thrust and his landing of the plane in the Hudson (Sullenberger and Zaslow 2009).[8]

Emphasize Learning Goals

Give equal attention to learning objectives alongside outcome objectives. Take, for example, Mel, an engineer aiming to obtain her professional license to transition into project management. She actively seeks additional project responsibilities to acquire the necessary skills for this role. Mel prioritizes a learning objective aimed at skill development, which will inevitably propel her career forward. Emphasizing goals inevitably unleashes the power of curiosity.

While companies naturally prioritize outcomes, they expect their employees to adhere strictly to the company's frameworks, processes, and protocols to achieve those outcomes. The implicit message conveyed to employees is that results are paramount more than anything else. Consequently, unthinkingly conforming to established systems stifles curiosity, which is the antithesis of being inquisitive.

It is the norm to focus on results, especially during tough times. Without taking one's eye off the bottom line, leaders can also encourage learning. Research shows that applied learning positively impacts goal achievement. For example, Gino (2018) studied U.S. Air Force personnel performing a demanding goal. The goal was to land the most planes within a set time limit. Nevertheless, the performance of pilots solely focused on the outcome declined compared to pilots who were encouraged to apply their newfound knowledge despite the additional time required.[9]

Southern Methodist University's Vande Walle (1999) researched sales professionals in another study. The product in this study was a high-priced piece of medical equipment. Sales reps received a generous bonus for each sale. Those who did nothing else but concentrate on meeting their sales targets did worse promoting a product. On the other hand, reps who were willing to learn, such as exploring ways to be better salespersons, performed better in selling the product.[10]

A practical starting point for learning is for a leader not to dismiss mediocre ideas instantly. Average ideas can serve as "plussing" *(Cleff 2014)*. Plussing involves building on ideas without judgment (Cleff 2014).[11] Instead of rejecting a sketch immediately, a director might say, "I like Woody's eyes, and what if we…?" Someone else might respond with another *plus*. Plussing allows people to remain curious, respect people's ideas, and promote active listening. Through employing this technique, various ideas that would typically be disregarded are investigated. With plussing, Pixar executives convey a distinct message emphasizing learning as the primary objective.

Explore Interests

Wherever possible, support team members in exploring and broadening their interests. Companies do this by giving employees time and resources to explore their curiosities. Google and 3M are famous for giving employees a percentage of their day to discuss their ideas with others. As I mentioned in the last chapter, Google has been renowned for its 20 % time policy, where employees devote 20 percent of their working hours to projects of their choosing. This learning initiative is the genesis of successful products, including *Gmail, Google Transit*, and *Google News*. This is a reminder that giving employees the scope to pursue their passions can lead to groundbreaking innovations.

Ask Open-Ended Questions

Another way to practice Being Curious is by asking thoughtful questions. *Why did we do this task this way? What if we reversed the process? How might we make this work?* Ask open-ended questions to spark curiosity.

Langer (2017) of MIT's Koch Institute for Integrative Cancer Research said he wants to "help people make the transition from giving good answers to asking good questions."[12] Langer tells his students that they can change the world and boost their curiosity by asking good questions.

Arranging a *Why?* day can yield significant advantages. When team members inquire *why* when confronted with a challenge, it can stimulate ideas. Intellectual Ventures, a company specializing in inventing, purchasing, and licensing patents, conducts *invention sessions*. These sessions bring together employees from diverse disciplines, backgrounds, and expertise levels to brainstorm potential solutions to complex problems. Such invention sessions enable the company to examine issues from multiple perspectives (Myhrvold 2010).[13]

Likewise, following Toyota's *5 Whys Approach*, also known as *Root Cause Analysis*, employees probe problems by repeatedly asking, *Why?* They continue this process, delving more deeply with each iteration until they have asked the *why* question five times. Such methods provide an alternative means to shift away from the conventional emphasis on results and toward a focus on learning within the company culture.

Consider implementing one or more of the following suggestions: prioritize hiring curious individuals, demonstrate curiosity yourself, underscore the importance of learning objectives, encourage exploration of interests, and pose open-ended questions. With consistent effort, you will undoubtedly ignite curiosity in yourself and others.

I would like you to take the Curiosity Inventory in Appendix G.

Top 10 Points

1. Interview for curiosity, like everything else you typically assess in a job applicant. Getting it right at the hiring stage can save you grief later.
2. Why are we reluctant to ask questions? We fear we will be judged incompetent, indecisive, or unintelligent.
3. Research findings indicate that when we demonstrate curiosity about others by asking questions, people like us more and view us as more competent.
4. Another way leaders can model curiosity is by acknowledging when they do not know the answer; that makes it clear that it is okay to be guided by curiosity.
5. When leaders concede that they do not know something, they show humility and openness.
6. Intellectual curiosity and continuous learning go together.
7. Focus on learning goals as much as outcome goals.
8. An excellent place to start learning is for a leader to take time to dismiss what seems like a mediocre idea.
9. Support team members in exploring and broadening their interests wherever possible.
10. Another way to practice Being Curious is by asking thoughtful questions.

Conclusion

In *Successful Self-Leadership: An Inside-Out Approach in Seven Steps*, we have explored self-leadership comprehensively, delving into seven practices categorized as The Inner Game and The Outer Game. As we conclude, let us briefly revisit each practice within the Self-Leadership Development Framework and explore their connections.

Your Inner Game is your mindset. The term comes from performance coach Timothy Gallwey (2001), who authored *The Inner Game of Work: Focus, Learning, Pleasure, and Mobility in the Workplace*. Gallwey describes The Inner Game as: "How you non-judgmentally observe the critical variables in your 'game of life' and adjust and correct those to achieve the best possible performance."[1] The four practices of The Inner Game are: Know Thyself, Discover True North, Build Strengths, and Keep Growing. These practices form the bedrock for effective self-leadership by aligning values, aspirations, and growth: The Inner Game.

Know Thyself emphasizes the importance of self-awareness and understanding one's values, beliefs, strengths, weaknesses, and motivations. Discover True North involves identifying one's purpose, vision, and long-term goals, providing a guiding compass for decision making and actions. Build Strengths emphasizes leveraging and using one's talents to excel in various aspects of life, including leading others. Lastly, Keep Growing is committed to continuous learning, personal development, and adaptation to embrace new challenges and opportunities.

The connection of these four practices of The Inner Game stresses the proper mindset for effective self-leadership. Knowing oneself lays the foundation for discovering one's true north. Understanding your values and aspirations guides the direction of personal growth and development. Building strengths becomes more focused and purposeful when aligned with one's true north. This maximizes potential and impact. Meanwhile, the commitment to continuous growth ensures that self-leadership remains dynamic and adaptable, allowing individuals to evolve in pursuit of their authentic selves and goals. Consequently, integrating these four practices cultivates a comprehensive approach for leadership to flourish. This empowers you to navigate life's complexities with clarity, purpose, and resilience.

The Outer Game refers to those self-leadership practices that directly impact those with whom the leader interacts. According to executive coach Slaven Drinovac (2023), in his article, *The Inner and The Outer Game of Leadership*, The Outer Game entails utilizing our knowledge, experience, and leadership competence to achieve results. Donovan says, "Most leaders spend most of their time in the all-consuming outer game because its daily demands are intense, and the learning curve is steep."[2] The three practices of The Outer Game are Show Intent, Self-Regulation, and Be Curious.

Show Intent involves being intentional and purposeful in one's actions, decisions, and interactions, aligning behaviors with personal values and goals. Self-regulation focuses on effectively managing emotions, impulses, and behaviors, exercising self-control and discipline to navigate challenges and achieve desired outcomes. Be Curious emphasizes the importance of curiosity and open-mindedness in seeking new experiences, knowledge, and perspectives. Curiosity promotes innovation, growth, and adaptability.

There is a clear connection between these three practices of self-leadership. Showing Intent requires Self-Regulation to ensure actions and decisions align with one's purpose and values, requiring discipline and control over impulses. Similarly, Self-Regulation begins with being curious about how we can respond appropriately to others and ourselves. Being open-minded allows individuals to regulate emotions effectively and approach situations with a growth mindset rather than reacting impulsively. Furthermore, curiosity fuels intent, as a curious mindset leads to exploring and discovering new goals and aspirations. Curiosity drives intentional actions and behaviors. So, these three practices of The Outer Game are interdependent. Each practice reinforces and complements others to support a well-rounded approach to leading others with purpose, discipline, and a thirst for knowledge.

I have good news and bad news.

The bad news is due to their interdependency; if any of these seven practices are underdeveloped, they will negatively impact other practices in the Self-Leadership Development Framework. However, the good news is that developing one of these practices will positively impact other practices.

So, start somewhere!

I trust *Successful Self-Leadership: An Inside-Out Approach in Seven Steps* has provided valuable insights and practical guidance for your leadership journey.

Appendixes

APPENDIX A

Are You a Peacock, Bull, Owl, or Lamb?

I indicated in Chapter 4 that completing a personality profile is one of the four strategies to improve self-awareness. Doing a personality profile can help you better understand yourself and identify your preferences, strengths, and growth opportunities. You may have completed a profile at work or elected to do one privately. Nevertheless, here is a chance for you to profile yourself.

The personality profile in Table A.1 is adapted from the work of Florence Littauer (1983) in her book *Personality Plus: How to Understand Others by Understanding Yourself*.[1] There are myriad personality profiles, diagnostics, and tests based on Carl Yung's personality type theory, including MBTI, DiSC, and others. This one is simple to complete and easy to understand. Instead of giving you an obscure set of letters or labels, this profile is based on four animals: *Peacock*, *Bull*, *Owl*, and *Lamb*. Although not validated by research, the profile is fun and gives you a sense of your dominant personality type. Please give it a go.

Instructions

In Table A.1, you are presented with 40 rows containing four descriptors. Look at each descriptor in each row and circle the one that best describes you. You may find it challenging to circle only answers. However, you can always validate your choice by asking someone who knows you well. Try not to have *analysis by paralysis*. In other words, do not think too hard about your answer. Go with your first impression. Select the descriptor that best describes you most of the time. Choose the word that describes you most of the time, not the one you would like to be described.

Table A.1 Personality scoring table

	PEACOCK	BULL	OWL	LAMB
1.	Animated	Adventurous	Analytical	Adaptable
2.	Playful	Persuasive	Persistent	Peaceful
3.	Sociable	Strong-willed	Self-sacrificing	Submissive
4.	Convincing	Competitive	Considerate	Controlled
5.	Refreshing	Resourceful	Respectful	Reserved
6.	Spirited	Self-reliant	Sensitive	Satisfied
7.	Promoter	Positive	Planner	Patient
8.	Spontaneous	Sure	Scheduled	Shy
9.	Optimistic	Outspoken	Orderly	Obliging
10.	Funny	Forceful	Faithful	Friendly
11.	Delightful	Daring	Detailed	Diplomatic
12.	Cheerful	Confident	Cultured	Consistent
13.	Inspiring	Independent	Idealistic	Inoffensive
14.	Demonstrative	Decisive	Deep	Dry Humor
15.	Mixes easily	Mover	Musical	Mediator
16.	Talker	Tenacious	Thoughtful	Tolerant
17.	Lively	Leader	Loyal	Listener
18.	Cute	Chief	Chart maker	Contented
19.	Popular	Productive	Perfectionist	Pleasant
20.	Bouncy	Bold	Behaved	Balanced
21.	Brassy	Bossy	Bashful	Blank
22.	Undisciplined	Unsympathetic	Unforgiving	Unenthusiastic
23.	Repetitious	Resistant	Resentful	Reticent
24.	Forgetful	Frank	Fussy	Fearful
25.	Interrupts	Impatient	Insecure	Indecisive
26.	Unpredictable	Unaffectionate	Unpopular	Uninvolved
27.	Haphazard	Headstrong	Hard to please	Hesitant
28.	Permissive	Proud	Pessimistic	Plain
29.	Angered easily	Argumentative	Alienated	Aimless
30.	Naive	Nervy	Negative attitude	Nonchalant
31.	Wants credit	Workaholic	Withdrawn	Worrier
32.	Talkative	Tactless	Too sensitive	Timid
33.	Disorganized	Domineering	Depressed	Doubtful
34.	Inconsistent	Intolerant	Introvert	Indifferent
35.	Messy	Manipulative	Moody	Mumbles

(Continued)

	PEACOCK	BULL	OWL	LAMB
36.	Show off	Stubborn	Skeptical	Slow
37.	Loud	Lord over others	Loner	Lazy
38.	Scatterbrained	Short-tempered	Suspicious	Sluggish
39.	Restless	Rash	Revengeful	Reluctant
40.	Changeable	Crafty	Critical	Compromising

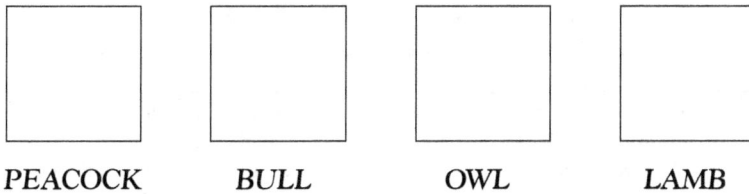

PEACOCK   BULL   OWL   LAMB

Interpretation

Add up the four columns and register your scores for each column. Now that you have four scores corresponding to the four animals, read the following interpretations. Because you probably have a distribution of scores for each column, you probably notice that aspects of your personality are covered in more than one of the personality types. However, if you scored 20 or more in one personality type, you would probably notice that the descriptor for that animal type rings true. After all, you calculated that at least 50 percent of your personality scores are in one column.

Peacock

Primary motivation: Being popular
Characteristics: Extrovert, talker, optimist
Strengths: Appealing personality, creative and colorful, energy and enthusiasm, inspiring
Famous people: Oprah Winfrey and Winston Churchill
Orientation: "Any publicity is good publicity."

Table A.2 Peacock characteristics

Strengths	Weaknesses
Emotions	
• Appealing personality • Talkative, storyteller • Life of the party • Good sense of humor • Enthusiastic and Expressive	• Compulsive talker • Exaggerates and elaborates • Cannot always remember names • Egotistical • So happy for some
At work	
• Volunteers for jobs • Thinks up new activities • Creative and colorful • Energy and Enthusiasm • Inspires others to join in	• Would rather talk than listen • Can be forgetful • Does not always follow through • Can be undisciplined • Easily distracted
As a parent	
• Makes home fun • Is liked by children's friends • Turns disasters into humor • Is the circus master	• Keeps home in a frenzy • Forgets children's appointments • Disorganized • Do not listen to the whole story
As a friend	
• Makes friends easily • Loves people • Thrives on compliments • Does not hold grudges • Likes spontaneous activities	• Hates to be alone • Needs to be center-stage • Wants to be popular • Looks for credit • Dominates conversations

Bull

Primary motivation: Being powerful

Characteristics: Extrovert, talker, optimist

Strengths: Comfortable leading, goal oriented, moves quickly to action

Famous people: Hillary Clinton and Jack Welsh

Orientation: "I am in control and willing to lead."

Table A.3 Bull characteristics

Strengths	Weaknesses
Emotions	
• Born leader • Dynamic and active • Strong-willed and decisive • Independent and self-sufficient • Not easily discouraged	• Bossy • Impatient • Quick-tempered • Cannot relax • Can be unsympathetic
At work	
• Goal oriented • Sees the whole picture • Organizes well • Seeks practical solutions • Moves quickly to action	• Little tolerance for mistakes • Does not analyze details • May make rash decisions • May be rude or tactless • Manipulates people
As a parent	
• Exerts sound leadership • Establishes goals • Motivates family into action • Knows the right answer • Organizes household	• Tends to dominate • Sometimes too busy for the family • Gives answers too quickly • Do not let children relax • Overbearing
As a friend	
• Has little need for friends • Will organize group activities • Will lead and organize • Is usually right • Excels in emergencies	• Tends to use people • Dominates others • Decides for others • Knows everything • Cannot say "I'm sorry"

Owl

Primary motivation: Being perfect

Characteristics: Introvert, thinker, pessimist

Strengths: Schedule-oriented, high standards, orderly and organized

Famous people: Angela Merkel and Tom Brady

Orientation: "How can I paint this perfect picture?

Table A.4 Owl characteristics

Strengths	Weaknesses
Emotions	
• Deep and thoughtful • Analytical • Serious and purposeful • Talented and creative • Sensitive to others	• Moody and prone to depression • Remembers the negatives • Guilt feelings • Off in another world • Self-centered
At work	
• Schedule oriented • High standards • Detail conscious • Persistent and thorough • Sees the problems	• Not people oriented • Depressed over imperfections • Hesitant to start projects • Spends too much time planning • Deep need for approval
As a parent	
• Sets high standards • Wants everything done right • Keeps home in good order • Encourages scholarship and talent • Picks up after children	• Puts goals beyond reach • May discourage children • May be too meticulous • Sulks over disagreements • Puts guilt upon children
As a friend	
• Faithful and devoted • Will listen to complaints • Can solve other's problems • Deep concern for other people • Moved to tears with compassion	• Insecure socially • Withdrawn and remote • Critical of others • Holds back affection • Suspicious of people

Lamb

Primary motivation: Being peaceful

Characteristics: Introvert, watcher, pessimist

Strengths: Competent and steady, peaceful and agreeable, mediates problems

Famous person: Mother Teresa and Nelson Mandela

Orientation: "Peace is the overriding objective."

Table A.5 Lamb characteristics

Strengths	Weaknesses
Emotions	
• Easy-going and relaxed • Calm, cool, and collected • Patient and well balanced • Consistent life • Sympathetic and kind	• Unenthusiastic • Fearful and worried • Indecisive • Avoids responsibility • Selfish
At work	
• Competent and steady • Peaceful and agreeable • Mediates problems • Avoids conflict • Finds the easy way	• Not goal-oriented • Lacks self-motivation • Resents being pushed • Would rather watch • Hard to get moving
As a parent	
• Makes a good parent • Takes time with children • Is not in a hurry • Can take the good with the bad • Does not get easily upset	• Lax on discipline • Fails to exercise discipline • Does not organize a home • Takes life too easily • Reluctant to provide direction
As a friend	
• Easy to get along with • Pleasant and enjoyable • Inoffensive • Good listener • Dry sense of humor	• Stays uninvolved • Low key • Indifferent to plans • Resists change • Dampens enthusiasm

Having completed this personality profile and read the interpretations, here are some questions that might assist you in your development:

- How accurate are the descriptors?
- What are your personality strengths, and how can you apply them in leadership?
- What do others think of these results?

APPENDIX B

Life Values Inventory

You complete the Life Values Inventory in Appendix B. Moreover, you will reflect on your results and consider how they apply to your life personally and professionally. As I suggested in Chapter 6, it may help you discover your True North—the second practice of self-leadership. Besides clarifying your values, the inventory can assist you in developing your leadership purpose statement. Being clear about one's values can guide you throughout life in the choices you make and the priorities you pursue.

Let us get underway.

Instructions

Table B.2 lists 42 values that guide people's behavior and assist them in making important decisions. Read each and then choose the response (1–5) that best describes how often that belief guides your behavior. Your choice need not be confined only to the workplace. Consider each value in general as it applies to your life overall.

Here is an example (Table B.1).

Table B.1 Guide for life values inventory

Values	Rarely guides my behavior	Occasionally guides my behavior	Sometimes guides my behavior	Most of the time guides my behavior	Almost always guides my behavior
2. Being liked by others.	1	2	3	4	5

If a belief of *Being liked by others* rarely guides your behavior, circle 1. Suppose *Being liked by others* almost always guides your behavior, circle 5. If a more accurate response is between 1 and 5, circle the number 2, 3, or 4. The main thing is to be consistent throughout your evaluation of each response.

Now, you are ready to begin. Read each value carefully and circle one response. Usually, your first idea is the best indicator of how you feel. Answer every item. There are no right or wrong answers. Remember to answer this with some detachment. You are answering how you are, not what you think you should be! Your choices should describe your values, not the values of others.

Table B.2 Life values inventory

Values	Rarely guides my behavior	Occasionally guides my behavior	Sometimes guides my behavior	Most of the time guides my behavior	Almost always guides my behavior
1. Challenging myself to achieve	1	2	3	4	5
2. Being liked by others	1	2	3	4	5
3. Protecting the environment	1	2	3	4	5
4. Being sensitive to others' needs	1	2	3	4	5
5. Coming up with new ideas	1	2	3	4	5
6. Having financial success	1	2	3	4	5
7. Taking care of my body	1	2	3	4	5
8. Downplaying compliments or praise	1	2	3	4	5
9. Being independent (doing things I want to do)	1	2	3	4	5
10. Accepting my place in my family or group	1	2	3	4	5
11. Having time to myself	1	2	3	4	5
12. Being dependable	1	2	3	4	5
13. Using science for progress	1	2	3	4	5
14. Believing in a higher power	1	2	3	4	5

(*Continued*)

Values	Rarely guides my behavior	Occasionally guides my behavior	Sometimes guides my behavior	Most of the time guides my behavior	Almost always guides my behavior
15. Improving my performance	1	2	3	4	5
16. Being accepted by others	1	2	3	4	5
17. Taking care of the environment	1	2	3	4	5
18. Helping others	1	2	3	4	5
19. Creating new things or ideas	1	2	3	4	5
20. Making money	1	2	3	4	5
21. Being in good physical shape	1	2	3	4	5
22. Being quiet about my success	1	2	3	4	5
23. 23. Giving my opinion	1	2	3	4	5
24. Respecting the traditions of my family or group	1	2	3	4	5
25. Having quiet time to think	1	2	3	4	5
26. Being trustworthy	1	2	3	4	5
27. Knowing things about science	1	2	3	4	5
28. Believing that there is something greater than ourselves	1	2	3	4	5
29. Working hard to do better	1	2	3	4	5
30. Feeling as though I belong	1	2	3	4	5
31. Appreciating the beauty of nature	1	2	3	4	5
32. Being concerned about the rights of others	1	2	3	4	5

(Continued)

Values	Rarely guides my behavior	Occasionally guides my behavior	Sometimes guides my behavior	Most of the time guides my behavior	Almost always guides my behavior
33. Discovering new things or ideas	1	2	3	4	5
34. Being wealthy	1	2	3	4	5
35. Being good at a sport	1	2	3	4	5
36. Avoid credit for my accomplishments	1	2	3	4	5
37. Having control over my time	1	2	3	4	5
38. Making decisions with my family or group in mind	1	2	3	4	5
39. Having a private place to go	1	2	3	4	5
40. Meeting my obligations	1	2	3	4	5
41. Knowing about numbers	1	2	3	4	5
42. Living in harmony with my spiritual beliefs	1	2	3	4	5

Transfer your scores to the below response summary (Table B.3). Add the ratings from all 42 statements. Record the total scores for each letter as follows. This will give you scores for this inventory's 15 central life values.

Table B.3 Life values inventory tabulation

A _____ H _____
Statements 1 + 15 + 29   Statements 8 + 22 + 36
B _____ I _____
Statements 2 + 16 + 30   Statements 9 + 23 + 37
C _____ J _____

(Continued)

Statements 3 + 17 + 31	Statements 10 + 24 + 38
D _____	K _____
Statements 4 + 18 + 32	Statements 11 + 25 + 39
E _____	L _____
Statements 5 + 19 + 33	Statements 12 + 26 + 40
F _____	M _____
Statements 6 + 20 + 34	Statements 13 + 27 + 41
G _____	N _____
Statements 7 + 21 + 35	Statements 14 + 28 + 42

Now record your answers in the boxes in Table B.4. This will give you your scores for the 15 central life values identified by this inventory.

Table B.4 Life values inventory results

A ACHIEVEMENT
☐ The belief in challenging yourself and working hard to improve.
B BELONGING
☐ The belief in being accepted by others and feeling included.
C CONCERN FOR THE ENVIRONMENT
☐ The belief in protecting and preserving the environment.
D CONCERN FOR OTHERS
☐ The belief in the importance of the well-being of others.
E CREATIVITY
☐ The belief in the value of new ideas or creating new things.
F FINANCIAL PROSPERITY
☐ The belief in the importance of being successful at making money.
G HEALTH AND ACTIVITY
☐ The belief in being healthy and physically active.
H HUMILITY
☐ The belief in being humble and modest about your accomplishments.
I INDEPENDENCE
☐ The belief in the importance of making decisions and doing things your way.

(*Continued*)

J LOYALTY TO FAMILY OR GROUP
☐ The belief in following the traditions and expectations of your family or group.
K PRIVACY
☐ The belief in the value of having time alone.
L RESPONSIBILITY
☐ The belief in being dependable and trustworthy.
M SCIENTIFIC UNDERSTANDING
☐ There is a belief in the importance of using scientific principles to understand and solve problems.
N SPIRITUALITY
☐ The belief in spiritual beliefs and that you are part of something greater than yourself.

Reflection

Now that you have completed the Life Values Inventory, here are some questions to ask yourself about your results. I suggest you take time to respond to each question in your journal before moving on. This reflection time is essential.

1. Did the results surprise you? If so, how?
2. Take a closer look. Are there any potential conflicts in your results? For example, you might have high scores for the values of ACHIEVEMENT and CONCERN FOR OTHERS. If you work in a sales environment, you compete with your colleagues for higher individual sales. Does this preference for achievement conflict with your concern for others? These potential conflicts can put stress on you without you realizing why. It could be a clash of values.
3. If there is a noticeable clash in beliefs, how can you reconcile these values in your current role?
4. What are the implications of the results for you and your leadership purpose? For example, if your two highest values are INDEPENDENCE and RESPONSIBILITY, then you would believe in allowing others to exercise their autonomy and independent judgment. Simultaneously, you could be prone to holding others accountable for their results. Furthermore, you would be a leader who likes to

lead by giving others a clear outcome of what you want and then allowing others to get on and do what they need to do to achieve that outcome.

5. Where are you vulnerable as a leader? When others do not share your values and have different beliefs, it can create tension and potential conflict. For example, if you scored high in SCIENTIFIC UNDERSTANDING, you look for logic and rational arguments to make decisions. Suppose one of your team members scored high in CONCERN FOR OTHERS. This might create a difference in point of view between you and your colleague. For example, you decide based on analysis, but this decision might infringe the rights of team members. Your colleague might disagree with your decision, regardless of its logic. This does not mean valuing data is counter to caring for people. Nonetheless, these two values (and others) are constantly being tested in the workplace.

6. If you have crafted a leadership purpose statement, are your results in this exercise congruent with that purpose? If you have not written your purpose statement yet, how can these results assist you in writing your leadership purpose statement?

APPENDIX C

Digital Leadership Development Profile

You complete the Digital Leadership Development Profile in Appendix C. On the following pages is a list of 100 statements related to the 10 attributes of digital leadership defined in Chapter 8. This profile will be easier to complete for those whose work is purely digital. However, if your work is only partially involved in the digital space, for example, in sales, some of the statements may not apply. I suggest marking them S (Sometimes) for consistency if this is the case.

Let's get underway.

Instructions

Here is an example in Table C.1 of statement #32 in the profile:

Table C.1 Guide for digital leadership profile

Statement	R	O	S	M	AA
32. I exhibit patience while engaging in digital dialogues, allowing others to express their ideas fully without interruption.	1	2	3	4	5

- **R** means Rarely
- **O** means Occasionally
- **S** means Sometimes
- **M** means Most of the Time
- **AA** means Almost Always

After immediately reading this statement, you Almost Always (**AA**) do circle 5 if you think this is something. On the other hand, if you acknowledge that you Rarely (**R**) exhibit patience, circle 1. Suppose your behavior in these circumstances varies between the two extremes, depending on what is being discussed and with whom, circle 3 (**S**). You can also select 3 when you are undecided; furthermore, if there is a tendency for you to favor one or the other, circle 2 or 4. The key here is to be consistent in your responses throughout the profile.

The focus here is working in leading in a digital environment. Depending on your industry and role, I understand there are varying degrees of digitalization. If an item does not apply to you, then circle 3.

Now, you are ready to begin. Read each item carefully and circle one response. Usually, your first idea is the best indicator of how you feel. Answer every item. Remember to answer this with some detachment. You are answering how you are, not what you think you should be! Your choices should describe your behavior, not the behavior of others.

Table C.2 Digital leadership profile

Statement	R	O	S	M	AA
1. I evaluate complex digital challenges from multiple perspectives before making decisions.	1	2	3	4	5
2. I confidently deliver engaging and articulate presentations in virtual settings, capturing my audience's attention.	1	2	3	4	5
3. I consistently demonstrate my commitment to active listening by providing thoughtful responses that show I have absorbed the digital discussions.	1	2	3	4	5
4. I adeptly use persuasion to shape digital discussions.	1	2	3	4	5
5. I consistently demonstrate a keen understanding of the digital landscape, staying current with trends and emerging dynamics.	1	2	3	4	5
6. I skillfully navigate virtual negotiations, finding common ground and win-win outcomes.	1	2	3	4	5
7. I consistently articulate an inspiring and motivating digital vision.	1	2	3	4	5
8. I possess a discerning eye for evaluating digital solutions and weighing the pros and cons to determine the best action.	1	2	3	4	5
9. I demonstrate a comprehensive understanding of the interconnected nature of digital systems and their impact on the organization.	1	2	3	4	5

(*Continued*)

Statement	R	O	S	M	AA
10. I actively seek new digital information sources and technologies to enhance my understanding of the evolving landscape.	1	2	3	4	5
11. I skillfully adapt my public speaking style to digital platforms like webinars, video conferences, and live streams.	1	2	3	4	5
12. In virtual meetings, I listen intently, ask pertinent questions, and seek clarification to deepen my understanding of digital topics.	1	2	3	4	5
13. I tailor my messages to resonate with the audience's values and priorities in virtual meetings.	1	2	3	4	5
14. In virtual interactions, I exhibit a solid ability to read between the lines and notice subtle cues to assess the emotional tone of the conversation accurately.	1	2	3	4	5
15. I employ effective communication strategies in digital discussions to influence decisions and reach mutually beneficial agreements.	1	2	3	4	5
16. I am known for envisioning innovative solutions and identifying emerging opportunities in discussions about digital strategies.	1	2	3	4	5
17. In discussions about digital issues, I am talented at breaking down problems into manageable components and identifying root causes.	1	2	3	4	5
18. Before moving forward, I thoroughly assess the proposed solutions' feasibility and potential impact on digital decision making.	1	2	3	4	5
19. In discussions about digital initiatives, I display a talent for evaluating how proposed changes may influence the larger ecosystem.	1	2	3	4	5
20. In discussions about digital strategies, I often identify potential risks and opportunities that others overlook.	1	2	3	4	5
21. In online meetings, I communicate complex ideas clearly and organized, making it easy for others to follow.	1	2	3	4	5

(Continued)

Statement	R	O	S	M	AA
22. I value diverse perspectives in digital conversations, often paraphrasing others' viewpoints to ensure accurate comprehension.	1	2	3	4	5
23. I skillfully leverage data and evidence in digital presentations to support my arguments.	1	2	3	4	5
24. I show genuine empathy and consideration for the well-being of team members in digital communications, even when working remotely.	1	2	3	4	5
25. I relish the challenge of negotiating through digital platforms and adapting my approach to different communication channels.	1	2	3	4	5
26. I enjoy brainstorming sessions where I can creatively envision the future of my organization's digital presence.	1	2	3	4	5
27. I enjoy tackling intricate digital puzzles, viewing obstacles as opportunities to innovate and find creative solutions.	1	2	3	4	5
28. I enjoy analyzing and comparing digital options to identify the most effective and efficient solution.	1	2	3	4	5
29. I enjoy exploring the intricacies of digital systems and analyzing their components, relationships, and potential bottlenecks.	1	2	3	4	5
30. I enjoy brainstorming sessions to explore innovative solutions to digital problems.	1	2	3	4	5
31. I display enthusiasm while speaking in digital forums, conveying a genuine passion for the topics I address.	1	2	3	4	5
32. I exhibit patience while engaging in digital dialogues, allowing others to express their ideas fully without interruption.	1	2	3	4	5
33. I enjoy the challenge of presenting compelling narratives in digital formats, capturing attention, and driving action.	1	2	3	4	5
34. I actively seek diverse perspectives from online discussions to enhance my awareness of various viewpoints and cultural nuances.	1	2	3	4	5
35. I demonstrate a thorough understanding of digital dynamics and leverage technology to enhance the negotiation process.	1	2	3	4	5

(Continued)

Statement	R	O	S	M	AA
36. I am knowledgeable about translating abstract digital concepts into tangible goals and actionable plans.	1	2	3	4	5
37. I actively encourage my team to think critically and explore different avenues when faced with digital roadblocks.	1	2	3	4	5
38. I actively seek input from team members and stakeholders when appraising digital solutions, valuing diverse perspectives.	1	2	3	4	5
39. I actively seek opportunities to optimize digital workflows and processes, focusing on improving the efficiency and effectiveness of systems.	1	2	3	4	5
40. When faced with a digital obstacle, I will experiment with different approaches before settling on a solution.	1	2	3	4	5
41. I use visual aids and multimedia elements thoughtfully to enhance my digital presentations and keep the audience engaged.	1	2	3	4	5
42. During online team collaborations, I practice empathetic listening, acknowledging the emotions and concerns expressed by my colleagues.	1	2	3	4	5
43. In online collaborations, I build rapport and trust with team members, developing an environment where my ideas carry significant weight.	1	2	3	4	5
44. In digital collaborations, I create a welcoming atmosphere where all voices are valued and respected, fostering a sense of inclusivity.	1	2	3	4	5
45. In virtual meetings, I manage conflicts and differing viewpoints effectively, guiding discussions toward resolution.	1	2	3	4	5
46. I effectively communicate my digital vision in virtual presentations, using engaging visuals and narratives to captivate the audience.	1	2	3	4	5
47. I contribute insightful ideas in virtual brainstorming sessions, demonstrating my digital problem-solving prowess.	1	2	3	4	5

(Continued)

Statement	R	O	S	M	AA
48. I am talented at identifying potential risks and mitigations associated with various solutions in virtual discussions.	1	2	3	4	5
49. In virtual collaborations, I excel at identifying opportunities for integrating different digital tools and platforms.	1	2	3	4	5
50. I encourage my team to question assumptions and explore alternative viewpoints when tackling digital projects.	1	2	3	4	5
51. I use storytelling techniques to make my digital presentations relatable and memorable to a diverse audience.	1	2	3	4	5
52. I employ nonverbal cues such as nodding and affirming language in digital interactions to indicate my attentiveness.	1	2	3	4	5
53. I engage in active networking and relationship-building through digital platforms to expand my circle of influence across various spheres.	1	2	3	4	5
54. I enjoy participating in digital networking and relationship-building, recognizing the importance of online connections for social awareness.	1	2	3	4	5
55. I am known for remaining composed and focused during tense digital negotiations, maintaining a positive and collaborative atmosphere.	1	2	3	4	5
56. I actively seek input from team members in shaping the digital vision, valuing diverse perspectives.	1	2	3	4	5
57. I use data-driven decision making in resolving digital issues, leveraging information to guide effective problem-solving strategies.	1	2	3	4	5
58. I excel at quantifying and qualifying the expected outcomes of digital solutions, using data-driven insights to inform their evaluation.	1	2	3	4	5
59. I use data analytics to evaluate the performance of digital systems, making informed decisions about adjustments and enhancements.	1	2	3	4	5
60. I frequently anticipate the potential long-term consequences of digital decisions and adjust my approach accordingly.	1	2	3	4	5

(*Continued*)

Statement	R	O	S	M	AA
61. My insights and opinions are expressed with clarity and confidence when participating in virtual panel discussions.	1	2	3	4	5
62. I am genuinely curious about others' viewpoints in virtual discussions.	1	2	3	4	5
63. I excel at anticipating potential objections in virtual discussions and proactively addressing them to overcome resistance to my ideas.	1	2	3	4	5
64. I use my social media presence thoughtfully, sharing content that promotes my industry.	1	2	3	4	5
65. I enjoy the strategic aspect of digital negotiations, analyzing data and trends to inform my negotiation tactics.	1	2	3	4	5
66. My enthusiasm for digital transformation is contagious, and I radiate excitement about the potential impact of my vision.	1	2	3	4	5
67. I seek feedback and perspectives from diverse sources in the digital realm to gain a well-rounded view of potential solutions.	1	2	3	4	5
68. My diligence in evaluating digital solutions ensures that even minor aspects are considered before making decisions.	1	2	3	4	5
69. I value continuous learning about emerging technologies and their potential impact.	1	2	3	4	5
70. I derive satisfaction from solving complex digital puzzles and take pride in my ability to connect unrelated concepts.	1	2	3	4	5
71. I seek opportunities to improve my digital public speaking skills through training, practice, and feedback.	1	2	3	4	5
72. I maintain consistent eye contact with the camera in video conferences, signaling my focused attention to the speaker.	1	2	3	4	5
73. I consistently provide thought leadership in digital forums, establishing myself as an authoritative voice and influential figure.	1	2	3	4	5
74. I frequently engage in digital conversations that foster a deeper understanding of diverse cultural backgrounds.	1	2	3	4	5
75. I actively seek opportunities to expand my digital network, recognizing the value of building relationships for future negotiations.	1	2	3	4	5

(Continued)

Statement	R	O	S	M	AA
76. I stay informed about the latest digital trends and technologies.	1	2	3	4	5
77. I exhibit a sense of perseverance in navigating digital challenges, showing determination to find solutions despite setbacks.	1	2	3	4	5
78. I appreciate the importance of continuous improvement and actively encourage reevaluation of digital solutions to optimize results over time.	1	2	3	4	5
79. I embrace an integrated approach to system evaluation, considering technical aspects, user experience, and business objectives.	1	2	3	4	5
80. I embrace digital storytelling techniques to craft narratives that resonate emotionally with my target audience.	1	2	3	4	5
81. In digital discussions, I am known for my ability to synthesize diverse information and distill it into actions.	1	2	3	4	5
82. I demonstrate a strong command of my virtual presence, including tone of voice, body language, and eye contact through the camera.	1	2	3	4	5
83. I actively avoid multitasking during digital conversations, focusing on the speaker's words and nuances.	1	2	3	4	5
84. I respond tactfully to digital conflicts, showing an ability to mediate and address disagreements while maintaining positive relationships.	1	2	3	4	5
85. I actively seek feedback on my digital strategies, demonstrating a commitment to continuous improvement.	1	2	3	4	5
86. I find satisfaction in successfully resolving digital problems, and my enthusiasm for overcoming challenges is contagious among my team.	1	2	3	4	5
87. I have a record of successfully inspiring, motivating, and influencing others through digital public speaking engagements.	1	2	3	4	5
88. I encourage the open sharing of ideas in virtual settings, creating an atmosphere where team members feel valued and heard.	1	2	3	4	5

(Continued)

Statement	R	O	S	M	AA
89. I actively seek feedback on my digital communication.	1	2	3	4	5
90. I am known for my ability to provide constructive feedback on digital proposals, helping others refine their ideas and solutions.	1	2	3	4	5
91. I actively engage with IT and digital teams to gather insights and feedback when evaluating and improving existing systems.	1	2	3	4	5
92. I actively participate in online communities and forums related to my industry.	1	2	3	4	5
93. My online presence reflects strong negotiation skills.	1	2	3	4	5
94. I foster a culture of continuous improvement by regularly revisiting and refining my digital vision in response to changing circumstances.	1	2	3	4	5
95. I am willing to experiment with negotiation techniques, continuously refining my approach for optimal results.	1	2	3	4	5
96. I embrace the iterative nature of digital visioning, finding joy in adjusting and evolving my plans as the digital landscape evolves.	1	2	3	4	5
97. I thrive in dynamic digital environments, adapting my problem-solving approach as circumstances evolve.	1	2	3	4	5
98. My capacity to synthesize complex information enables me to make informed judgments about the suitability of digital solutions.	1	2	3	4	5
99. I proactively identify potential vulnerabilities in digital systems, working to enhance cybersecurity and data protection measures.	1	2	3	4	5
100. I approach complex digital challenges with a systematic and analytical problem-solving mindset.	1	2	3	4	5

Scoring

Now, transfer your scores to the following response summary. Add your 10 ratings for each attribute to get a total score for each attribute.

Cognitive Leadership

- Critical Thinking 1+ 10 + 20 + 30 + 40 + 50 + 60 + 70 + 81 + 85 = ____
- Public Speaking 2+ 11 + 21 + 31 + 41 + 51 + 61 + 71 + 82 + 87 = ____
- Active Listening 3+ 12 + 22 + 32 + 42 + 52 + 62 + 72 + 83 + 88 = ____

Interpersonal Leadership

- Influencing 4 + 13 + 23 + 33 + 43 + 53 + 63 + 73 + 80 + 89 = ____
- Social Awareness 5 +14 + 24 + 34 + 44 + 54 + 64 + 74 + 84 + 92 = ____
- Negotiating 6 +15 + 25 +35 + 45 + 55 + 65 + 76 + 93 + 95 = ____

Strategic Leadership

- Visioning 7 + 16 + 26 + 36 + 46 + 56 + 66 + 76 + 94 + 96 = ____
- Problem Solving 17 + 27 + 37 + 47 + 57 + 67 + 77 + 86 + 97 + 100 = ____
- Solution Appraisal 8 + 18 + 28 + 38 + 48 + 58 + 68 + 78 + 90 + 98 = ____
- System Evaluation 9 + 19 + 29 + 39 + 49 + 59 + 69 + 79 + 91 + 99 = ____

To illustrate your profile visually, include your scores on the Digital Leadership Strengths Profile in Figure C.1.

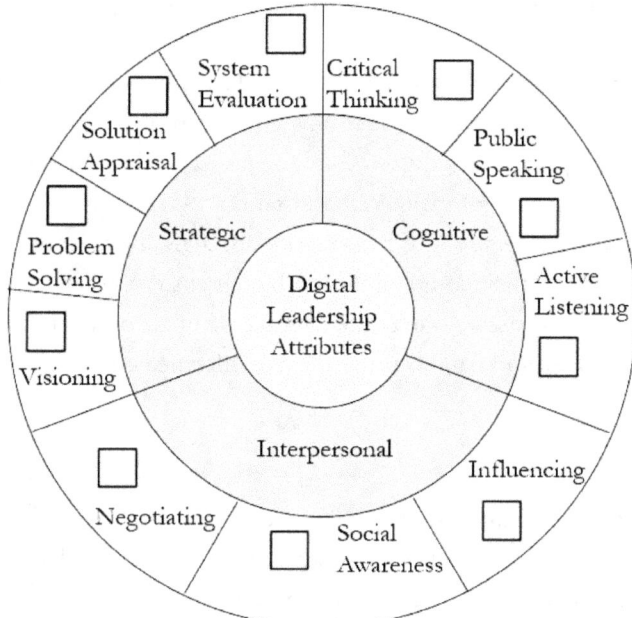

Figure C.1 Digital leadership development profile

Following are five suggestions and ideas for developing your talents, as illustrated in the Digital Leadership Development Profile above. I suggest you start with the top three scores from the profile.

We start with Critical Thinking and go clockwise on the model.

Critical Thinking

1. *Evaluating Information*: Critically assess the validity and reliability of digital information before making decisions or sharing it with your team. Verify sources, fact-check data, and consider potential biases to ensure you base your actions on accurate information.
2. *Problem-Solving*: Encourage your team to engage in collaborative digital brainstorming sessions where you analyze challenges from various angles. Challenge assumptions, encourage diverse perspectives, and guide discussions toward innovative solutions.
3. *Data Analysis:* Utilize data analytics tools to interpret digital metrics and trends. Analyze patterns, identify correlations, and draw

meaningful insights from the data to inform strategic decisions and optimize processes.
4. *Scenario Planning*: Develop scenarios based on digital trends and potential outcomes. Consider how changes in the digital landscape could impact your industry, team, or projects, allowing you to prepare proactively for various circumstances.
5. *Technology Assessment*: When considering new digital tools or platforms, assess their compatibility with your current systems, potential benefits, and risks. Analyze the long-term impact on workflows, user experiences, and data security to make informed choices.

Public Speaking

1. *Virtual Town Hall Meetings*: Conduct regular virtual town hall meetings to address the entire team, where you can share updates, convey the company's vision, and answer questions.
2. *Effective Video Conferencing*: During video conferences, use effective body language, maintain eye contact with the camera, and enunciate clearly to enhance your message's impact. Encourage active participation by allowing team members to ask questions or provide feedback.
3. *Podcasts or Webinars*: Host (or be a guest) podcasts or webinars where you discuss industry trends, share insights, or address familiar challenges. These platforms allow you to demonstrate expertise and establish a leadership presence while honing your speaking skills for digital audiences.
4. *Team Messages and E-mails*: Craft well-structured, concise e-mails and messages to communicate important updates, instructions, or appreciation to your team. Use an empathetic tone and clear language to ensure your messages are easily understood and resonate with recipients.
5. *Virtual Presentations*: When giving virtual presentations, employ visual aids like slides or interactive tools to complement your spoken content. Practice dynamic delivery, incorporate storytelling, and encourage interaction through Q&A sessions or polls to keep your audience engaged and receptive.

Active Listening

1. *Virtual Team Meetings*: Actively listen during virtual team meetings by giving your full attention to each speaker. Use nonverbal cues such as nodding or video to show your engagement and processing shared information.
2. *One-on-One Virtual Check-Ins*: During virtual check-ins with team members, focus on their words, tone, and emotions. Ask open-ended questions to encourage them to share their thoughts and concerns, and avoid interrupting or multitasking to demonstrate your commitment to active listening.
3. *Online Discussion Forums*: Participate in online discussion forums or chat platforms where team members share ideas, feedback, or challenges. Please read the messages carefully, respond thoughtfully, and acknowledge their contributions to show that you value their input.
4. *Feedback Sessions*: When providing feedback to team members, summarize their points to ensure you understand their perspective accurately. Then, offer your insights and suggestions while remaining open to their reactions and additional input.
5. *Reflective Summaries*: Send a follow-up message summarizing the key points and decisions made after a virtual meeting or discussion. This demonstrates your active listening skills and ensures everyone is on the same page and understands the outcomes.

Influencing

1. *Thought Leadership Content*: Share thought-provoking articles, blog posts, or videos on digital platforms to highlight your expertise and perspective. Engage with comments and discussions to further influence industry conversations.
2. *Virtual Presentations*: Host webinars or online workshops where you can present innovative ideas, strategies, or insights to a broad audience. Craft your presentation to be engaging, informative, and tailored to your target audience's interests.
3. *Social Media Engagement*: Participate in relevant social media discussions, sharing valuable insights and fostering connections. Respond

to comments or share relevant content and position yourself as a knowledgeable and influential voice in your field.
4. *Online Networking*: Join professional digital networking groups, forums, or LinkedIn communities to connect with peers and industry leaders. Engage in meaningful discussions, share insights, and build relationships that can lead to collaborative opportunities.
5. *Effective Communication*: Craft persuasive and well-structured e-mails, messages, or presentations when communicating with stakeholders. Use data, compelling narratives, and clear reasoning to influence decision making and garner support for your initiatives.

Social Awareness

1. *Cultural Sensitivity*: Show awareness of cultural differences when interacting with virtual teams from diverse backgrounds. Be mindful of customs, communication styles, and special days to foster a respectful and inclusive environment.
2. *Virtual Team Building*: Organize virtual team-building activities that promote social interaction and strengthen team bonds. Acknowledge team member's accomplishments and milestones, fostering a sense of camaraderie despite physical distance.
3. *Active Listening in Virtual Discussions*: Closely to nonverbal cues, tones, and subtleties during virtual discussions to understand team members' emotions and perspectives. Acknowledge and validate their feelings to show empathy.
4. *Inclusivity in Online Communication*: Use inclusive language in written communications to ensure all team members feel valued and included. Address everyone's input and concerns, promoting a sense of belonging.
5. *Digital Conflict Resolution*: Address conflicts or misunderstandings in virtual environments promptly and privately. Employ EQ to navigate challenging conversations and find solutions that preserve team relationships.

Negotiation

1. *Virtual Negotiation Sessions*: Conduct negotiation sessions through video conferencing tools, where you can discuss terms, exchange proposals, and address concerns in real time with remote counterparts.
2. *Structured Online Communication*: Outline negotiation points using e-mail or messaging platforms, ensuring clear and documented communication. This minimizes misunderstandings and provides a reference for discussions.
3. *Collaborative Document Sharing*: Utilize cloud-based platforms for collaborative document editing during negotiations. This allows both parties to make real-time changes, track revisions, and ensure transparency.
4. *Video Message Rebuttals*: If a negotiation requires counteroffers or responses, use video messages to personalize your communication. Express your points, clarify your position, and show sincerity through facial expressions and tone.
5. *Data-Driven Persuasion*: Present data, analytics, and market trends to support your negotiation points, making your position more persuasive and informed.

Visioning

1. *Strategic Roadmaps*: Develop digital transformation roadmaps that outline the organization's long-term vision for leveraging technology. Define milestones, initiatives, and goals that align with your digital future.
2. *Innovative Ideation Sessions*: Host virtual brainstorming sessions where your team generates ideas and concepts for digital innovation. Encourage thinking beyond current limitations and explore new possibilities.
3. *Digital Product Development*: Based on your vision, lead the creation of new digital products or services. Guide the development process, ensuring the result aligns with the envisioned digital experience.

4. *Change Management Strategies*: Develop strategies for implementing digital changes within your organization. Outline how your vision will be communicated, the steps to adopt new technologies, and the expected outcomes.
5. *Thought Leadership Content*: Share your digital vision through thought leadership articles, webinars, or podcasts. Articulate the future you see and inspire others to embrace it, encouraging a culture of digital innovation.

Problem-Solving

1. *Root Cause Analysis Tools*: Utilize digital tools and software for root cause analysis. These tools can help you systematically identify underlying factors contributing to challenges or issues within your team or projects.
2. *Online Surveys and Feedback*: Create digital surveys or feedback forms to gather insights from team members. Ask open-ended questions to encourage them to share their perspectives on potential causes of problems or inefficiencies.
3. *Collaborative Brainstorming Sessions*: Host virtual brainstorming sessions using video conferencing or collaboration tools. Encourage team members to contribute their thoughts on the possible causes of specific challenges and collaborate on solutions.
4. *Data Analytics and Reporting*: Leverage data analytics platforms to analyze digital metrics and patterns. Look for trends, anomalies, or correlations that could reveal underlying causes of issues related to performance, engagement, or other factors.
5. *Virtual Focus Groups*: Create virtual focus groups or discussion forums where team members can openly discuss potential causes of challenges. These online forums encourage candid conversations and diverse perspectives, aiding in cause identification.

Solution Appraisal

1. *Digital Tool Selection*: Evaluate various digital tools or software options to address specific challenges within your team. Consider

factors such as functionality, integration capabilities, user-friendliness, and scalability.
2. *Digital Transformation Initiatives*: Assess potential solutions for broader digital transformation initiatives. Determine how different solutions align with your business's strategic goals and their potential impact on workflows and processes.
3. *Data-Driven Decision Making*: Utilize data analytics to appraise the effectiveness of digital solutions. Analyze metrics and KPIs to measure the outcomes of implemented solutions and identify areas for improvement.
4. *User Feedback Analysis*: Gather feedback from team members about the effectiveness of current digital solutions. Use their insights to identify pain points, challenges, and potential enhancements.
5. *Pilot Programs*: Implement pilot programs for testing new digital solutions on a smaller scale before full deployment. Evaluate the outcomes, user experiences, and feedback to inform your decision on broader implementation.

System Evaluation

1. *Software and Tool Assessment*: Regularly evaluate the effectiveness of digital tools and software used by your team. Consider factors such as usability, functionality, and alignment with your goals.
2. *Process Audits*: Conduct audits of digital workflows and processes to identify bottlenecks, redundancies, or areas for improvement. Use digital process mapping tools to visualize and analyze these workflows.
3. *User Experience Testing*: Involve team members in user experience testing of digital platforms or applications. Gather feedback on usability, user-friendliness, and any challenges they encounter during their interactions.
4. *Cybersecurity Audits*: Perform regular cybersecurity audits to assess the robustness of your digital security measures. Evaluate encryption protocols, access controls, and data protection procedures.
5. *Data Management Review*: Evaluate how your digital systems collect, store, and manage data. Ensure compliance with data privacy regulations and assess data quality and integrity.

APPENDIX D

Influencing Capabilities Profile

You complete the Influencing Capabilities Profile[2] in Appendix D. Following these instructions are 64 statements. You are to respond to each statement in a work context. More specifically, answer each statement in terms of what you believe you do in situations where you need to influence others at work. You do not have to identify specific examples. You can go with your gut feeling or first reaction for many statements. In other words, there is no need to overanalyze each statement and your behavior.

Instructions

Home and work are entirely different contexts. Your strategies to influence people at work differ from how you persuade family at home. We have a separate set of relationships on the one hand. The issues are entirely different. Try, therefore, to separate work from home when responding to the following statements. Only consider the statements from a work-related perspective.

Although gut feeling can often be the best way to answer these statements, sometimes you may need to think deeper about some statements. If you find you have difficulty with a rating for a statement, focus on a situation where you need to be influential. By considering specific circumstances, you can put the statement in context. For example, this may include dealing with your manager or dealing with conflict. If you are unsure, ask someone who knows you at work for their opinion. As a last resort, mark the statement as a *0*.

In your responses, be as objective as you can. This is easier said than done. The profile will be of little or no value to you unless you provide an accurate and objective description of yourself.

Apart from being objective, be consistent. By consistently, I mean maintaining a certain self-assessment standard throughout. If you are reasonably self-critical, do this for all 64 statements. Then again, if you will be easier on yourself, do so from start to finish. The result is a comparative analysis between four influencing strategies and 16 supporting capabilities, so consistency in scoring is helpful.

Scoring

For each profile statement, enter on the scoring sheet the number corresponding with your choice from the following five alternatives:

+2 *Definitely Agree* that the statement always describes your behavior.
+1 *Inclined to Agree* if the statement describes your behavior sometimes.
 0 *Neutral* if you cannot decide whether the statement applies to your behavior.
−1 *Inclined to Disagree* if the statement describes your behavior occasionally.
−2 *Definitely Disagree* if the statement does not describe your behavior at all.

Profile Statements

1. I strive to put together a logical argument for my point of view.
2. I do not hesitate to point out others' mistakes as a way of changing their behavior.
3. I help others become aware of the strengths and advantages they can have by pulling together.
4. I think others would consider me a trustworthy person.
5. I usually provide detailed plans for implementing an idea.
6. I quickly praise another's performance to reinforce their behavior.
7. I foster an esprit de corps where others sense a common purpose.
8. I encourage others to participate in decision making.
9. I produce evidence in support of my proposals.
10. I pass on worthy praise and constructive criticism I have heard to others.
11. I help others I work with and feel personally involved and responsible for the project's success.

12. I help others to express themselves.
13. I like to gather the facts before convincing others of a proposal.
14. People can readily tell if I disapprove of what they do or say.
15. I help others to see how they can achieve more by working together.
16. I accept criticism without becoming defensive.
17. I put forward ideas and plans that I have thought through.
18. I will articulate the pros of a new proposal.
19. When working with others, I communicate my belief in the value and importance of joint tasks.
20. I listen to and try to use the ideas raised by others.
21. It is not unusual for me to stick my neck out with ideas and suggestions.
22. When striving to change people's opinions, I explain the pitfalls of the current situation.
23. I articulate a sharp vision of what could be.
24. I usually listen with understanding if others become angry or upset.
25. My focus is to persuade others of my ideas rather than listen to the ideas of others.
26. When deciding, I like to weigh up the advantages and disadvantages of a particular approach.
27. I am skillful at articulating the aims and goals people have in common.
28. I am a good listener.
29. I enjoy putting solutions on the table to resolve problems.
30. I enjoy articulating the strengths and weaknesses of various approaches.
31. I strive to develop in those with whom I work a sense of unity and common purpose against the outside world.
32. I empathize with people who do not share my point of view.
33. I put much energy into arguing my case.
34. I am prepared to offer bargains or exchange favors to get what I want from others.
35. I can put into words the hopes, aspirations, and fears others are feeling.
36. I hand essential tasks over to others even when they may be personally criticized if they are not done well.
37. I push my ideas vigorously.

38. I clarify what I am willing to give in return for what I want.
39. I am skillful at using images and figures of speech to present exciting possibilities.
40. I encourage people to produce their own solutions to solve problems.
41. I defend my ideas energetically.
42. I enjoy bargaining based on people's positions' relevant strengths and weaknesses.
43. I appeal to their values, emotions, and feelings when persuading others.
44. I put as much effort into developing the ideas of others as I do my own.
45. I frequently disregard the ideas of others in favor of my proposals.
46. I will make concessions if it means getting what I want.
47. I use emotionally charged language to generate enthusiasm.
48. I support and work with people to assist them to be empowered.
49. I anticipate objections to my point of view and am ready with a counterargument.
50. I like to communicate standards that others ought to meet.
51. When others become uncertain or discouraged, I carry people with my enthusiasm.
52. I am open to being influenced by others.
53. I draw attention to inconsistencies in the ideas of others.
54. I let people know the standards by which their performance will be judged.
55. I can bring others to see the exciting future possibilities in a situation.
56. I am receptive to the ideas and suggestions of others.
57. I am quick to come forward with an alternative argument when opposed.
58. I sometimes use my power and authority to make others comply with standards.
59. My way of speaking conveys a sense of enthusiasm to others.
60. I am quick to admit my own mistakes and errors.
61. I put my ideas clearly and convincingly.
62. I give frequent and specific feedback on whether my requirements are being met.
63. My passion is contagious.
64. I readily admit my lack of knowledge and expertise.

Scoring

Enter the score you assign to each question (–2, –1, 0, +1, +2) in the space in Table D.1. Please note: The item numbers progress from left to right across the page.

Table D.1 Influencing capabilities scoring sheet

1.	2.	3.	4.
5.	6.	7.	8.
9.	10.	11.	12.
13.	14.	15.	16.
The sum of positive numbers:	The sum of positive numbers:	The sum of positive numbers:	The sum of positive numbers:
The sum of negative numbers:	The sum of negative numbers:	The sum of negative numbers:	The sum of negative numbers:
Subtotal:	Subtotal:	Subtotal:	Subtotal:
Gather Evidence	**Provide Feedback**	**Build Morale**	**Build Trust**
17.	18.	19.	20.
21.	22.	23.	24.
25.	26.	27.	28.
29.	30.	31.	32.
The sum of positive numbers:	The sum of positive numbers:	The sum of positive numbers:	The sum of positive numbers:
The sum of negative numbers:	The sum of negative numbers:	The sum of negative numbers:	The sum of negative numbers:
Subtotal:	Subtotal:	Subtotal:	Subtotal:
Generate Ideas	**Weigh Options**	**Communicate Vision**	**Listen Actively**
33.	34.	35.	36.
37.	38.	39.	40.
41.	42.	43.	44.
45.	46.	47.	48.
The sum of positive numbers:	The sum of positive numbers:	The sum of positive numbers:	The sum of positive numbers:
The sum of negative numbers:	The sum of negative numbers:	The sum of negative numbers:	The sum of negative numbers:

(*Continued*)

Subtotal:	Subtotal:	Subtotal:	Subtotal:
Assert Ideas	Offer Concessions	Connect Emotionally	Share Ownership
49.	50.	51.	52.
53.	54.	55.	56.
57.	58.	59.	60.
61.	62.	63.	64.
The sum of positive numbers:	The sum of positive numbers:	The sum of positive numbers:	The sum of positive numbers:
The sum of negative numbers:	The sum of negative numbers:	The sum of negative numbers:	The sum of negative numbers:
Subtotal:	Subtotal:	Subtotal:	Subtotal:
Counter Arguments	Communicate Standards	Generate Enthusiasm	Communicate Openly
Total:	Total:	Total:	Total:
Investigation	Calculation	Motivation	Collaboration

Now, transfer your result from the scoring sheet to the Influencing Capabilities Profile in Table D.2. The scores for the four supporting capabilities should add to the total score for the corresponding strategy: Investigation, Calculation, Motivation, and Collaboration. For example, Gather Evidence, Counter Arguments, Assert Ideas, and Generate Ideas are added to Investigation.

Your Push Style score is the total for Investigation and Motivation in the top row, and Your Pull Style score is the total for Calculation and Collaboration.

On the right-hand side of the profile, your score for the logical approach is the combined total of Investigation and Calculation. Your score for the Emotional Approach is the combined total of Motivation and Collaboration.

Table D.2 Influencing capabilities profile

Push Style ☐		Pull Style ☐		
Gather Evidence ☐	Counter Arguments ☐	Weigh Options ☐	Offer Concessions ☐	**Logical Approach**
INVESTIGATION ☐		**CALCULATION** ☐		☐
Generate Ideas ☐	Assert Ideas ☐	Communicate Standards ☐	Provide Feedback ☐	
Build Morale ☐	Connect Emotionally ☐	Build Trust ☐	Share Ownership ☐	**Emotional Approach**
MOTIVATION ☐		**COLLABORATION** ☐		☐
Communicate Vision ☐	Generate Enthusiasm ☐	Listen Actively ☐	Communicate Openly ☐	

*This material is the intellectual property of Dr. Tim Baker. Further use of this material can be sought by contacting the author at tim@winnersatwork.com.au.

Brief Understanding of the Profile

Investigation and Calculation use logic to influence.

More specifically, the Investigation strategy relies on gathering and presenting the facts logically and convincingly. A coherent and assertive argument based on well-founded research is a powerful persuasion in the right circumstances.

Calculation relies on communicating the pitfalls of the current state and promoting the benefits of a new solution. This strategy sharpens the distinction between an argument's pros and cons and the pros of not adopting it.

Motivation and Collaboration use emotion to influence.

The Motivation strategy associates an idea or proposal with a compelling future vision. People who can paint a convincing picture of the future and sell that vision are generally inspirational and motivating.

Finally, the collaboration strategy involves others in the proposal. Collaboration builds trust and shared ownership. By collaborating with others, a leader invites the team to be involved in the change.

There are 16 capabilities in the profile, four supporting each influencing strategy. Look at your profile and identify your highest score for the 16 capabilities. Your highest score suggests that this capability comes naturally to you. What's more, you probably use it often, perhaps too often. You might overuse it, given that you are comfortable with the capability. Be aware of this, and make sure you do not rely too heavily on it.

Now, look at your lowest score for the 16 capabilities. This is the capability that you feel uncomfortable using. So, you do not use it very often, if at all very least. Practice using it. Be conscious of applying it when the opportunity arises.

Here are four questions you can ask yourself about your profile:

1. What influencing strategies are you most and least comfortable using?
2. How does your profile shape the way you engage and influence others at work?
3. What are the key influencing capabilities of the people you work with?
4. What are the best ways of communicating with influence with your manager, colleagues, team members, and stakeholders?

If you want more information about improving your influencing capabilities, check out my book, *The New Influencing Toolkit: Capabilities for Communicating with Influence*.[3] There are over 100 practical tools to develop your ability to influence in the book.

The key to being more influential is extending your communication style to include these four strategies in the right place, at the right time, with the right people. This means you will be more adaptable to a range of different situations and with people who are influenced in ways that are different from you. If Plan A fails, be ready to try Plan B, and so on.

APPENDIX E

Reflections on Leadership Intention

In Appendix E, you can assess your ability to lead with intent. In Chapter 12, I shared eight characteristics of the practice of Show Intent. Following are five questions for each characteristic. These questions help reflect on your behavior.

Instructions

Answer each question in the context of the workplace. If you cannot think of an example, consider what you could not do in that circumstance.

If you are using a journal, as discussed in Chapter 4, write your answers in your journal. If not, you can write the answers down on paper or type them on a Word document.

By going through this exercise, you reflect on your ability to Show Intent. This reflection can be helpful for your growth and development for this and other practices in the Self-Leadership Development Framework.

Reflective Questions

1. **Be a Better Communicator**
    1.1. How do you ensure your team members and stakeholders effectively understand your messages?
    1.2. Can you provide an example of a recent communication challenge you faced in the workplace and how you addressed it?
    1.3. How do you tailor your communication style to different individuals or situations to maximize understanding and engagement?
    1.4. What steps do you take to solicit feedback on your communication effectiveness and make necessary adjustments?
    1.5. How do you manage difficult conversations or conflicts while maintaining open and transparent communication?

2. **Look to the Future**
    2.1. How do you stay informed about industry trends and changes that could impact your organization?
    2.2. Can you describe a recent initiative you led that focused on long-term goals and objectives?
    2.3. How do you encourage your team members to think strategically and anticipate future challenges and opportunities?
    2.4. What strategies do you use to foster innovation and forward-thinking within your team?
    2.5. How do you ensure your plans and strategies align with your organization's long-term vision and goals?
3. **Build on People's Strengths**
    3.1. How do you identify the unique strengths and talents of individuals within your team?
    3.2. Can you explain how you have leveraged someone's strengths to achieve a specific goal or project outcome?
    3.3. What measures do you take to create a culture that values and celebrates individual strengths and contributions?
    3.4. How do you support and encourage team members to further develop and utilize their strengths?
    3.5. How do you ensure equitable distribution of tasks and responsibilities based on individual strengths and capabilities?
4. **Develop Emotional Intelligence**
    4.1. How do you recognize and manage your emotions in the workplace, especially during challenging situations?
    4.2. Can you describe when you effectively used empathy to understand and address a colleague's or team member's emotions?
    4.3. How do you foster a positive and emotionally supportive work environment?
    4.4. How do you provide feedback or address conflicts in a way that considers the emotions and well-being of others?
    4.5. How do you continuously improve your emotional intelligence skills and self-awareness?
5. **Give Constructive Feedback**
    5.1 How do you approach giving feedback to team members to ensure it is constructive and well received?

5.2. Can you provide an example of when you delivered feedback that led to positive changes in a team member's performance or behavior?
5.3. What strategies do you use to ensure that feedback is specific, actionable, and focused on behavior rather than personality?
5.4. How do you handle resistance or defensiveness from team members when providing feedback?
5.5. How do you follow up on feedback to ensure it is understood and implemented effectively?

6. **Actively Listen**
   6.1. How do you demonstrate active listening during team meetings or one-on-one discussions?
   6.2. Can you describe when you effectively resolved a misunderstanding or conflict by actively listening to all perspectives?
   6.3. What techniques do you use to show empathy and understanding when listening to team members' concerns or ideas?
   6.4. How do you encourage participation and ensure all voices are heard during discussions?
   6.5. How do you follow up on conversations or feedback to demonstrate your listening and understanding?

7. **Define Responsibilities**
   7.1. How do you ensure your team or department's roles and responsibilities are clearly defined?
   7.2. Can you provide an example of when ambiguity around responsibilities led to confusion or inefficiency, and how did you address it?
   7.3. How do you effectively communicate expectations regarding tasks and projects?
   7.4. How do you ensure that each team member understands their responsibilities, and how they contribute to the overall goals?
   7.5. How do you adjust responsibilities as needed to accommodate changes in priorities or resources?

8. **Encourage Others to be Their Best and Healthiest Self**
   8.1. How do you support your team members' professional development and growth?

8.2. Can you describe when you provided mentorship or guidance to help someone achieve their career goals?

8.3. What strategies do you use to promote work–life balance and overall well-being within your team?

8.4. How do you recognize and celebrate the achievements and successes of your team members?

8.5. How do you foster a continuous learning and self-improvement culture among your team?

Further Reflection

Take time to reflect on your responses. To assist you, here are some questions:

- What did you discover about yourself?
- Where do you need to make changes?
- How will you do this?

APPENDIX F

Self-Regulation Appraisal

Here is a self-regulation test to evaluate how effectively you manage your behaviors, emotions, and thoughts in work and home environments.

Instructions

The test includes a variety of statements that you rate on a scale from 1 to 5, where:

- 1 = Strongly Disagree
- 2 = Disagree
- 3 = Neither Agree nor Disagree
- 4 = Agree
- 5 = Strongly Agree.

The Self-Regulation Appraisal follows Table F.1.

Please read each statement carefully and indicate the number that best represents your agreement with each statement as it applies to you in the last month in both work and home contexts.

Self-Regulation Appraisal

Table F.1 Self-regulation appraisal

Statement	Strongly Disagree	Disagree	Neither Agree nor Disagree	Agree	Strongly Disagree
1. I can keep distractions to a minimum when focusing on a task.	1	2	3	4	5

(Continued)

Statement	Strongly Disagree	Disagree	Neither Agree nor Disagree	Agree	Strongly Disagree
2. I set clear goals for myself at work and home.	1	2	3	4	5
3. I manage my emotions well in stressful situations.	1	2	3	4	5
4. I can resist temptations that prevent me from completing my tasks.	1	2	3	4	5
5. I can work or perform tasks independently without constant reassurance.	1	2	3	4	5
6. I regularly review my progress toward my goals.	1	2	3	4	5
7. I can adapt my plans if unexpected issues arise.	1	2	3	4	5
8. I prioritize my tasks effectively.	1	2	3	4	5
9. I maintain a healthy balance between work and personal life.	1	2	3	4	5
10. I can calm myself down when I get upset or angry.	1	2	3	4	5
11. I avoid procrastination when I have important tasks to complete.	1	2	3	4	5
12. I seek feedback to improve my performance and behavior.	1	2	3	4	5
13. I take breaks when needed to avoid burnout.	1	2	3	4	5

(Continued)

Statement	Strongly Disagree	Disagree	Neither Agree nor Disagree	Agree	Strongly Disagree
14. I am aware of my emotional triggers and know how to manage them.	1	2	3	4	5
15. I can say no to additional responsibilities when overloaded.	1	2	3	4	5
16. I reflect on my mistakes and learn from them.	1	2	3	4	5
17. I practice patience in challenging situations.	1	2	3	4	5
18. I communicate my needs effectively at work and home.	1	2	3	4	5
19. I manage my time efficiently.	1	2	3	4	5
20. I can adjust my behavior based on the feedback I receive.	1	2	3	4	5
21. I remain focused on tasks even when I encounter difficulties.	1	2	3	4	5
22. I make healthy choices for myself daily.	1	2	3	4	5
23. I handle criticism without becoming defensive.	1	2	3	4	5
24. I maintain a positive outlook even in challenging circumstances.	1	2	3	4	5
25. I balance my needs with the needs of others effectively.	1	2	3	4	5

(Continued)

Statement	Strongly Disagree	Disagree	Neither Agree nor Disagree	Agree	Strongly Disagree
26. I recognize when I need help and am not afraid to ask for it.	1	2	3	4	5
27. I can stay motivated over extended periods, even without immediate rewards.	1	2	3	4	5
28. I control impulses that lead me to engage in unhealthy behaviors.	1	2	3	4	5
29. I maintain discipline in my daily routines.	1	2	3	4	5
30. I effectively manage stress through healthy activities and relaxation techniques.	1	2	3	4	5

Scoring Scale

To score the assessment, add the total points from all the items. The maximum score is 150, and the minimum score is 30.

- 120–150: *High self-regulation*. You can effectively manage your thoughts, emotions, and behaviors at work and home. You find it easier to achieve your goals and maintain a balanced life.
- 90–119: *Moderate self-regulation*. You manage yourself well but may have specific areas to improve. Identifying and focusing on these areas can enhance your self-regulation skills.
- 60–89: *Low self-regulation*. In some situations, you may struggle with managing your emotions, behaviors, or thoughts. Consider some strategies we covered in Chapter 14 or support developing more vital self-regulation skills.

- Below 60: *Deficient self-regulation.* You might often find it challenging to control impulses, manage stress, or stay motivated. Seeking guidance through resources or professional help could be beneficial in developing better self-regulation strategies.

Remember, this assessment is for personal insight and development. It can highlight areas of strength and potential growth, but it is not a diagnostic tool. To further explore your self-regulation abilities, invite someone who knows you well at home and work. Also, your results can fluctuate occasionally, depending on what is happening in your life. Nevertheless, it is a rough guide to developing self-awareness of situations when maintaining self-control is relatively challenging. You can also consult a psychologist or a professional coach to assist you in developing strategies for better self-regulation.

APPENDIX G

Curiosity Inventory

The Curiosity Inventory consists of five elements: *Asking Questions, Exploring New Ideas, Embracing Ambiguity, Pursuing Continuous Learning,* and *Challenging Assumptions*. The inventory offers you the opportunity to assess yourself against each element. By comparing your ratings for each component, you can identify where you find it easier to display curiosity and where you do not. This can give you insight to improve your ability to Be Curious. At the end of this chapter, I provide practical ways to exercise each of the five elements of the inventory.

Instructions

In Table G.1 are 25 statements about curiosity. The five-point scale asks you to describe how much you agree or disagree with each statement. The scale consists of the following:

+2 = Strongly Agree

+1 = Moderately Agree

0 = Neither Agree nor Disagree

−1 = Moderately Agree

−2 = Strongly Disagree

The scoring scale follows Table G.1.

Table G.1 Curiosity assessment

Statement	+2	+1	0	−1	−2
1. I frequently inquire about topics to gain a deeper understanding.					
2. I often actively seek opinions and viewpoints different from mine.					
3. In uncertain situations, I can stay calm.					

(Continued)

Statement	+2	+1	0	–1	–2
4. I actively seek out new knowledge or skills to continuously learn.					
5. I critically evaluate commonly accepted ideas or beliefs.					
6. I actively seek clarification when encountering something I do not understand.					
7. I am open to considering alternative solutions or approaches to problems.					
8. I tolerate ambiguity without feeling anxious or overwhelmed.					
9. I am motivated to learn about topics outside my expertise.					
10. I am willing to challenge authority or tradition when I believe it is necessary.					
11. I am comfortable asking questions, even if they might challenge existing knowledge or beliefs.					
12. I discuss with people with different beliefs or perspectives.					
13. I see uncertainty as an opportunity for growth and exploration.					
14. I set aside time regularly for personal or professional development.					
15. I often question the reasons behind societal norms or cultural practices.					
16. I prioritize seeking answers to my questions, even if they require effort or research.					
17. I am flexible in accepting innovative ideas.					
18. I am comfortable with ambiguity.					
19. I am committed to lifelong learning.					
20. I am willing to challenge assumptions.					
21. I often want to know more about subjects outside my expertise.					
22. I am comfortable changing your mind when presented with compelling evidence or arguments.					
23. I embrace ambiguity as a natural part of life rather than striving for certainty in every situation.					
24. I challenge myself to explore areas where I lack knowledge or expertise.					
25. I am open to considering alternative perspectives contradicting my beliefs or values.					

Scoring Scale

Now add up your scores under the following five elements:

Asking Questions: Seeking understanding and knowledge.
- 1 + 6 + 11 + 16 + 21 = ____

Exploring New Ideas: Being open to different perspectives.
- 2 + 7 + 12 + 17+ 22 = ____

Embracing Ambiguity: Being comfortable with uncertainty.
- 3 + 8 + 13 + 18 + 23 = ____

Pursuing Continuous Learning: Never being satisfied with what is known.
- 4 + 9 + 14 + 19 + 24 = ____

Challenging Assumptions: Questioning established norms and beliefs.
- 5 + 10 + 15 + 20 + 25 = ____

Curiosity Inventory

Figure G.1 is the Curiosity Inventory. The Curiosity Inventory gives you an illustration of the five elements. You can place your totals for the five elements below.

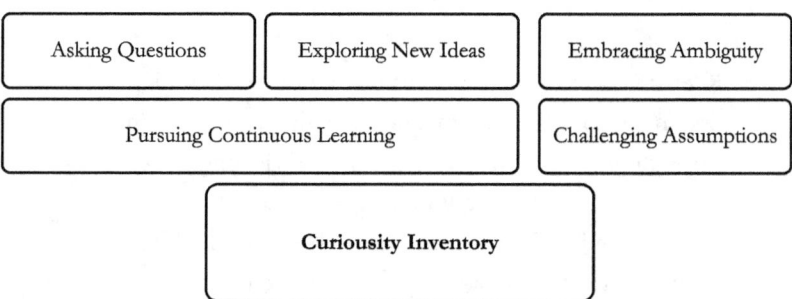

Figure G.1 Curiosity inventory

Following are reflective questions that you might like to ask yourself about the results.

Reflective Questions

Now that you have a score for each of the five elements in the Curiosity Inventory, here are four questions to ponder:

1. Which element scored highest?
2. What general assumptions and beliefs do you carry about this element of the Curiosity Inventory that might explain this high score? For example, my highest score is for *Pursuing Continuous Learning*. I believe that developing my innate talents into strengths is my responsibility for having this talent.
3. Which was your lowest score?
4. What assumptions and beliefs about this element might keep you from being more curious? For example, my lowest score is *Embracing Ambiguity*. I have always felt secure when I don't have a plan. However, I am aware that life is unpredictable and that great opportunities can come from dealing with uncertainty—provided I am willing to embrace ambiguity.

Following are three practical suggestions to boost each of the five elements of the Curiosity Inventory.

Practical Strategies

Asking Questions

- Keep a Curiosity Journal. Dedicate a notebook or digital document to jot down any questions that come to mind throughout your day. Make a habit of reviewing and expanding upon these questions regularly.
- Practice the Five Whys Technique. When faced with a problem or situation, ask *why* five times to delve deeper into the underlying causes or motivations.
- Engage in Socratic Dialogues. Seek conversations with others where you can ask open-ended questions and explore different perspectives.

Exploring New Ideas

- Diversify Your Reading. Make a conscious effort to read books, articles, and content from various genres, disciplines, and viewpoints.

- Attend Workshops and Seminars. Participate in workshops or seminars on topics that are unfamiliar to you. This exposes you to the latest ideas and allows for direct learning experiences.
- Experiment with Hobbies. Start new hobbies or interests regularly to explore diverse ways of thinking and problem-solving.

Embracing Ambiguity

- Practice Mindfulness. Engage in mindfulness exercises to become more comfortable with uncertainty and ambiguity. This can help you develop patience and clarity of thought.
- Seek Feedback. Regularly seek feedback from peers, mentors, or experts in various fields. Embracing feedback can help you see ambiguity as an opportunity for growth rather than a barrier.
- Explore Contradictory Views. Deliberately seek out perspectives that challenge your existing beliefs or opinions. This can help you become more adaptable and open-minded.

Pursuing Continuous Learning

- Set Learning Goals. Identify specific areas or skills you want to improve and set measurable goals for your learning. Regularly review and adjust these goals as needed.
- Utilize Online Courses and Resources. Access courses and educational materials using online learning platforms and resources.
- Join a Learning Community. Participate in learning communities or groups where members share resources and insights and support each other's learning journeys.

Challenging Assumptions

- Practice Devil's Advocacy. When evaluating ideas or making decisions, deliberately take on the role of a devil's advocate to challenge assumptions and explore alternative viewpoints.
- Encourage Constructive Debate. Promote an environment where constructive debate and disagreement can flourish. This encourages critical thinking and helps uncover hidden assumptions.
- Conduct Experiments. Design and conduct experiments to assess assumptions and hypotheses in your life or work. This empirical approach can lead to new insights and discoveries.

Notes

Introduction

1. Frankl, *Man's Search for Meaning*.
2. Manz, "Self-Leadership: Toward an Expanded Theory of Self-Influence Processes in Organizations," 585–600.

Chapter 1

1. Nielsen and Sirke, *Presidential Leadership: Learning From United States Presidential Libraries and Museums*.
2. Clance, and Imes, "The Imposter Phenomenon in High Achieving Women: Dynamics and Therapeutic Intervention," 241–247.
3. Carnegie, *How to Win Friends & Influence People: The Only Book You Need to Lead You to Success*.
4. White, *200 Inspirational Leadership Action Quotes*.
5. Bryant, and Kazan, *Self-Leadership: How to Become a More Successful, Efficient, and Effective Leader From the Inside Out*.
6. Rotter, "Cognates of Personal Control: Locus of Control, Self-efficacy, and Explanatory Style: Comment," 127–129.

Chapter 2

1. Meier, *The Power of Personal Leadership*.
2. Dweck, *Mindset: The New Psychology of Success*.
3. Wright, and Wigmore, "VUCA (Volatility, Uncertainty, Complexity and Ambiguity)."

Chapter 3

1. Kinni, "Leader, Know Thyself. Strategy + Business: PWC."
2. Fleming, *Know Thyself: The Science of Self-Awareness*.
3. Franklin, *Poor Richard's Almanack*.
4. Haselton, Nettle, and Andrews, *The Evolution of Cognitive Bias*, 724–746.
5. Kahneman, and Tversky, "Subjective Probability: A Judgment of Representativeness."
6. Kahneman, *Thinking, Fast and Slow*.
7. Black, "Thinking About Thinking About Leadership: Metacognitive Ability and Leader Developmental Readiness," 85–95.
8. Fubini, *Hidden Truths: What Leaders Need to Hear but Are Rarely Told*.
9. Vinney, "Understanding Maslow's Theory of Self-Actualization."
10. Couture, Desrosiers, and Leclerc, "Self-Actualization and Poststroke Rehabilitation," 111–117.
11. Boyatzis, "An Overview of Intentional Change From a Complexity Perspective," 607–623.
12. Boyatzis, "The Five Stages of Intentional Change Theory."

Chapter 4

1. Feldman, "The Power of Journaling."
2. Baikie, and Wilhelm, "Emotional and Physical Health Benefits of Expressive Writing," 338–346; Cameron, *The Artist's Way: A Spiritual Path to Higher Creativity*; Emmons and McCullough, "Counting Blessings Versus Burdens: Experimental Studies of Gratitude and Subjective Well-being," 377–389; Krizan and Herlache, "Sleep Diary and Polysomnographic Studies of Sleep Disturbance Following a Written Disclosure Intervention for Worry," 1506–1514; Mehl, Pennebaker, Crow, Dabbs, and Price, "The Electronically Activated Recorder (EAR): A Device for Sampling Naturalistic Daily Activities and Conversations," 513–521; Pennebaker and Beall, "Confronting a Traumatic Event: Toward an Understanding of Inhibition and

Disease," 274–281; Smyth, "Written Emotional Expression: Effect Sizes, Outcome Types, and Moderating Variables," 174–184.
3. Fain, "Author Natalie Goldberg on the Zen of Living, Writing and Eating."
4. Heimbigner, "Why You Need to Start Journaling in 2024."
5. Andersen, "The Healing Power of Journaling: Ten Benefits for Self-Discovery and Growth."
6. Günel, "The Power of Journaling."
7. Pennebaker and Smyth, *Opening Up by Writing It Down: How Expressive Writing Improves Health and Eases Emotional Pain.*
8. Tolle, *The Power of Now: A Guide to Spiritual Enlightenment.*
9. Kinni, "Leader, Know Thyself. Strategy + Business PWC publication."
10. Engel, "The Third Commandment of Highly Effective Leadership: Know Thyself and Others."
11. Littauer, *Personality Plus: How to Understand Others by Understanding Yourself.*

Chapter 5

1. George, *Discover Your True North: Becoming an Authentic Leader.*
2. Craig and Snook, "From Purpose to Impact."
3. Hill, and Turiano, "Purpose in Life as a Predictor of Mortality Across Adulthood," 1482–1486.
4. Craig and Snook, "From Purpose to Impact."
5. Ibid.
6. Goffee and Jones, "Why Should Anyone Be Led by You?"
7. Craig and Snook, "From Purpose to Impact."

Chapter 6

1. Goffee and Jones, "Why Should Anyone Be Led by You?"
2. Yang and Hu, "Role of Job Mobility Frequency in Job Satisfaction Changes: The Mediation Mechanism of Job-Related Social Capital and Person–Job Match," 156.
3. Zimmerman, "Resiliency Theory: A Strengths-Based Approach to Research and Practice for Adolescent Health."

4. Sorenson, "How Employees' Strengths Make Your Company Stronger."
5. Brown and Kelly, "Life Values Inventory."

Chapter 7

1. Baker, *The New Influencing Toolkit: Capabilities for Communicating With Influence.*
2. Rath, *Strengths Finder 2.0.*
3. Ibid.
4. Ibid.
5. Ibid.
6. Simpson, *Touching the Void: The True Story of One Man.*
7. Campbell, "Strengths-Based Development Requires a Growth Mindset."
8. Ibid.
9. Lopez and Louis, "The Principles of Strengths-Based Education," 4.
10. Ibid.
11. Rath, *Strengths Finder 2.0.*
12. Campbell, "Strengths-Based Development Requires a Growth Mindset."

Chapter 8

1. Church, *Writing a New Leadership Playbook.*
2. Readytech, "What Is a Digital Leader (and Do You Need to Be One)?"
3. Guzmán, Muschard, Gerolamo, Kohl and Rozenfield, "Characteristics and Skills of Leadership in the Context of Industry 4.0, 543–550.

Chapter 9

1. Dweck, *Mindset: The New Psychology of Success.*
2. Salovey and Mayer, "Emotional Intelligence."
3. Goleman, "Emotional Intelligence: Why It Can Matter More than IQ."

4. Cox, "5 Experts Answer: Can Your IQ Change?"
5. Goleman, "Emotional Intelligence: Why It Can Matter More Than IQ."
6. Kraut and Korman, *Evolving Practices in Human Resource Management*, 3–22.
7. Whitener, "The Value of a Growth Mindset and How to Develop One."
8. Mateos-Aparicio and Rodríguez-Moreno,. "The Impact of Studying Brain Plasticity."
9. Hendry, "7 Epic Fails Brought to You by the Genius Mind of Thomas Edison."
10. Whitener, "The Value of a Growth Mindset and How to Develop One."

Chapter 10

1. Confino, "Paul Polman: The Power Is in the Hands of the Consumer."
2. Baker, *The New Influencing Toolkit: Capabilities for Communicating With Influence*.
3. Ibid.
4. Scott and Jaffe, "Survive and Thrive in Times of Change."
5. Kübler-Ross, *On Death and Dying: What the Dying Have to Teach Doctors, Nurses, Clergy and Their Own Families*.
6. Baker, *Mastering Change: A Practical Guide for Better Leadership Conversations*.
7. Stephens, "The Psychology of Roller Coasters."
8. Baker, *Mastering Change: A Practical Guide for Better Leadership Conversations*.
9. Ibid.
10. Goodwin, *Leadership: In Turbulent Times*.
11. Sloan, "How to Become More Empathetic—Because, Yes, Empathy Is a Quality You Can Grow."
12. Ibid.
13. Ibid.
14. Kettlewell, *Skin Games*; Walsh, *Treating Self-Injury: A Practical Guide*.

15. Harter, "U.S. Employee Engagement Data Hold Steady in First Half of 2021."
16. Dogru, McGinley, Sharma, Isik, and Hanks, "Employee Turnover Dynamics in the Hospitality Industry vs. the Overall Economy."
17. Hetler, "The Great Resignation: Everything You Need to Know."
18. Telford, "U.S. Workers Have Gotten Way Less Productive. No One Is Sure Why."
19. Holbeche, "How Good Leaders Inspire and Motivate Others. Business Leadership Today."
20. Grint, "Problems, Problems, Problems: The Social Construction of Leadership."
21. Qualtrics, "The 5 Trends Transforming Employee Experience."

Chapter 11

1. Covey, *The 7 Habits of Highly Effective People*.
2. Greenfield, *Servant Leadership: A Journey Into the Nature of Legitimate Power and Greatness*.
3. Sipe and Frick, *Seven Pillars of Servant Leadership: Practicing the Wisdom of Leading by Serving*.
4. Stazesky, "Genius in Leadership."
5. Petkovic,. "Reward-Based Leadership vs Responsibility-Based Leadership."
6. Lencioni, *The Motive: Why So Many Leaders Abdicate Their Most Important Responsibilities*.
7. Pink, *Drive: The Surprising Truth About What Motivates Us*.
8. Eubanks, "Why Leadership Intent Matters."
9. McCracken, "Lead by Intent if You Want to Empower Your People."

Chapter 12

1. Craig, "8 Ways to Lead Employees With Intent-based Leadership."
2. Manzoni and Barsoux, "New Leaders: Stop Downward Performance Spirals Before They Start."
3. Goman, "Why First Impressions Stick: And What You Can Do About It."

4. Sluss, "Stepping Into a Leadership Role? Be Ready to Tell Your Story."
5. Sluss, Ployhart, Cobb, and Ashforth, "Generalizing Newcomers' Relational and Organizational Identifications: Processes and Prototypicality."
6. Kouzes and Posner, *Credibility: How Leaders Gain and Lose It, Why People Demand It.*
7. Sluss, "Stepping Into a Leadership Role? Be Ready to Tell Your Story."
8. Ibid.
9. Crosby, "How Great Leaders Get Employees Motivated by Explaining Intent."
10. Ibid.
11. Ewen, Smith, and Hulin, "An Empirical Test of the Herzberg Two-Factor Theory." 544–550.
12. Crosby, "How Great Leaders Get Employees Motivated by Explaining Intent."
13. Sinek, *Start With Why: How Great Leaders Inspire Everyone to Take Action.*
14. Lai, "Motivating Employees Is Not About Carrots or Sticks."
15. Nevogt, "Employee Productivity: The Only Guide You'll Ever Need."
16. Crosby, "How Great Leaders Get Employees Motivated by Explaining Intent."

Chapter 13

1. Goleman, "Self-Regulation: A Star Leader's Secret Weapon."
2. Wallbridge, "Self-Regulation: How to Develop It and Become a Better Leader."
3. Yeow and Martin, "The Role of Self-regulation in Developing Leaders: A Longitudinal Field Experiment," 625–637.
4. Latham and Locke, "Self-Regulation Through Goal Setting," 212–247.
5. Goleman, "Self-Regulation: A Star Leader's Secret Weapon."

6. De Ridder, Lensvelt-Mulders, and Baumeister, "Taking Stock of Self-Control: A Meta-Analysis of How Trait Self-Control Relates to a Wide Range of Behaviors."
7. Yam, Fehr, Keng-Highberger, Klotz, and Reynolds, "Out of Control: A Self-Control Perspective on the Link Between Surface Acting and Abusive Supervision," 292–301.
8. Byrne, Dionisi, Barling, Akers, Robertson, Lys, Wylie, and Dupre, "The Depleted Leader: The Influence of Leaders' Diminished Psychological Resources on Leadership Behaviors," 344–357.
9. Yam, Fehr, Keng-Highberger, Klotz, and Reynolds, "Out of Control: A Self-Control Perspective on the Link Between Surface Acting and Abusive Supervision," 292–301.
10. Ibid.
11. Grissinger, "Disrespectful Behavior in Health Care," 73–75.
12. Yam, Chen, and Reynolds, "Ego Depletion and Its Paradoxical Effects on Ethical Decision Making," 204–214.
13. Barnes, Schaubroeck, Huth, and Ghumman, "Lack of Sleep and Unethical Conduct," 169–180.
14. Frankl, *Man's Search for Meaning*.

Chapter 14

1. Yam, Lian, Ferris, and Brown, "Leadership Takes Self-Control. Here's What We Know About It."
2. Ibid.
3. Ibid.
4. Larson and Yao, "Clinical Empathy as Emotional Labor in the Patient-Physician Relationship," 1100–1106.
5. Neuhaus, "What Is Self-Leadership? Models, Theory, and Examples."
6. Miller, "What Is Self-Control Theory in Psychology?"
7. Hülsheger, Alberts, Feinholdt, and Lang, "Benefits of Mindfulness at Work: The Role of Mindfulness in Emotion Regulation, Emotional Exhaustion, and Job Satisfaction," 310–325.
8. Arch and Craske, "Mechanisms of Mindfulness: Emotion Regulation Following a Focused Breathing Induction," 1849–1848.

9. Gosserand and Diefendorff, "Emotional Display Rules and Emotional Labor: The Moderating Role of Commitment," 1256–1264.
10. Kross, Bruehlman-Senecal, Park, Burson, Dougherty, Shablack, Bremner, "Self-Talk as a Regulatory Mechanism: How You Do it Matters," 304–324.
11. Bargh and Williams, *Handbook of Emotion Regulation*, 429–445.
12. Lewis, Hopper, and Healion, "Partners in Recovery: Social Support and Accountability in a Consumer-Run Mental Health Center," 61–65.

Chapter 15

1. Gino, "The Business Case for Curiosity."
2. Gersch, "Google's Best New Innovation: Rules Around '20% Time'."
3. Gino, "The Business Case for Curiosity."
4. Miller, "Memoirs of William Miller. Life Magazine."
5. Bashar, "How the Art of Curiosity Transforms Leadership."
6. Ibid.
7. Goleman, *Distraction Is the New Normal*.

Chapter 16

1. John, "The Surprising Power of Questions."
2. Wale, "Shaped Skills."
3. Gino, "The Business Case for Curiosity."
4. Ibid.
5. Catmull, "How Pixar Fosters Collective Creativity."
6. Porter, Elnakouri, Shibayama, Jayawickreme and Grossmann, "Predictors and Consequences of Intellectual Humility," 524–536.
7. Sullenberger and Zaslow, "Highest Duty: My Search for What Matters."
8. Ibid.
9. Gino, "The Business Case for Curiosity."
10. Vandewalle, Steven, Brown, Cron, and Slocum, "The Influence of Goal Orientation and Self-Regulation Tactics on Sales Performance: A Longitudinal Field Test," 249–259.

11. Cleff, "'Plussing'—Learning and Working in a Collaborative Environment."
12. Prokesch, "The Edison of Medicine."
13. Myhrvold, "The Big Idea: Funding Eureka!"

Conclusion

1. Gallwey, *The Inner Game of Work: Focus, Learning, Pleasure, and Mobility in the Workplace.*
2. Drinovac, "The Inner and The Outer Game of Leadership."

Appendix

1. Littauer, *Personality Plus: How to Understand Others by Understanding Yourself.*
2. Baker, *The New Influencing Toolkit: Capabilities for Communicating With Influence.*
3. Ibid.

References

Andersen, B. 2023. "The Healing Power of Journaling: Ten Benefits for Self-Discovery and Growth." *LinkedIn*. www.linkedin.com/pulse/healing-power-journaling-ten-benefits-self-discovery-growth-andersen/.

Arch, J.J. and M.G. Craske. 2015. "Mechanisms of Mindfulness: Emotion Regulation Following a Focused Breathing Induction." *Behaviour Research and Theory* 44(12): 1849–1848.

Baikie, K.A. and K. Wilhelm. 2005. "Emotional and Physical Health Benefits of Expressive Writing." *Advances in Psychiatric Treatment* 11(5): 338–346.

Baker, T. 2015. *The New Influencing Toolkit: Capabilities for Communicating With Influence*. London: Palgrave Macmillan.

Baker, T. 2023. *Mastering Change: A Practical Guide for Better Leadership Conversations*. Brisbane: WINNERS-at-WORK.

Bargh, J.A. and L.E. Williams. 2007. "The Nonconscious Regulation of Emotion." *In Handbook of Emotion Regulation*, J.J. edited by Gross, eds. 429–445. The Guilford Press.

Barnes, C.M., J. Schaubroeck., M. Huth., and S. Ghumman. 2011. "Lack of Sleep and Unethical Conduct." 115(2): 169–180. www.sciencedirect.com/science/article/abs/pii/S0749597811000239.

Bashar, C. 2023. "How the Art of Curiosity Transforms Leadership." *Forbes*.

Black, H. 2016. "Thinking About Thinking About Leadership: Metacognitive Ability and Leader Developmental Readiness." *New Directions for Student Leadership* 149: 85–95.

Boyatzis, R.E. 2006. "An Overview of Intentional Change From a Complexity Perspective." *Journal of Management Development* 25(7): 607–623. https://doi.org/10.1108/02621710610678445.

Boyatzis, R.E. n.d. "The Five Stages of Intentional Change Theory." www.keystepmedia.com/intentional-change-theory/.

Brown, D. and C. Kelly. 1996. "Life Values Inventory." *Life Values Resources*.

Bryant, A. and A. Kazan. 2012. *Self-Leadership: How to Become a More Successful, Efficient, and Effective Leader From the Inside Out*. McGraw-Hill.

Byrne, A., A.M. Dionisi., J. Barling., A. Akers., J. Robertson., R. Lys., and J. Wylie, et al. 2015. "The Depleted Leader: The Influence of Leaders' Diminished Psychological Resources on Leadership Behaviors." *The Leadership Quarterly* 25(2): 344–357.

Cameron, J. 1992. *The Artist's Way: A Spiritual Path to Higher Creativity*. TarcherPerigee.

Campbell, K. 2021. *Strengths-Based Development Requires a Growth Mindset.* Noomii. www.noomii.com/articles/11643-strengthsbased-development-requires-a-growth-mindset.

Carnegie, D. 1998. *How to Win Friends and Influence People: The Only Book You Need to Lead You to Success (Revised edition).* Pocketbooks.

Cassam, Q. 2014. *Self-Knowledge for Humans.* Oxford University Press.

Catmull, E. 2008. "How Pixar Fosters Collective Creativity." *Harvard Business Review.*

Church, Z. 2020. "Writing a New Leadership Playbook." *MIT Management.*

Clance, P.R. and S.A. Imes. 1978. "The Imposter Phenomenon in High Achieving Women: Dynamics and Therapeutic Intervention." *Psychotherapy: Theory, Research & Practice* 15(3): 241–247. https://doi.org/10.1037/h0086006.

Cleff, A. 2014 "Plussing"—Learning and Working in a Collaborative Environment. www.accme.org/sites/default/files/2018-12/plussing_.pdf.

Clance, P.R. and S.A. Imes. 1978. "The Imposter Phenomenon in High Achieving Women: Dynamics and Therapeutic Intervention." *Psychotherapy: Theory, Research & Practice* 15(3): 241–247. https://doi.org/10.1037/h0086006.

Cohen, A. R. and D.L. 2011. Bradford. *Influence Without Authority.* Wiley.

Confino, J. 2011. "Paul Polman: The Power Is in the Hands of the Consumer." *Guardian.* www.theguardian.com/sustainable-business/unilever-ceo-paul-polman-interview.

Couture, M., J. Desrosiers., and G. Leclerc. 2007. "Self-actualization and Poststroke Rehabilitation." *International Journal of Rehabilitation Research* 30(2): 111–117.

Covey, S. 2020. *The 7 Habits of Highly Effective People.* NY, New York, NY: Simon & Shuster.

Cox, L. 2013. "5 Experts Answer: Can Your IQ Change?" www.livescience.com/36143-iq-change-time.html.

Craig, N. and S.A. Snook. 2014. "From Purpose to Impact." *Harvard Business Review,* May.

Craig, W. 2019. "8 Ways to Lead Employees With Intent-based Leadership." *Forbes.*

Crosby, P. 2018. "How Great Leaders Get Employees Motivated by Explaining Intent." www.theuncommonleague.com/blog/2018813/sz1pp6mq4id96lfi3fjfg5remghodf.

Crosby, P. 2018. "How Great Leaders Get Employees Motivated by Explaining Intent." *The Uncommon League.*

Cynthia, V. 2024. *Understanding Maslow's Theory of Self-Actualization.* Thought Co.www.thoughtco.com/maslow-theory-self-actualization-4169662.

De Ridder, D.T.D., G. Lensvelt-Mulders and R.F. Baumeister. 2011. "Taking Stock of Self-Control: A Meta-Analysis of How Trait Self-Control Relates to a Wide Range of Behaviors." *Sage* 16(1): https://journals.sagepub.com/doi/abs/10.1177/1088868311418749

Dogru, T., S. McGinley., A. Sharma., C. Isik., and L. Hanks. December, 2023. "Employee Turnover Dynamics in the Hospitality Industry vs. the Overall Economy." *Tourism Management* 99.

Drinovac, S. 2023 The Inner and The Outer Game of Leadership. *LinkedIn.*

Dweck, C. 2008. *Mindset: The New Psychology of Success. Ballantine Books.*

Emmons, R.A. and M.E McCullough. 2003. "Counting Blessings Versus Burdens: Experimental Studies of Gratitude and Subjective Well-being." *Journal of Personality and Social Psychology* 84(2): 377–389.

Engel, J.M. 2019. "The Third Commandment of Highly Effective Leadership: Know Thyself and Others." *Forbes.*

Eubanks, J. 2022. "Why Leadership Intent Matters." *Forbes.*

Ewen, R.B., P.C. Smith., and C.L. Hulin. 1996. "An Empirical Test of the Herzberg Two-Factor Theory." *Journal of Applied Psychology* 50(6): 544–550. https://doi.org/10.1037/h0024042.

Ewenstein, B., W. Smith, and A. Sologar. 2015. Changing Change Management. McKinsey.

Fain, J. 2017. "Author Natalie Goldberg on the Zen of Living, Writing and Eating." www.huffpost.com/entry/writing-wellbeing_b_2800728.

Feldman, D.B. 2020. "The Power of Journaling." *Psychology Today.* www.psychologytoday.com/au/blog/supersurvivors/202009/the-power-journaling.

First; Kettlewell, C. 2000. *Skin Games.* St Martin's Griffin; Walsh, B. 2012. *Treating Self-Injury: A Practical Guide*, 2nd ed. Guilford Press.

Fleming, S.M. 2021. *Know Thyself: The Science of Self-awareness.* , New York, NY: Basic Books.

Frankl, V.E. *Man's Search for Meaning.* Beacon. 2006.

Franklin, B. 2018. *Poor Richard's Almanack (Illustrated Edition).* Martino Fine Books.

Fubini, D. 2020. *Hidden Truths: What Leaders Need to Hear but Are Rarely Told.* New Jersey, NJ: Wiley.

Gallwey, T.W. 2001. *The Inner Game of Work: Focus, Learning, Pleasure, and Mobility in the Workplace.* Random House.

Geurts, S.A. and S. Sonnentag. 2006. "Recovery as an Explanatory Mechanism in the Relation Between Acute Stress Reactions and Chronic Health Impairment." *Scandinavian Journal of Work, Environment & Health* 32: 482–492.

George, B. 2015. *Discover Your True North: Becoming an Authentic Leader.* Jossey-Bass.

Gersch, K. 2013. *"Google's Best New Innovation: Rules Around "20% Time".* Forbes.

Gino, F. 2018. "The Business Case for Curiosity". *Harvard Business Review.*

Goffee, R. and Jones, G. 2000. "Why Should Anyone Be Led by You?" *Harvard Business Review.*

Goleman, D. 1995. *Emotional Intelligence: Why It Can Matter More than IQ.* , New York, NY: Bloomsbury.

Goleman, D. 2013. "Distraction is the New Normal." *YouTube.*

Goleman, D. 2015. "Self-Regulation: A Star Leader's Secret Weapon." *LinkedIn.* www.linkedin.com/pulse/self-regulation-star-leaders-secret-weapon-daniel-goleman/.

Goman, C. 2015. "Why First Impressions Stick: And What You Can Do About It." *Forbes.*

Goodwin, D.K. 2018. *Leadership: In Turbulent Times.* , New YorkNew York, NY: Simon & Schuster.

Gosserand, R.H. and J.M. Diefendorff. 2005. "Emotional Display Rules and Emotional Labor: The Moderating Role of Commitment." *Journal of Applied Psychology* (6): 1256–1264.

Greenfield, R.K. 1977. *Servant Leadership: A Journey into the Nature of Legitimate Power and Greatness.* New Jersey: Paulist Press.

Grint, K. 2005. "Problems, Problems, Problems: The Social Construction of Leadership." *Human Relations* 58(11).

Grissinger, M. 2017. "Disrespectful Behavior in Health Care." *P & T* 42(2): 73–75. www.ncbi.nlm.nih.gov/pmc/articles/PMC5265230/.

Günel, S. 2018. "The Power of Journaling." *Ascent.* https://medium.com/the-ascent/the-power-of-journaling-d8654060c7a7.

Guzmán, V.E., B. Muschard., M. Gerolamo., H. Kohl., and H. Rozenfield. 2020. "Characteristics and Skills of Leadership in the Context of Industry 4.0." *17th Global Conference on Sustainable Manufacturing* 43: 543–50.

Harter, J. 2021. "U.S. Employee Engagement Data Hold Steady in First Half of 2021." *Gallup.*

Haselton, M.G., D. Nettle., and P.W. Andrews. 2015. "The Evolution of Cognitive Bias." In *The Handbook of Evolutionary Psychology*, edited by Buss, D.M, 724–746. Hoboken, NJ: John Wiley & Sons.

Heimbigner, J.R. 2023. "Why You Need to Start Journaling in 2024." *Medium.* https://medium.com/readers-digests/why-you-need-to-start-journaling-in-2024-ba28df411b0e.

Hendry, E.R. 2013. "7 Epic Fails Brought to You by the Genius Mind of Thomas Edison." www.smithsonianmag.com/innovation/7-epic-fails-brought-to-you-by-the-genius-mind-of-thomas-edison-180947786/.

Hetler, A. 2023. "The Great Resignation: Everything you need to know." www.techtarget.com/whatis/feature/The-Great-Resignation-Everything-you-need-to-know.

Hill, P.L. and N.A. Turiano. 2014. "Purpose in Life as a Predictor of Mortality Across Adulthood." *Psychological Science* 25(7): 1482–1486. https://doi.org/10.1177/0956797614531799.

Holbeche, L. n.d. "How Good Leaders Inspire and Motivate Others." *Business Leadership Today.* https://businessleadershiptoday.com/how-do-good-leaders-inspire-and-motivate-others/.

Hülsheger, U.R., H.J.E.M. Alberts., A. Feinholdt., and J.W.B. Lang. 2013. "Benefits of Mindfulness at Work: The Role of Mindfulness in Emotion Regulation, Emotional Exhaustion, and Job Satisfaction." *Journal of Applied Psychology* 98(2): 310–325. https://doi.org/10.1037/a0031313.

John, L.K. 2018. "The Surprising Power of Questions." *Harvard Business Review.*

Jung, C.G. 2016. *Psychological Types or the Psychology of Individuation.* Princeton.

Kahneman, D. 2011. *Thinking, Fast and Slow.* US: Penguin.

Kahneman, D., and A. Tversky. 1972. "Subjective Probability: A Judgment of Representativeness." *Cognitive Psychology* 3(3).

Keyne Petkovic, K. 2020. "Reward-based Leadership vs Responsibility-based Leadership." www.assuredstrategy.com/reward-based-leadership-vs-responsibility-based-leadership/.

Kinni, T. 2021. "Leader, Know Thyself. Strategy + Business PWC publication." www.strategy-business.com/blog/Leader-know-thyself.

Kouzes, J.M. and B.Z. Posner. 2011. *Credibility: How Leaders Gain and Lose It, Why People Demand It.* San Francisco: Wiley.

Kraut, A.I., and A.K. Korman. 1999. "The "DELTA Forces" Causing Change in Human Resource Management." In *Evolving Practices in Human Resource Management*, edited by Kraut, A.I and Korman, A.K, 3–22. San Francisco: Jossey-Bass Publishers.

Krizan, Z., and A.D. Herlache. 2017. "Sleep Diary and Polysomnographic Studies of Sleep Disturbance Following a Written Disclosure Intervention for Worry." *Journal of Experimental Psychology: General* 146(10): 1506–1514.

Kross, E., E. Bruehlman-Senecal., J. Park., A. Burson., A. Dougherty., H. Shablack, R. Bremner., and J. Moser., et al. 2014. "Self-talk as a Regulatory Mechanism: How You Do it Matters." *Journal of Personality and Social Psychology* 106(2): 304. https://doi.org/10.1037/a0035173.

Kübler-Ross, E. 1969. "On Death and Dying: What the Dying Have to Teach Doctors, Nurses, Clergy and Their Own Families." *Scribner.*

Lai, L. 2017. "Motivating Employees Is Not About Carrots or Sticks." *Harvard Business Review.*

Larson, E.B. and Yao, X. 2005. "Clinical Empathy as Emotional Labor in the Patient-Physician Relationship." *JAMA* 293(9): 1100–1106.

Latham, G. and Edwin Locke, E. A. 1991. *Theory of Goal Setting and Task Performance.* Pearson.

Latham, G. P. and Locke, E. A. 1991. "Self-regulation Through Goal setting." *Organizational Behavior and Human Decision Processes* 50(2): 212–247. https://doi.org/10.1016/0749-5978(91)90021-K.

Lencioni, P. 2020. *The Motive: Why So Many Leaders Abdicate Their Most Important Responsibilities.* New Jersey: Jossey Bass.

Lewis, S.E., K. Hopper and E. Healion, E. 2012. "Partners in Recovery: Social Support and Accountability in a Consumer-Run Mental Health Center." *Psychiatric Services* 63(1). 61–65. www.ncbi.nlm.nih.gov/pmc/articles/PMC4547771/pdf/nihms700208.pdf.

Littauer, F. 1983. *Personality Plus: How to Understand Others by Understanding Yourself.* New York, NY: Baker Book House.

Lopez, S.J. and M.C. Louis. 2009. "The Principles of Strengths-Based Education." *Journal of College and Character*, X, 4.

Manz, C.C. 1986. "Self-Leadership: Toward an Expanded Theory of Self-Influence Processes in Organizations." *The Academy of Management Review* 11(3): 585–600.

Manzoni, J-F. and J-L. Barsoux. 2009. "New Leaders: Stop Downward Performance Spirals Before They Start." *Harvard Business Review.*

Mateos-Aparicio, P. and A. Rod Rodríguez-Moreno. 2019. "The Impact of Studying Brain Plasticity." *Frontiers in Cellular Neuroscience* 18. www.frontiersin.org/articles/10.3389/fncel.2019.00066/full.

McCracken, G. 2020. "Lead by Intent if You Want to Empower Your People." *Management Today.*

Mehl, M.R., J.W. Pennebaker., D.M. Crow., J. Dabbs and J.H. Price. 2006. "The Electronically Activated Recorder (EAR): A Device for Sampling Naturalistic Daily Activities and Conversations." *Behavior Research Methods* 38(2): 513–521.

Meier, J.D. n.d. "The Power of Personal Leadership." https://sourcesofinsight.com/the-power-of-personal-leadership/.

Meijman TF, Mulder G. 1998. "Psychological aspects of workload." In *Handbook of work and organizational psychology 2 Work Psychology*, edited by Drenth P.J.D, H. Thierr., and de Wolff C.J. Psychol Press.

Michels, D. 2017. "Because I Said So: Lessons In Parenting and Change Management." *Forbes.*

Miller, K. 2020. "What Is Self-Control Theory in Psychology?" *Positive Psychology.* https://positivepsychology.com/self-control-theory/.

Miller, W. 1955. "LIFE magazine." *May* 2, 1955: 281.

Myhrvold, N. 2010. "The Big Idea: Funding Eureka!" *Harvard Business Review.*

Neuhaus, M. 2020. "What is Self-Leadership?" *Models, Theory, and Examples. Positive Psychology.* https://positivepsychology.com/self-leadership/.

Nevogt, D. 2022. "Employee Productivity: The Only Guide You'll Ever Need." https://blog.hubstaff.com/employee-productivity/.

Nielsen, D. and E. Sirke. 2016. "Presidential Leadership: Learning From United States Presidential Libraries and Museums." *Dan Nielsen Company*.

Pennebaker, J. and J. Smyth. 2016. "Opening Up by Writing It Down: How Expressive Writing Improves Health and Eases Emotional Pain." 3rd ed. , New YorkNew York, NY, NY: Guilford.

Pennebaker, J.W. and S.K. Beall, S. K. 1986. "Confronting a Traumatic Event: Toward an Understanding of Inhibition and Disease." *Journal of Abnormal Psychology* 95(3): 274–281.

Pink, D. 2018. *Drive: The Surprising Truth About What Motivates Us*. NY, New York, NY: Riverhead.

Porter, T., A. Elnakouri., T. Shibayama., E. Jayawickreme., and I. Grossmann. 2022. "Predictors and Consequences of Intellectual Humility." *Nature Reviews Psychology* 1: 524–536.

Prokesch, S. 2017. "The Edison of Medicine." *Harvard Business Review*.

Qualtrics "The 5 Trends Transforming Employee Experience." 2024. www.qualtrics.com/ebooks-guides/employee-experience-trends-2021/.

Rath, T. 2007. *Strengths Finder 2.0*. NY, New York, NY: Gallup.

Rotter, J. B. 1992. "Cognates of Personal Control: Locus of Control, Self-efficacy, and Explanatory Style: Comment." *Applied & Preventive Psychology* 1(2): 127–129. https://doi.org/10.1016/S0962-1849(05)80154-4.

Salovey, P. and J.D. 1990. "Emotional Intelligence." Sage 9(3): https://doi.org/10.2190/DUGG-P24E-52WK-6CDG.

Scott, C.D. and D.T. Jaffe. 1998. "Survive and Thrive in Times of Change." *Training & Development Journal* 42(4).

Simpson, J. 1998. *Touching the Void: The True Story of One Man*. NY, New York, NY: HarperCollins.

Sinek, S. 2011. *Start With Why: How Great Leaders Inspire Everyone to Take Action*. UK: Penguin.

Sipe, J.W. and D.M. Frick. 2015. *Seven Pillars of Servant Leadership: Practicing the Wisdom of Leading by Serving*. New Jersey, NJ: Paulist Press.

Sloan, E. 2023. "How To Become More Empathetic—Because, Yes, Empathy Is a Quality You Can Grow." www.wellandgood.com/how-to-become-more-empathetic/.

Sluss, D. 2020. "Stepping Into a Leadership Role? Be Ready to Tell Your Story." *Harvard Business Review*.

Sluss, D., R.E. Ployhart., M.G. Cobb, and B.E. Ashforth. 2012. "Generalizing Newcomers' Relational and Organizational Identifications: Processes and Prototypicality". *Academy of Management* 55(4).

Smyth, J.M. 1998. "Written Emotional Expression: Effect Sizes, Outcome Types, and Moderating Variables." *Journal of Consulting and Clinical Psychology* 66(1), 174–184.

Sorenson, S. 2014. "How Employees' Strengths Make Your Company Stronger." *Gallup*. https://news.gallup.com/businessjournal/167462/employees-strengths-company-stronger.aspx.

Stazesky, R.C. 2000. "George Washington, Genius in Leadership." https://washingtonpapers.org/resources/articles/george-washington-genius-in-leadership/.

Stephens, R. 2018. "The Psychology of Roller Coasters." https://theconversation.com/the-psychology-of-roller-coasters-99166.

Sullenberger, C.B. and J. Zaslow, J. 2009. *Highest Duty: My Search for What Matters*. HarperCollins.

Telford, T. 2022. "U.S. Workers Have Gotten Way Less Productive. No One is Sure Why." *The Washington Post*. www.washingtonpost.com/business/2022/10/31/productivity-down-employers-worried-recession/.

Tolle, E. 2004. *The Power of Now: A Guide to Spiritual Enlightenment*. Tolle, Eckhart.

Vandewalle, V., P. Steven., S.P. Brown., W.L. Cron., and J. Slocum. 1999. "The Influence of Goal Orientation and Self-Regulation Tactics on Sales Performance: A Longitudinal Field Test." *Journal of Applied Psychology* 84(2): 249–259.

Vinney, C. 2018. "Understanding Maslow's Theory of Self-Actualization." *ThoughtCo*. www.thoughtco.com/maslow-theory-self-actualization-4169662.

Wale, H. "T-Shaped Skills." https://corporatefinanceinstitute.com/resources/management/t-shaped-skills/.

Wallbridge, A. 2023. "Self-Regulation: How to Develop It and Become a Better Leader." *TSW Training*. www.tsw.co.uk/blog/leadership-and-management/self-regulation/.

Westerman, G., D. Bonnet, and A. McAfee. 2014. "Leading Digital: Turning Technology Into Business Transformation." *Harvard Business Review*.

"What is a Digital Leader (and Do You need to be One)?" *Readytech* www.readytech.com.au/news-and-views/blog/what-is-a-digital-leader-and-do-you-need-to-be-one/.

White, J. 2023. *200 Inspirational Leadership Action Quotes*. www.consultclarity.org/post/leadership-action-quotes#google_vignette.

Whitener, S. 2021. "The Value of a Growth Mindset. And How to Develop One." *Forbes*.

Wright, G. and Wigmore, I. n.d. "VUCA (Volatility, Uncertainty, Complexity and Ambiguity)". *TechTarget*. www.techtarget.com/whatis/definition/VUCA-volatility-uncertainty-complexity-and-ambiguity.

Yam, K.C., R. Fehr., F.T. Keng-Highberger., A.C. Klotz., and S.J. Reynolds. 2016. "Out of Control: A Self-control Perspective on the Link Between Surface Acting and Abusive Supervision." *Journal of Applied Psychology* 101(2): 292–301. https://doi.org/10.1037/apl0000043.

Yam, K.C., Z-P Chen., and S.J. Reynolds. 2014. "Ego Depletion and its Paradoxical Effects on Ethical Decision Making." *Organizational Behavior and Human Decision Processes* 124(2): 204–214. www.sciencedirect.com/science/article/abs/pii/S0749597814000284.

Yam, K.C., H. Lian., D.L. Ferris and D. Brown, D. 2017. "Leadership Takes Self-Control. Here's What We Know About It." *Harvard Business Review.*

Yang, H. and P. Hu. 2023. "Role of Job Mobility Frequency in Job Satisfaction Changes: The Mediation Mechanism of Job-related Social Capital and Person–job Match." *Humanities and Social Sciences Communications* 10: 156.

Yam, K.C., R. Fehr, F.T. Keng-Highberger, A.C. Klotz, and S.J. Reynolds. 2016. "Out of Control: A Self-control Perspective on the Link Between Surface Acting and Abusive Supervision." *Journal of Applied Psychology* 101(2): 292–301. https://doi.org/10.1037/apl0000043.

Yeow, J and R. Martin. 2013. "The Role of Self-Regulation in Developing Leaders: A Longitudinal Field Experiment." *The Leadership Quarterly* 24(5): 625–637.

Zimmerman, M.A. 2013. "Resiliency Theory: A Strengths-based Approach to Research and Practice for Adolescent Health." *Health Educ Behav* 40(4).

About the Author

Dr. Tim Baker is an esteemed thought leader, international consultant, and accomplished author. He is the managing director of WINNERS-at-WORK Pty Ltd., which specializes in leadership development and performance improvement. Their website is www.winnersatwork.com.au.

The World HRD Congress recently recognized Dr. Baker as one of the most talented global training and development leaders. The award is given by a distinguished international panel of professionals *who are doing extraordinary work* in HRD. Additionally, he was named a finalist in the Learning Professional of the Year category for the Asia Pacific Institute of Learning Professionals Awards in 2018. HR Tech Outlook also listed his consulting firm, WINNERS-at-WORK, as one of the Top 10 Change Management Consulting Service Companies in APAC 2020.

In 2005, Dr. Baker completed his doctoral degree at QUT, where he also served on the QUT Council for over 11 years.

He has conducted over 2,530 seminars, workshops, and keynote addresses for over 47,000 people in 14 countries across 21 industry groups. Dr. Baker also regularly contributes his writing to the HR industry press.

Dr. Baker resides in Brisbane, Australia, with his wife, Carol, and has two daughters. If you would like to contact him, please e-mail him at tim@winnersatwork.com.au.

Index

Letters '*b*', '*f*' and '*t*' after locators indicate 'box', 'figure' and 'table', respectively.

Active listening, 77, 82, 203
    feedback sessions, 203
    one-on-one virtual check-ins, 203
    online discussion forums, 203
    reflective summaries, 203
    virtual team meetings, 203
Adams, John, 7
Adams, John Quincy, 7
Aptitude, 43
Attention control, 129
Authenticity, 33

Be Curious, 22–23, 92, 172
    as a trait, 149, 157
    asking thoughtful questions, 168, 169
    barriers to curiosity, 155–156
    benefits of, 152–153
    curiosity, hiring for, 159–161, 169
    curious leader, 150, 157
    exploring of interests, 167, 169
    growth mindset and curiosity, 151, 157
    inquisitiveness, modelling of, 161–162
    intellectual humility, 165
    intentional curiosity, 153–155, 158
    leading by example, 156–157
    learning goals and importance, 166–167, 169
    questioning and open to learning, 162–166, 169
Because I Said So: Lessons in Parenting and Change Management, 125
Beliefs, 171
Blanchard, Ken, 97
Body scan, 40
Breathing/breathwork, 143–144
Briggs, Katharine Cook, 43
Bryant, Andrew, 8

Buddha, Gautama, 48
Buffett, Warren, 48
Build Strengths, 15, 17–18, 171
    overcoming weaknesses, obsession with, 65–68, 71
    societal conditioning, 64–65, 71
    turning talents into strengths, 68–71
The Business Case for Curiosity, 151, 161
Butler, Bill, 13

Cain, Herman, 48
Change Grid, 99
Characteristics and Skills of Leadership in the Context of Industry, 74
Chilon, 15
Cincinatus, Lucius Quinctius, 112*b*
Clarity, 46, 49, 52
Cloud Land Systems, 82
Cognitive bias, 29, 42
Cognitive leadership, 74, 75*f*, 76–78
Collaborative brainstorming sessions, 206
Collaborative document sharing, 205
Comfort zone, 92
Communication, 20, 21, 42, 77, 115, 121–124, 127, 152, 204, 205
Consistency, 20
Covey, Stephen, 8
Credibility: How Leaders Gain and Lose It, Why People Demand It, 120
Critical thinking, 76, 82, 201–202
    data analysis, 201–202
    information evaluation, 201
    problem-solving, 201
    scenario planning, 202
    technology assessment, 202
Cultural sensitivity, 204

Curiosity, 172
Curiosity inventory, 225–230
　asking questions, 228
　challenging assumptions, 230
　continuous learning, pursuit of, 229
　elements, 227f
　embracing ambiguity, 229
　exploring new ideas, 228–229
Cybersecurity audits, 207

Dalai Lama, 48
Data analysis, 201–202
Data analytics and reporting, 206
Data management review, 207
Data-driven decision making, 207
Data-driven persuasion, 205
Decision-making, 16–17, 19, 21, 30, 76, 80, 115, 150, 171, 207
Devil's advocacy, 230
Digital conflict resolution, 204
Digital leader, 73
Digital leadership. *See also* Digital Leadership Development Profile
　attributes, 73b–74b
　cognitive leadership, 74, 75f, 76–78
　and digital economy, 73
　interpersonal leadership, 74, 75f, 78–79
　leadership types, 74, 75f
　strategic leadership, 74, 75f, 79–82
　strength model, 74, 75f
Digital Leadership Development Profile, 191–201. *See also* Digital leadership
　active listening, 203
　critical thinking, 201–202
　influencing, 203–204
　negotiation, 205
　problem-solving, 206
　public speaking, 202
　social awareness, 204
　solution appraisal, 206–207
　system evaluation, 207
　visioning, 205–206
Digital leadership strengths model, 74, 75f

Digital product development, 205
Digital tool selection, 206–207
Digital transformation initiatives, 207
Discipline, 172
Discover True North, 16–17, 45–46, 171
　leadership purpose statement, 50–52
　purpose and forms of, 46–48, 52
　purpose-driven leadership, 49–50
Divergent thinking, 150
Dopamine, 152
Drinovac, Slaven, 172
Drive: The Surprising Truth About What Motivates Us, 113
Drucker, Peter, 8, 13, 47, 134b
Dweck, Carol, 88
Dyke, Greg, 161

E-mails, 202
Edison, Thomas, 92
Ego, 30, 90, 93
Einstein, Albert, 154
Emerson, Ralph Waldo, 47
Emotional display rule, 144–145
Emotional Intelligence, 87
Emotional intelligence (EQ), 16, 21, 33, 61, 86–88, 129, 147, 150, 204
Emotional Intelligence: Why it Can Matter More than IQ, 87
Emotional regulation, 129
Emotional resilience, 21
Emotional self-regulation, practicing. *See also* Self-Regulation/ Regulate
　awareness of physiological cues, 142
　breathing and pausing, 143–144
　educating yourself, 147
　emotional display rule, 144–145
　emotions, being in touch with, 140–141, 147
　exercise, 141, 147
　journaling, 146, 147
　mindfulness meditation, 144, 147
　proper sleep, 140, 147
　seeking feedback, 146–147
　self-care, 139–140

INDEX

Emotions, 140–141
Empathy
  definition, 101
  qualities of, 102
  vs. sympathy, 102
Employee Experience Trends Report, 105
Engel, Jacob, 43
Evaluating information, 201
Exercise, 141, 147
External locus of control, 9

Feedback, x, xi, 18, 33, 42–43, 44, 61, 146–147, 203, 206, 207, 229
Ferry, Korn, 122
Fixed mindset, 18, 69, 88, 151
Frankl, Viktor E., ix, 134*b*

Gallwey, Timothy, 171
George, Bill, 45, 46
Gmail, 167
Goal setting, x, 129
Google, 140, 150, 160, 167
Google News, 167
Google Transit, 167
Great Resignation, 104
Growth mindset, 7, 10, 18, 68, 69, 71, 88–91, 140, 151
  cultivating, 91–93
  and self-belief, 88
  vs. fixed mindset, 88–89, 90
Guide to Engaging and Retaining Employees (Gallup, 2023), 151

Hawking, Stephen, 6
Hemingway, Ernest, 85
Herzberg, Frederick, 122
Hidden Truths: What Leaders Need to Hear but Are Rarely Told, 30
Hierarchy, 115
Holbeche, Linda, 104
Holmes, Oliver Wendell, 50
Holocaust, ix
Honesty, 3
How Good Leaders Inspire and Motivate Others, 104
How Great Leaders Get Employees Motivated by Explaining Intent, 122

How the Art of Curiosity Transforms Leadership, 155
How to Win Friends & Influence People, 7
Hubstaff, 126

Ideal self, 31
IDEO, 160
Imposter syndrome, 5
Impulse control, 129
Influence/influencing, 78, 83, 203–204. *See also* Influencing capabilities framework
  building, 96–98
  capabilities framework, 97*f*
  effective communication, 204
  online networking, 204
  positive, 96
  social media engagement, 203–204
  thought leadership content, 203
  variables in, 98
  virtual presentations, 203
Influencing capabilities framework, 97*f*, 98
Influencing capabilities profile, 208–215
The Inner and The Outer Game of Leadership, 172
The Inner Game, xi, 4, 13, 14, 15, 46, 86, 171
The Inner Game of Work: Focus, Learning, Pleasure, and Mobility in the Workplace, 171
Internal locus of control, 9
Innovation, 22, 115, 150, 172
Innovative ideation sessions, 205
Inquisitiveness, modeling of, 161–162
Inside-out leadership, 6
Inspiration/inspiring, 103–106
  engagement/disengagement, 103–104
  importance of, 104
  practical considerations for, 104–106
Integrity, 3, 134
Intellectual humility, 165
Intellectual Ventures, 168
Intent-based leadership, 110, 123*b*. *See also* Intentional Leaders,

characteristics; Leadership growth framework characteristics, 114–116, 117
Intentional curiosity, 153–155
Intentional Leaders, characteristics, 119. *See also* Intent-based leadership; Leadership growth framework
  communication of intentions, 121–124, 127
  engagement and collaborations, 125–126
  first impressions, importance of, 120–121
  job purpose, 124–125, 128
  look to the future, 127
  performance traits, 120
Interpersonal leadership, 74, 75*f*, 78–79
Interpersonal self-leadership practices, 14

Job purpose, 124–125, 128
Jobs, Steve, 47
Journaling, 38–39, 146, 228
Jung, Carl, 43, 44, 177

Keep growing, 16, 18–20, 171. *See also* Growth mindset; Leadership growth framework
  emotional intelligence, 86–88, 93
  growth mindset, 88–91
  growth mindset, cultivating, 91–93
  leadership growth framework, 96*f*, 106
  and personal growth, 85
Kennedy, John F., 45
Kinni, Theodore, 43
Know Thyself, 15–16, 27–28, 34, 171. *See also* Knowing oneself, dimensions in
  being true to oneself, 31–32
  knowing oneself, dimensions in, 32–34
  metacognition, 28–30, 34
Know Thyself: The Science of Self-Awareness, 28

Knowing oneself, dimensions in. *See also* Know Thyself
  authenticity, 33, 35
  emotional intelligence, 33, 35
  resilience, 34, 35
  self-awareness, 32, 35
  self-improvement, 33, 35
Kübler-Ross, Elisabeth, 99

Leader Know Thyself, 43
Leadership, xi, 3, 4, 7, 31, 120, 135. *See also* Intent-based leadership; Intentional leaders, characteristics; Leadership growth framework; Self-leadership
  intent-based, 110
  purpose statement, 50–52
  purpose-driven, 49–50
  responsibility-based *vs.* reward-based, 113–114
Leadership growth framework, 96*f. See also* Self-leadership development framework
  building influence, 96–98, 106
  developing empathy, 101–103, 106
  elements, 96, 96*f*
  inspiring others, 103–106
  leadership as interpersonal vocation, 95
  managing change, 99–101
Leadership intention, 216–219
Leadership, purpose-driven, 49–50
Leadership purpose statement, 50–52
  characteristics, 58
  crafting, 58–62
  life story, reflecting on, 56–57, 62
  tips for, 61–62
  values and beliefs, 57–58, 62
Leadership: In Turbulent Times, 102
Leadership types, 74, 75*f*
Leading Digital: Turning Technology into Business Transformation, 74
Life Values Inventory, 58, 59, 184–190
Lincoln, Abraham, 3
LinkedIn, 204
Locus of control, 9–10

Man's Search for Meaning, ix, 136
Management strategies, 206
Managing change
   Change Grid, 99
   importance of, 99
   workplace rollercoaster model, 99–100, 100*f*
Mandela, Nelson, 6, 47
Manufacturers' Alliance for Productivity and Innovation (MAPI), 123
Manz, Charles C., ix, 134*b*
Marquet, Captain David, 123*b*
Maslow, Abraham, 31
Mastering Change: A Practical Guide for Better Leadership Conversations, 101
The Matrix (Film), 28
Meditation, 144
Meier, J.D., 13
Metacognition, 28–30
Mindful breathing, 40
Mindful eating, 41
Mindful leadership, 40, 44
Mindful observation, 41
Mindfulness, 40–42
Mindfulness meditation, 41, 144, 147, 229
Mindfulness walking, 41
Motivating Employees Is Not About Carrots or Sticks, 126
Motivation, 171
The Motive: Why So Many Leaders Abdicate Their Most Important Responsibilities, 113
Myers–Briggs Types Indicator (MBTI), 43
Myers, Isabel Briggs, 43

Negotiation, 205
   collaborative document sharing, 205
   data-driven persuasion, 205
   structured online communication, 205
   video message rebuttals, 205
   virtual sessions, 205
Negotiation skills, 79, 83
The New Influencing Toolkit, 97

The New Influencing Toolkit: Capabilities for Communicating with Influence, 215

One-on-one virtual check-ins, 203
Online communication, inclusivity in, 204
Online communication, structured, 205
Online discussion forums, 203
Online networking, 204
Online surveys, 206
The Outer Game, xi, 4, 14, 15, 46, 109, 129, 171, 172
Overcoming weaknesses, obsession with, 65–68, 71

Pausing, 143–144
Performance traits, 120
Perseverance, 69
Personal growth, 85
Personal self-leadership practices, 14
Personal vision, 79
Personality Plus: How to Understand Others by Understanding Yourself, 177
Personality profile/profiling, 43–44
   bull personality type, 180, 181*t*
   lamb personality type, 182, 183*t*
   owl personality type, 181, 182*t*
   peacock personality type, 179, 180*t*
   personality scoring table, 178*t*–179*t*
Personality Types, 43
Pilot programs, 207
Pinnacle CodeWorks, 81
Pixar, 164
Plato, 134*b*
Plussing, 167
Podcasts, 202
Poor Richard's Almanack, 29
The Power of Now: A Guide to Spiritual Enlightenment, 40
Problem-solving, 80–81, 83, 201
   collaborative brainstorming sessions, 206
   data analytics and reporting, 206
   online surveys and feedback, 206

root cause analysis tools, 206
virtual focus groups, 206
Problems, Problems: The Social Construction of Leadership, 105
Process audits, 207
Psychological curiosity, 153
Public speaking, 76–77, 82, 202
  effective video conferencing, 202
  podcasts and webinars, 202
  team messages and e-mails, 202
  virtual presentations, 202
  virtual town hall meetings, 202
Purpose statement, 50–52
Pythagoras, 15

QuantumLeap Innovations, 80
Quiet quitting, 104

Reason for being, 46, 52
Red mist, 142
Reflective summaries, 203
Resilience, 34
Responsibility-based leadership, 113–114
Reward-based leadership, 113–114
Rogers, Will, 120
Root Cause Analysis, 168
Root cause analysis tools, 206
Rowling, J. K., 6

Scenario planning, 202
Schmidt, Eric, 160
Schweitzer, Albert, 48
Self-actualization, 31
Self-affirmation, 17
Self-awareness, ix, 9, 10, 15–16, 28–30, 32, 171
  journaling, 38–39, 44
  mindfulness, 40–42, 44
  personality profiling, 43–44
  seeking feedback, 42–43, 44
  ways of developing, 37, 44
Self-belief, 88
Self-care, 139–140
Self-confidence, 5, 9
Self-control, 135, 140, 141b, 147, 172
Self-cruelty, 140
Self-discipline, 9, 135
Self-discovery, 16, 28
Self-improvement, 33
Self-influence, ix
Self-kindness, 140
Self-knowledge, 30, 32
Self-leadership, ix, 3, 8, 46, 171.
    See also Intent-based leadership; Intentional leaders, characteristics; Leadership growth framework; Self-leadership development framework
  Be Curious, 22–23
  benefits for managers, x–xi
  Build Strengths, 17–18
  central tenets of, ix–x
  characteristics of, ix
  concept of, ix
  definition, 4
  development framework, 14f
  Discover True North, 16–17
  habits for, x
  Keep Growing, 18–20
  Know Thyself, 15–16
  and leadership skills, 10, 11
  locus of control, 9–10
  and management, x
  overcoming obstacles, 5–7, 11
  personal *vs.* interpersonal practices, 14
  Self-Regulation, 21–22
  Show Intent, 20–21
  successful life, basis of, 8–9
Self-leadership development framework, xi, 14f, 173.
    See also Leadership growth framework
  Be Curious, 22–23
  Build Strengths, 17–18
  Discover True North, 16–17
  Keep Growing, 18–20
  Know Thyself, 15–16
  outer *vs.* inner game, 14, 15
  personal *vs.* interpersonal practices, 14
  Self-Regulation, 21–22

Show Intent, 20–21
Self-learning, 5
Self-mastery, 28
Self-motivation, ix, x, 9
Self-reflect/reflection, x, 152
Self-Regulation/Regulate, ix, x, 16, 21–22, 172. *See also* Emotional self-regulation, practicing
   benefit for leaders, 133–136, 137
   definition, 129–130
   and emotional intelligence, 129, 137
   factors in, 129, 137
   learning, 131–133, 137
   natural *vs.* effective, 132
   responding/reacting, 130–131, 137
   as a skill, 132–133, 137
Self-regulation appraisal, 220–224
Self-talk, 145
Self-understanding, ix, 5, 16, 30, 34
The Servant as Leader, 111
Servant leadership, 111–113
   goals of, 111
   vs. intent leadership, 111–112, 116–117
The 7 Habits of Highly Effective People: Be Proactive and Begin with the End in Mind, 109
Seven Pillars of Servant Leadership: Practicing the Wisdom of Leading by Serving, 112
Show Intent, 16, 20–21, 46, 172
   benefits of, 110
   definition, 109–110
   intent-based leaders, characteristics of, 114–116, 117
   intent-based leadership, 110
   responsibility-based leadership approaches, 113–114
   servant leadership, 111–113, 116–117
Sinek, Simon, 8
Sleep, proper, 140, 147
Social awareness, 78, 83, 204
   active listening in virtual discussions, 204
   cultural sensitivity, 204
   digital conflict resolution, 204
   inclusivity and online communication, 204
   virtual team building, 204
Social media engagement, 203–204
Societal conditioning, 64–65, 71
Socrates, 15, 27, 34
Software and tool assessment, 207
Solution appraisal, 81, 83, 206–207
   data-driven decision making, 207
   digital tool selection, 206–207
   digital transformation initiatives, 207
   pilot programs, 207
   user feedback analysis, 207
Start with Why: How Great Leaders Inspire Everyone to Take Action, 125
Stepping into a Leadership Role? Be Ready to Tell Your Story, 122
Strategic leadership, 74, 75*f,* 79–82
Strategic purpose, 46, 52
Strategic roadmaps, 205
Strategic vision, 79
Strength, 68
Strength Finder 2.0, 64, 70
Strength-based development programs, 69, 71
Strength-based Development Requires a Growth Mindset, 68
Strengths-based approach, 57
Sullenberger, Captain Sully, 165
Sustainable behavior change, 5
System evaluation, 82, 83, 207
   cybersecurity audits, 207
   data management review, 207
   process audits, 207
   software and tool assessment, 207
   user experience testing, 207

T-shaped employees, 160
Talent identification programs, 69
Talents, 65, 68–71, 171
Taylor-Klaus, David, 135*b*
Team messages, 202
Technology assessment, 202
Thinking, Fast and Slow, 29

260   INDEX

The Third Commandment of Highly Effective Leadership: Know Thyself and Others, 43
Thought leadership content, 203, 206
3M, 167
Three P principles, 60
Toastmasters International, 7, 66
Touching the Void, 66
Toyota's 5 Whys Approach, 168
Trust, 20, 163
Twain, Mark, 47
20 percent-time policy, 150, 167
Tze, Lao, 134*b*

U.S. Centers for Disease Control and Prevention (CDC), 37
User experience testing, 207
User feedback analysis, 207

Value-based leadership, 57
The Value of a Growth Mindset and How to Develop One, 89*b*
Values, 3, 32, 57–58, 62, 171
Video conferencing, 202
Video message rebuttals, 205
Virtual discussions, active listening in, 204
Virtual focus groups, 206
Virtual negotiation sessions, 205
Virtual presentations, 202, 203
Virtual team building, 204
Virtual team meetings, 203
Virtual town hall meeting, 202
Visioning, 79–80, 83, 205–206
    change management strategies, 206
    digital product development, 205
    innovative ideation sessions, 205
    strategic roadmaps, 205
    thought leadership content, 206
Volatility, uncertainty, complexity, and ambiguity (VUCA), 22, 34, 49, 52, 85
VUCA, 88, 105, 115
Vujicic, Nick, 6

Washington, George, 112*b*
WebFX, 119
Webinars, 202
Why First Impressions Stick: And What You Can Do About It, 120
Why Should Anyone Be Led by You?, 55
Workplace Rollercoaster Model, 99–101, 100*f*
World Health Organization (WHO), 37

Yousafzai, Malala, 5

ZenithTech Labs, 79

OTHER TITLES IN THE HUMAN RESOURCE MANAGEMENT AND ORGANIZATIONAL BEHAVIOR COLLECTION

Michael J. Provitera and Michael Edmondson, Editors

- *Nice Guys Finish Last And Other Workplace Lies,* by John Ruffa
- *Understanding and Using AI* by Daniel O. Livvarcin and Yacouba Traoré
- *The Leadership Edge* by Michael B. Ross and Mike Shaw
- *Business and Management in the Age of Intangible Capitalism* by Hamid Yeganeh
- *Ignite All* by The Fusion Team
- *(Re)Value* by Adam Wallace and Adam Wallace
- *Dysfunctional Organizations* by David D. Van Fleet
- *The Negotiation Edge* by Michael Saksa
- *Applied Leadership* by Sam Altawil
- *Forging Dynasty Businesses* by Chuck Violand
- *How the Harvard Business School Changed the Way We View Organizations* by Jay W. Lorsch
- *Managing Millennials* by Jacqueline Cripps
- *Personal Effectiveness* by Lucia Strazzeri
- *Catalyzing Transformation* by Sandra Waddock
- *Nurturing Equanimity* by Michael Edmondson

Concise and Applied Business Books

The Collection listed above is one of 30 business subject collections that Business Expert Press has grown to make BEP a premiere publisher of print and digital books. Our concise and applied books are for...

- Professionals and Practitioners
- Faculty who adopt our books for courses
- Librarians who know that BEP's Digital Libraries are a unique way to offer students ebooks to download, not restricted with any digital rights management
- Executive Training Course Leaders
- Business Seminar Organizers

Business Expert Press books are for anyone who needs to dig deeper on business ideas, goals, and solutions to everyday problems. Whether one print book, one ebook, or buying a digital library of 110 ebooks, we remain the affordable and smart way to be business smart. For more information, please visit www.businessexpertpress.com, or contact sales@businessexpertpress.com.

www.ingramcontent.com/pod-product-compliance
Lightning Source LLC
Chambersburg PA
CBHW050136240426
43673CB00043B/1690